Better Homes and Gardens®

Treasures
from
Throwaways

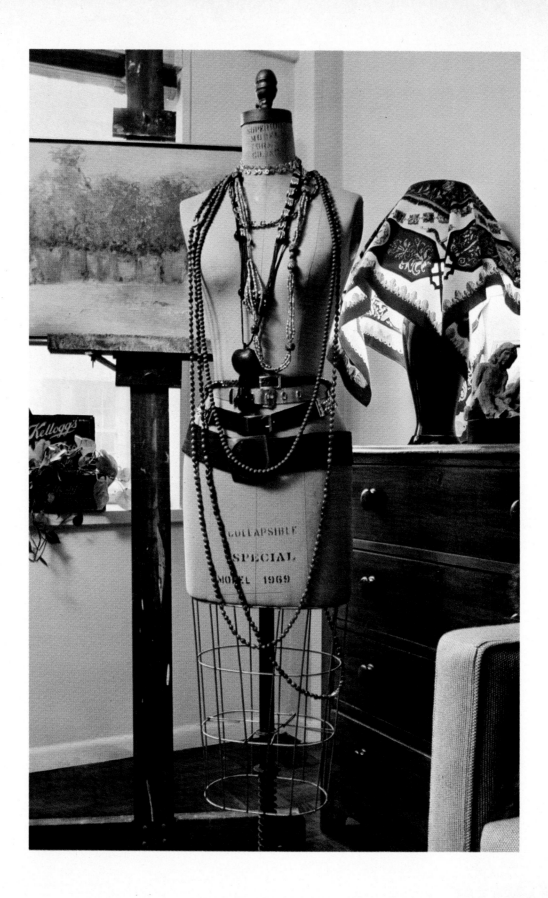

Contents

BETTER HOMES AND GARDENS BOOKS

Editorial Director: Don Dooley
Managing Editor: Malcolm E. Robinson   Art Director: John Berg
Production and Copy Chief: Lawrence D. Clayton   Asst. Art Director: Randall Yontz
Senior Writer: Sharyl Heiken   Associate Editors: Jo Moore Stewart, Marie Schulz
Designers: Harijs Priekulis, Candy Carleton, Faith Berven, Sheryl Veenschoten
Contributing Editor: Jean LemMon   Technical Editor: David Ashe

One person's trash is another person's treasure...

If beauty is in the eye of the beholder—so is the ability to see potential in castoffs. Only a true "pack rat" can look at a carefully collected pile of junk and visualize wonderful things. *Treasures from Throwaways* is aimed at these "pack rats." If you like dragging home odds and ends with the hopes of someday doing something with them, read on. On the following pages, you'll see imaginative ideas backed up by complete how-to instructions.

But in case your attic isn't already bulging with raw materials for your reincarnation projects, here are some likely sources:

Flea markets are a good bet if what you're looking for is reclaimable furniture and accessories. Check your newspaper classifieds for locations and plan to browse without any preconceived notions of what you want to buy. Shopping the secondhand market is always most successful if you approach your outlet with an open mind. Finding a real "treasure" is as much serendipity as shopping skill. And don't be afraid to haggle over price. It's part of the fun.

Country auctions can produce some spectacular finds, providing you have a little moxie. Examine items carefully before bidding to make sure the piece is as good as it looks. Carry a little notebook and jot down the prices you're willing to pay. Then stick to them. Don't let your emotions control your bidding. And keep your eyes open for odd-lot boxes. They usually go for very little and there may be one or two things in a box that make the purchase well worth what you paid. And if you're buying big, keep cartage costs in mind. A big freight bill can turn a bargain into something less.

Garage, rummage, and house sales can be a good source for all sorts of recyclable things. You may find costs a bit higher at house sales than garage sales. But then, the quality of the items may be higher, too. Check your newspaper for current sales.

Antique shops don't have to be considered off-limits to bargain hunters, either. Usually, you'll pay more than you would at a secondhand store, but you may pay less than at an auction. To be on the safe side, get to know the antique dealers in your area. They may be willing to let you know when they have some good buys. And whenever you buy used items, no matter what the source, check their condition thoroughly. Take along a flashlight. It can illuminate dark corners of furniture that might reveal imperfections. And watch out for strategically placed price tags that may cover damaged areas.

Station wagon sales are nothing more than open-air garage sales—a group of people in a parking lot or open field, with each person selling discards from his own station wagon. This might be a good place to look for salvageable smaller items, but it's usually no source for furniture.

Wrecking companies sometimes unearth nice architectural parts that you can turn into exquisite treasures. Check the Yellow Pages for salvage yards and watch your newspaper for announcements of sales in old commercial buildings about to succumb to the wrecking ball.

Used furniture stores such as Salvation Army, Goodwill, and some privately owned operations are good spots to check for recyclables. The stock varies from month to month, so plan a periodic stop at these junktique places.

Free junk is the best kind of all. So keep your eye open for sidewalk castoffs. If you're lucky, you can beat the disposal sanitation engineer to a real find. When you're alert and have an open mind, there's no end to the priceless treasures around.

Tin Can Creations

No one expects a whole lot from a tin can. Once it has done its job, that's it—usually. That's not true of the tin cans featured in this chapter, though. Each of them signs a new lease on life as part of an eye-catching project that's fun to make and equally enjoyable for you to display.

Tin Can Owls

Remember those flattened tin cans you used to kick along as you walked down the street? Cans similar to those rusty, creased, environmental eyesores provided the inspiration for these striking owls shown on the opposite page as well as in the mobile on page 8. The trick regarding this type of artistry is to use your imagination and study the creases and wrinkles and folds of each can for features to fall into place on the owl.

Materials
(for single and mobile)
- Rusty flattened beverage cans
- White charcoal pencil
- Acrylic paints
- Rusty nails
- Liquid solder, epoxy, or plastic steel
- Assorted lengths of reinforcement rods, or straight edge of coat hanger
- Fine wire
- Piece of driftwood, weathered wood, or a wood block
- Rings from beverage can pop tops
- Shallow metal saucer for mobile top
- Core solder
- Swag hook toggle bolt

Tools
- Hammer
- Small paintbrush
- Steel wool
- Soldering iron

Directions
Single owl **1.** Scrub the flattened tin can to remove any dirt or loose rust particles. Let dry thoroughly. (**Note:** Whatever rust is left will add to the natural coloring of the owl. The rust will work with the paint to create texture as well as a very realistic and rustic look and finish.)
2. Find the fold where the top of the can is smashed against the body of the can. (This fold is a guideline for placement of the owl's eyes.)
3. Using the basic face of the owl shown, at left, proceed as follows:
- Sketch the eyes on or below the fold of the can with the white charcoal pencil (drawing is erasable in case you want to make some changes).
- Sketch the rest of the owl's face.
- Paint in basic face, following sketch. Let dry.
- For a more realistic appearance, paint in feather details. Let dry.

4. Display the single owl in any of the following ways:
- Drill a hole in a wooden base and insert a short

(continued on next page)

piece of coat hanger, securing with liquid solder or epoxy. Mount owl on rod with liquid solder, plastic steel, or epoxy. Let dry.

• Attach a ring from a beverage can pop top to the back of owl with liquid solder or epoxy. Let dry completely. Hang on wall with nail.

• Punch a nail through the can into the wall. (**Note:** A rusty nail looks best, since it blends in well with the coloring of owl.)

• Solder a pile of rusty nails together. Use liquid solder or epoxy to attach the owl to the nail base. Let dry.

• Mount the owl on a piece of weathered wood or driftwood with epoxy glue. Let dry.

Owl mobile   **1.** Prepare each owl in the same way as given in steps 1, 2, and 3 of the single owl instructions.

2. Bend the reinforcement rods to simulate branches (see photograph below).

3. Arrange rods as desired, remembering that the mobile must balance.

4. Wrap reinforcement rods at joints with wire.

5. Solder the rods at the wire-wrapped joints.

6. To attach the owls to the mobile:

• Using steel wool, polish the back of the owl and the surface of the reinforcement rod where they will touch when attached.

• Attach the owls to the rods with liquid solder or epoxy. Let dry completely. (An odd number of tin can owls on the mobile usually gives a more pleasing appearance.) Test the balance of the mobile and add or subtract owls.

7. Solder the metal saucer to the top of the mobile, as shown in the photograph. Let dry.

8. Solder a chain to the top of the mobile.

9. Drill a hole in the ceiling.

10. Screw swag hook into ceiling for hollow wall rather than joist, use a toggle bolt).

11. Hang the mobile from the swag hook.

Coffee Can Canisters

If you've been searching for a good-looking, yet inexpensive canister set, look no further. The set pictured here satisfies both requirements. Coffee cans were used here.

Materials

Three coffee cans (1-, 2-, and 3-pound sizes)
60 feet ¼-inch sisal rope
Three bridle rings (graduated sizes)
Belt leather (real or synthetic) 1⅛ to 1½
    inches wide, in sufficient length to go
    around cans, plus 4 inches
Three medium-size rivets
Scraps of 1-inch plywood
½-inch plywood scraps
Three #12 sheet metal screws (⅝ inch thick)
Flat black paint
Contact cement

Tools

Saber saw
Paintbrush
Punch
Drill
½-inch dowel

Directions

1. From plywood cut a one-inch-thick circle to fit inside the bottom rim; a one-inch-thick circle to fit top outer rim; and a ½-inch-thick circle the size of the opening.

2. Glue cutouts together with contact cement, making sure inner circle is centered on outer circle and fits easily into can. Let dry.

3. Paint wood tops and bases black. Let dry.

4. Fit leather around cans, paint edges, and dry. Set aside for later use.

5. Wrap sections of can with rope:

• Cut off length needed to go around 6 or 7 times plus about three extra inches. Fray about one inch on starting end.

• Spread contact cement on one area to be covered with rope. Start rope at back seam of can. Press frayed end into glue below dent. Flatten frayed ends and spread out.

• Wrap around the can and over frayed section. Continue wrapping rope tightly, with the last row in indented area.

• Allowing 1 to 1½ inches for tuck-under, cut off excess. Fray end and work end under wrapped section at back seam of can.

6. Cement leather to can, starting and ending at back seam of can. Secure with rubber bands. Remove rubber bands when dry.

7. Drill hole through center of the bottom of the cans. Make the hole large enough to receive the sheet metal screws.

8. Screw wood base in place on bottom of can.

9. Drill ½-inch hole through the center top circles.

10. Make three leather holders or tops:

• Dampen and roll leather around ½-inch dowel,

• Slip off dowel.

• Punch holes for rivets.

• Set rivets. Let dampened leather dry.

11. To assemble the tops,

• Cut two 20-inch pieces of rope.

• For small ring, slip rope through ring, then push ends through leather loop and top. Knot to hold in place. Cut off excess rope.

• Repeat procedure on remaining tops but wrap rope two turns around on medium ring and three times around on largest ring before finishing.

Tin-Topped Table

Set against a background of glowing embers, the coffee table pictured above looks like an expensive import. Take a closer look. The imported part is correct, since the tabletop is made of olive oil cans that were imported. But the expensive appraisal of this work-of-art table is wrong. An assortment of cans with printed surfaces and an old rectangular table (the one shown in the photo above was originally an old library table) will give you the same fine results.

Materials

    Rectangular table
    Black paint with a satin finish
    Empty olive oil cans (**Note:** It is important to wash out these cans thoroughly as soon as they are empty in order to avoid a rancid odor. Olive oil cans are available in ½-pint, pint, quart, ½-gallon, and gallon sizes. If you need the larger sizes, ask someone at a restaurant to save a few used olive oil cans for you.)
    Small brass nails
    ¼-inch plate glass (cut to fit the tabletop)
    1⅜x1⅜-inch corner bead molding
    Finishing nails

Tools

    Saw
    Paintbrush
    Can opener
    Tin snips
    Two pieces of scrap plywood
    Hammer
    Awl
    Miter box

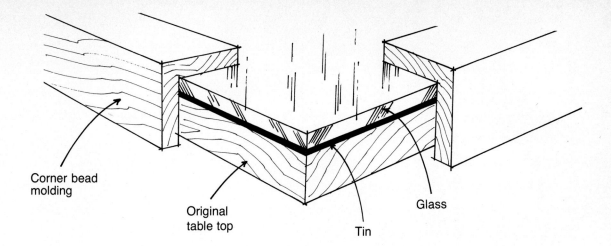

Corner bead molding

Original table top

Tin

Glass

Directions

1. If necessary, cut off legs of table to make coffee table height (about 16 inches high).

2. Paint the table black. Let dry.

3. Remove the top and bottom of the olive oil cans with a can opener. Cut along the seam of each can with tin snips.

4. Flatten cans by placing them between two pieces of plywood and pounding with hammer.

5. Arrange the sides and ends of cans on tabletop to create the desired design. Place the cans edge to edge without overlapping, as shown in the photograph on the opposite page.

6. Use an awl to make pilot holes through the olive oil cans and into the tabletop.

7. Use brass nails to nail the cans in place.

8. Place the piece of plate glass atop the cans. (The glass makes the table level and protects the cans from water spills.)

9. Cut molding to fit around tabletop. Using miter box, miter molding for table corners.

10. Paint molding black to match the rest of the table. Let dry thoroughly before proceeding.

11. Nail the molding in place along the edges of the tabletop, making sure it rests flush against edges of glass top and sides of the table.

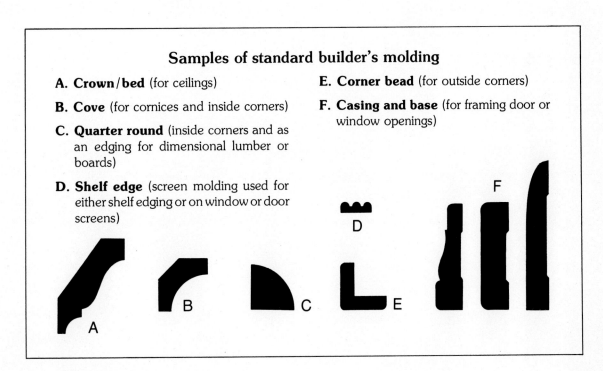

Samples of standard builder's molding

A. Crown/bed (for ceilings)

B. Cove (for cornices and inside corners)

C. Quarter round (inside corners and as an edging for dimensional lumber or boards)

D. Shelf edge (screen molding used for either shelf edging or on window or door screens)

E. Corner bead (for outside corners)

F. Casing and base (for framing door or window openings)

Tennis Ball Can Vases

There's as much bounce to empty tennis ball cans as there is to the balls they contained when you turn them into whimsical flower vases like shown here. If tennis isn't your game, you can net the same results using empty potato chip or cleanser cans. And in case your tennis arm outranks your artistic hand, you may want to substitute some magazine clippings for the ink drawings.

Add some fluffy tissue paper flowers and you've got a combination that's a real winner.

Materials
Vases
    Three empty tennis ball cans
    One package of white watercolor paper
    One yard clear self-adhesive paper (for three cans)
    Acrylic paints (white and black)
    India ink
Tissue paper flowers
    White tissue paper
    One 2-ounce bundle of 12-16 gauge cut wire (it comes in 18-inch lengths)
    Cellophane or florist's tape
    Scraps of yellow construction paper
    Glue

Tools
    Wire cutter
    Scissors
    Ink pen

Directions
Vases **1.** Cut white watercolor paper the height of the tennis ball can (less the top and bottom rims) and wide enough to overlap ¼ inch. (Be sure to fit under the edges of the rim of the cans.)
2. Lay the paper flat, and with pen and India ink draw the figures of the women as shown in the grid patterns on page 14. Let the ink dry.
3. Paint the rims of the can black or white, using acrylic paint to match design. Let dry.
4. Cut a piece of clear self-adhesive paper slightly larger than the paper with the ink drawings.
5. Lay the self-adhesive paper on the table, sticky side up.
6. Carefully lay design with drawings face down, smoothing out from center to avoid air bubbles.

7. Trim away the self-adhesive paper from the top and bottom and one of the edges.
8. Wrap the design around the tennis ball can.
9. Use the overlap of self-adhesive paper to ''tape'' the design to the can.

Tissue paper flowers **1.** Fold up several sheets of tissue paper to obtain many folds.
2. Make cardboard patterns from designs in sketch below.
3. Cut out tissue flowers, using either pattern.
4. Cut wire into 11-inch lengths.
5. Hold each flower firmly and poke a wire into the center of it.
6. Bend the top of the wire into a loop so the tissue can't slide off.
7. Let the tissue slip down the wire a bit.
8. Separate each tissue layer, sliding it up the wire until it hits the bent wire end.
9. Crunch each layer in your hand.
10. Wrap a strip of cellophane or florist's tape around the base of the flower to prevent it from sliding down the wire.
11. Cut out round centers, if desired.
12. Glue them to the tissue flowers. Let dry.

(continued on next page)

Recycled Containers

Coffee cans, soda cans, and juice cans all take to the wall in this easygoing organizer that gives you efficiency at a price that even college students easily can afford.

Materials
Tin cans (assorted sizes)
5-minute epoxy
Enamel paint (yellow and orange)
One common nail or toggle bolt

Tools
Hammer

Directions
1. Remove the labels from the cans.
2. Arrange cans in small groupings that please.
3. Glue cans in each group together. Let dry.
4. Paint each group of cans a different color. Let dry.

5. Glue groups of cans together. Let dry.
6. Attach the unit to the wall with a nail through the cans into a stud, or with a toggle bolt if the wall is hollow.

Ham Can Lanterns

These bold lanterns will add a festive touch to any party. Hang them, as shown in the photo, or use them as a centerpiece for the table. These same lanterns also provide great atmosphere lighting for patio picnics and recreation room gatherings.

Materials
(For each lantern)

Ham can—1-, 3-, or 5-pound size (use a can opener rather than the key provided on the can to open the can. Also, remove can bottom with can opener.)

One small potted meat or deviled ham can (remove the top only)

Vinegar water

Wooden block for base (about 2x3x6 inches)

Two stove bolts with two nuts and two washers to fit

Masking tape

One large wooden bead

One wooden drapery ring

Primer

Latex enamel paint

One votive candle

Candle stubs

Colorful twine or fine rope

Tools

Can opener

Saber saw

Drill

Wrench

Steel wool

Paintbrush

Knife

Directions

1. Wash the cans thoroughly and rinse with vinegar water.

2. Cut out a wooden base. (Measurements of the base will vary with the can size. The dimensions shown in the sketch are for 5-pound ham can.)

3. In the center of the wooden base, drill a vertical hole large enough to accommodate bolt.

4. Drill hole in the center bottom of the small meat can.

5. Drill hole through the center of the bottom and top surfaces of the ham can.

6. Drill a hole through the drapery ring.

7. Steel-wool the outside of the ham can. Dust well.

8. Cover the inside of the ham can completely with masking tape.

9. To assemble the lantern for painting,

• Run one bolt through the wood base and the bottom of the ham can.

• Add the washer and screw on nut to secure, but don't tighten completely.

• Put the second bolt through the drapery ring, wooden bead, and the top of the ham can.

• Add a washer and nut, and tighten.

10. Prime the assembled ham can and the small candle holder can. Let dry.

11. Paint both units. Let dry.

12. Remove the masking tape.

13. Remove nut and washer in base of lantern and slide candle holder can onto bolt.

14. Add the washer, then replace the nut and tighten.

15. Melt candle stubs in a container set in a pan of water.

16. Cut into the center of the bottom of the voltive candle enough to make it fit over the bolt in the bottom of the candle holder can.

17. Pour a small amount of the melted wax from the candle stubs into the bottom of the candle holder can.

18. Set the votive candle in place while the wax is soft. Let stand till hardened.

19. To hang the lantern, tie fine rope or twine through the drapery ring and hang from a tree limb, light fixture, or other sturdy fixture.

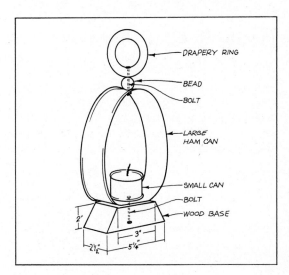

Hanging-Can Planters

What better way to give your special plants their own place in the sun than in these distinctive, yet inexpensive hanging planters? The design for each planter is made by gluing vinyl pieces atop each other. Fill the bottom of the cans with pebbles to ensure drainage.

Materials
  Three tin cans in varied sizes (large juice cans, coffee cans, and shortening cans work especially well)
  Vinyl material (black, brown, and gold)
  White glue

  Buckskin strips (or leather and suede scraps)
  "S" hooks

Tools
  Scissors to cut vinyl
  Large and small paper punches
  One large nail

Directions
1. Remove the labels and glue from the tin cans. (An overnight soaking makes this easy.)
2. Wash and dry the cans thoroughly.
3. Cut a paper pattern to fit around each can between the top and bottom rims.
4. Cut a vinyl covering for each can, using the

paper pattern. (Use black vinyl for tall can at left and brown vinyl for other two cans.)

5. Spread white glue around the cans at the top and bottom rims and along the vertical seams.

6. Press the vinyl material smoothly onto the cans. Trim at seam, if necessary, to make a neat fit. (Secure the vinyl to the cans with masking tape until the glue is thoroughly dry, then remove the tape.)

7. Cut a 1½-inch-wide strip of brown vinyl to fit around tall can at left. Cut a 3-inch-wide strip of gold vinyl to fit around center can. Cut a 2-inch-wide strip of gold vinyl to fit around can at right.

8. For left can and center can, position these vinyl strips at bottom rim of can and glue in place. For can at right, position the gold vinyl strip 1 inch up from bottom rim and glue in place.

9. Glue buckskin strips in place at top and bottom rims of each can and at top and bottom of each vinyl strip. (Wash off any excess glue immediately.) Let dry.

10. Enlarge border patterns as shown on grid. (See page 209 for grid instructions.)

11. Use paper punches to cut circles from vinyl. (G stands for gold vinyl and B for brown vinyl.)

12. Cut paper patterns for remaining shapes, then cut the vinyl pieces, using the paper patterns as a guide.

13. Position largest vinyl border pieces on cans as shown, spacing evenly around can. (Cut more pieces as needed to go around can.) Mark position, then glue each piece in place. Let dry completely before proceeding.

14. Glue remaining pieces in place as shown. Let dry thoroughly.

15. Using the nail, punch three holes 1¼ inches or more apart on one side of each can. (The space between the holes will depend on the diameter of the can you select.) Punch three more holes on opposite side of each can.

16. Cut three buckskin strips for hangers.

17. Thread a buckskin strip through one hole, threading from inside of can to outside. Thread same strip through hole on opposite side of can. Repeat with remaining buckskin strips.

18. Knot the strips on the outside of the can, as shown in the sketch.

19. Place a dot of glue on each knot. Let dry.

20. Clip the knotted ends of the strips short.

21. Hang the planters from the "S" hooks that are hung over curtain rod, as shown in photo.

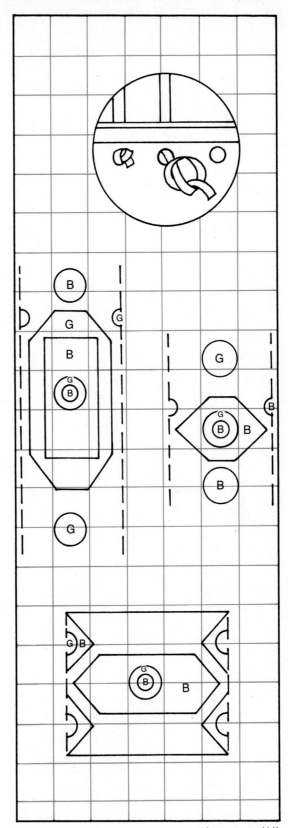

1 square = ½''

Tin-Turned Toys

Kick the can is old stuff. What's really new in the play department is tin cans converted to toys. Here's a lovable dragon made of five one-pound coffee cans. Humpty Dumpty is a ham can turned bank. And the tin man? Well, he's just that—some things can't be improved.

Materials

Tin man

Six small juice cans
Two small spray can lids
One large stew can
One large spray can lid
One baking powder can with lid
One small funnel
Four 1½-inch bolts with nuts to fit
Two 6-inch threaded steel rods with washers and hex nuts to fit
One 9-inch threaded steel rod with washer, hex nut, and washer to fit
Two wooden circles
Scrap piece of wood
Blue paint
Scraps of self-adhesive paper (black and red)

Humpty-Dumpty bank

One 5-pound ham can
One 8x10-inch piece of 1-inch-thick wood
Four ¾-inch wood screws
One piece of cardboard
Two 20-inch chenille stems
Two 20-inch pieces of wire
½ yard black adhesive-backed paper
Scraps of white adhesive-backed paper
1 yard adhesive-backed burlap paper
White paint
Glue
Black vinyl tape
Red ribbon for bow

Dragon pull toy

Five 1-pound coffee cans (12½ inches wide)
Red, black, and blue yarn scraps
1¾ yards green terry cloth
1 yard aqua terry cloth
One large red bead
Polyester stuffing

Tools

File
Punch
Paintbrush
Saber saw
Drill
Compound-action tinsnips
Screwdriver
Scissors
Pliers
Coarse-grade sandpaper
Sewing machine
Large darning or crewel embroidery needle

(continued on next page)

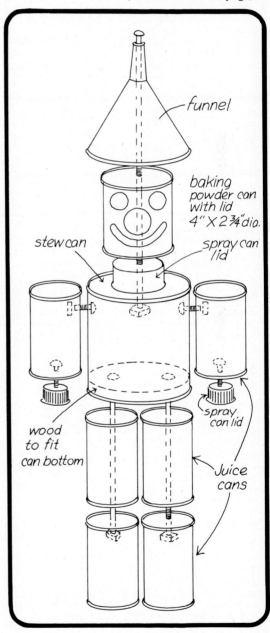

funnel

baking powder can with lid 4" X 2¾" dia.

stew can

spray can lid

wood to fit can bottom

spray can lid

Juice cans

21

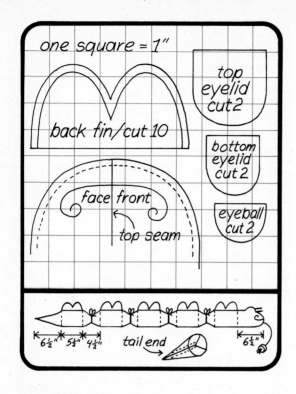

one square = 1"

top eyelid cut 2

back fin/cut 10

bottom eyelid cut 2

face front

top seam

eyeball cut 2

6½" 5½" 4½"

tail end

Directions

Tin Man **1.** Make holes in centers of all cans.
2. Make holes in sides of two juice cans and stew can. (See drawing on page 21 for location.)
3. Paint large spray can lid and all the cans except the baking powder can. Let dry.
4. Place nut on top end of 9-inch rod. Run rod through funnel, baking powder can, and spray can lid.
5. Secure with washer nut below top of stew can.
6. Draw a circle on wood scrap the diameter of the stew can. Cut out with saber saw.
7. Drill two holes in circle for leg rods.
8. Run 6-inch rods through the holes of the wooden circle and run them through the cans.
9. Tighten with nuts at bottom of rods.
10. Attach spray can lid to arm with 1½-inch bolt. Put bolt through lid into closed end of can. Hold nut in place with pliers. Tighten.
11. Bolt arms to body in the same manner.
12. Cut out eyes and mouth from black adhesive-backed paper. Cut nose from red.
13. Position cutouts on baking powder can.

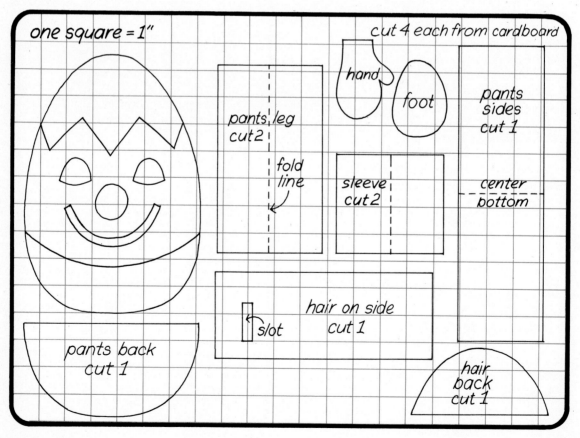

one square = 1"

cut 4 each from cardboard

hand

foot

pants sides cut 1

pants leg cut 2

fold line

sleeve cut 2

center bottom

hair on side cut 1

slot

pants back cut 1

hair back cut 1

Humpty-Dumpty bank **1.** Punch hole in the side of the can. Use tinsnips to enlarge hole to form money slot. File edges smooth.

2. Paint can and lid white. Let dry.

3. Draw ham can lid on 1-inch-thick wood. Cut out with saber saw. Sand edges smooth.

4. Attach wood to inside of lid, using screws.

5. Using pattern on page 22, cut four hands and four feet from cardboard. Cut sleeves and pant pieces from adhesive-backed burlap.

6. Cover hands with white adhesive-backed paper; feet with black adhesive vinyl tape.

7. For arms, fold two 20-inch chenille stems in half. Glue each stem between two hands. Dry.

8. Fold sleeve in half over stem.

9. For legs, bend 20-inch wire in hairpin shape.

10. Drill holes at base. Push wire ends through.

11. Fold burlap pant legs over wire. Glue feet to wire ends. Let dry.

12. Apply burlap to can to form pants.

13. Drill hole in can side at center top of pant edge. Push arm stem through hole.

14. Cut facial features and hair from red and black self-adhesive paper. Position on can.

15. Tie red bow. Glue on can and let dry.

16. Use black vinyl tape to secure lid.

Dragon pull toy **1.** Cut ten fins from aqua terry cloth (see sketch on page 22).

2. Place two together. Stitch curved edges. Clip.

3. Turn and topstitch curved edge. Make five.

4. Cut body piece of green terry cloth: 14½ inches wide x 1¾ yards long.

5. Measure in 6½ inches from end of body strip. Pin back fin into seam allowance.

6. Measure 4½ inches down. Pin in next fin. Continue down length of tube.

7. Stitch back seam, using ⅝-inch seam allowance. Don't turn. At one end, center back seam.

8. Cut face according to sketch. Stitch and turn tube right side out. Stuff head.

9. Put 1-pound coffee cans in body tube.

10. Tie yarn between cans.

11. Stitch tail end to a point.

12. Embroider details on dragon, using a chain stitch for mouth and satin stitch for eyeballs. Add two rows of rya stitch lashes. Use a running stitch on the top edge of fins. Sew on a fringe of yarn scraps for the hair.

13. Crochet or braid pull cord. Sew to front.

14. Loop cord through wooden bead and tie.

Tin Totem Pole Hat Rack

Every family needs a totem pole! At least, that's what the Indians of the Northwest thought when they carved totems to record stories and legends. In case you haven't figured it out, the story on the 44-inch totem pole shown here is that it's made of coffee cans and designed as a rack for hats—or war bonnets.

Materials

Six 3-pound coffee cans
One 44-inch threaded metal rod
One cap nut
Six threaded washers and nuts to fit
Primer
Model paint (orange, yellow, white, and blue)
Black spray paint
Cardboard
Contact glue
Nine sheet metal screws
One 16x11-inch piece of 1-inch pine
One 12x18-inch piece of 2-inch oak
Carbon paper
Plain wrapping paper
Coarse-grade sandpaper

(continued on next page)

Tools
   Drill
   Saber saw
   Paintbrush

Directions
1. Drill holes in center of each 3-pound coffee can to fit threaded rod.
2. Paint all six cans black. Let dry.
3. Cut cardboard circles to fit inside solid ends of five cans.
4. Build up enough cardboard to form a plug to fit in open can ends.
5. Glue cardboard together. Let dry completely.
6. Make a hole at center of cardboard.
7. Adhere cardboard circles to can with contact glue. Let dry.
8. Enlarge designs in sketch on wrapping paper.
9. Tape the wrapping paper over carbon paper; trace pattern on cans.

10. Brush designs on cans with model paint. Let dry completely.
11. Cut the wings and beak from piece of pine with saber saw.
12. Sand the wings and beak until smooth.
13. Cut two circles—6 and 12 inches in diameter—from the piece of oak. Use saber saw.
14. Prime all the wood pieces except the 6-inch diameter circle base. Let dry.
15. Paint the wings blue, the beak yellow, and the 12-inch base black. Let dry.
16. Glue the 6-inch circle to the center of the 12-inch circle. Let dry.
17. Drill two holes for screws in wings and beak areas of top two cans.
18. Screw the wing and beak in place with sheet metal screws.
19. Beginning at top of cans, put one washer and cap nut on end of rod.
20. Thread through top of can 1.
21. Set this can on next one.
22. Push open end down on cardboard circle.
23. Push rod through holes.
24. Add washer and thread on nut. Tighten.
25. Continue in same way with other four cans.
26. To put assembled pole on base,
• Drill three evenly spaced holes through can into wood circle (the 6-inch diameter circle inside bottom can).
• Screw pole to base with sheet metal screws.

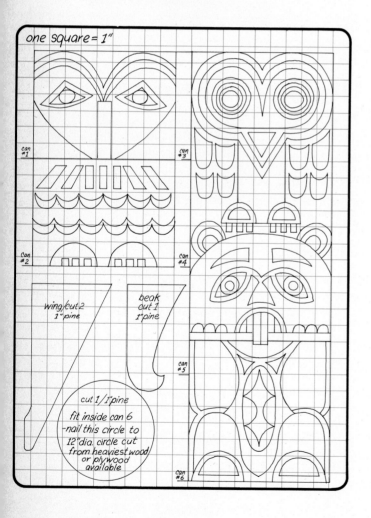

one square = 1"

can #1

can #2

can #3

can #4

wing, cut 2
1" pine

beak
cut 1
1" pine

can #5

cut 1/1" pine
fit inside can 6
—nail this circle to
12" dia. circle cut
from heaviest wood
or plywood
available

can #6

How to attach metal to metal

Make metal-to-metal bonds by using epoxy, rivets, bolts, sheet metal screws, and soldering or welding techniques.

Epoxy takes several hours to cure to full strength, but 5-minute curing types are on the market. *Rivets* (soft metal pins) are bolt-type fasteners that join metal firmly, simply, quickly, and inexpensively. A non-heat method, rivets are a clean connection.

Bolts are used to join metal that may have to be taken apart later. *Sheet metal screws* are made of hardened steel and cut their own threads as turned. *Soldering* joins metal to wires with the use of a soldering iron. *Welding* joins metals by melting electrically or by gas.

24

Yarn-Wrapped Can Lamp

Attractive table lamps need not be expensive, as illustrated by this project. Except for electrical parts, almost everything used in the project is a throwaway—juice cans, yarn, wood scraps, and a wooden thread spool. In addition to economical virtues, it's easy to make.

Materials

Two 46-ounce juice cans (with tops removed)
Cotton rug yarn in harmonious colors (leftover scraps totaling about 40 yards)
Epoxy
Paint with flat finish (black plus a color that harmonizes with the yarn)
½-inch pine (5x15 inches)
1-inch pine (6x6 inches)
Unpainted wooden lamp base
Pebbles or coarse gravel
Paraffin
1½-inch wooden thread spool (or purchased lamp riser)
Vase cap (optional)
⅛-inch all-thread lamp pipe (length determined by total length of assembled lamp)
Four lock nuts to fit pipe
Two steel washers to fit pipe
Two lock washers to fit pipe (use to ensure a wobble-free assembly)
Electrical parts (socket, cord, and plug)
8-inch harp
Lamp shade

Tools

Drill with ⅜-inch wood bit and ½-inch metal bit (or, use hammer and chisel instead of metal bit)
Saber saw
Paintbrushes
Toothpick

Directions

1. Cut three 4¼-inch-diameter disks from the ½-inch pine.
2. Cut one 5¼-inch-diameter disk from the 1-inch pine.
3. Drill a ⅜-inch hole in center of each disk.
4. Sand the disks until smooth.
5. Paint the 4¼-inch disks to blend with the yarn colors you have. Let dry.
6. Paint the 5¼-inch disk, the lamp base, the spool (or riser), and vase cap flat black. Let them dry completely before proceeding.
7. In the center of the can bottoms, drill a ½-inch hole or punch out an equivalent opening with a hammer and a chisel.
8. Wash and dry the cans.
9. To cover cans with yarn,
• Starting at the bottom rim, spread a thin bead of white glue around the can.
• Press the yarn into glue, adjusting the cut end so the second row will cover it.
• Continue gluing and winding until the can is completely covered. (When one length of yarn runs out, start with another yarn length, overlapping ends. Trim ends and glue securely in place. Every inch or so, use a toothpick to slide rows downward so that they fit closely together and are evenly horizontal.)
• Vary yarn colors to create design and let dry.
10. Start the final assembly at the bottom by gluing the 5¼-inch black wooden disk to the painted lamp base, being sure to match up center holes. Let dry completely.
11. Glue one of the 4¼-inch disks atop the 5¼-inch disk, matching center holes. Let dry.

(continued on next page)

12. Spread glue on bottom rim of one can and position atop glued disks, matching holes. Dry.
13. Slip the lamp pipe through holes in base and wooden disks, and secure temporarily under the base with a nut.
14. Keeping the pipe perpendicular to base, fill can with pebbles or coarse gravel. (**Note:** Don't use sand, as it will sift out.)
15. Melt paraffin in container set in pan of water. Cool to point of partial fluidity.
16. Pour a cup of paraffin over pebbles or gravel to secure it. Let stand till hardened.
17. Apply glue to the top rim of the can.
18. Thread a 4¼-inch disk on pipe. Press disk onto glued can rim. Let dry.
19. Thread the second can atop, as shown in photograph. Glue in place. Thread the remaining 4¼-inch disk onto pipe and glue in place atop second can. Let dry.
20. Thread the vase cap atop disk. Glue in place. Thread wooden spool atop vase cap; glue. (If not using vase cap, glue spool directly to disk.) Let dry before proceeding.
21. Wire the socket and assemble the lamp parts as shown in diagram. (See pages 252 and 253 for wiring instructions.)
22. Glue one row of yarn over the exposed can rims. Let dry completely.

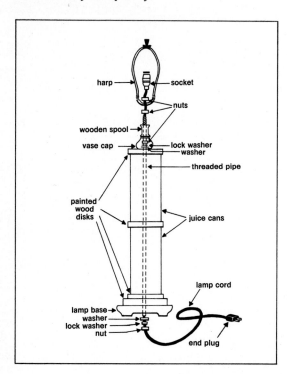

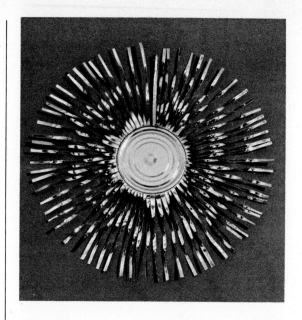

Tin Can Sunburst

With just the right twist, you can turn even the grubbiest tin can into a dazzling sunburst. Hang the bright sunburst design in a window to sparkle in the sunlight, or use it on your Christmas tree to reflect the glitter of tree lights.

Materials
Tin can with gold interior
Nail polish remover

Tools
Tin shears
Can opener
Pliers

Directions
1. Erase any printing on the outside of the can, using nail polish remover.
2. Remove the top of the can with a can opener.
3. With a pair of tin shears, remove top rim.
4. Cut the can to the base in strips of varied widths according to the design wanted.
5. Spread the strips flat.
6. Twist each strip twice into the design wanted, using the pliers.
(**Note:** See top photograph on page 40 for how to cut tin cans as well as the tip box about the dangers of handling tin on the same page.)

Beer Can Table

Here's a coffee table that's a unique pop-art approach to ecology. With patience, you can collect the 147 required beverage cans over a period of time. Impetuous table-makers, however, will have to schedule a pre-construction party to acquire the raw materials.

Materials
147 beverage cans without dents

One 2x2-foot piece of sheet plastic
Epoxy

Directions
1. Rinse out the cans thoroughly. Let dry completely before proceeding.
2. Arrange the cans in desired pattern. (Here, a variety of labels was used. If you want a stronger color effect, use one kind of can.)
3. Glue the cans together with epoxy. Let dry.
4. Place the sheet of plastic on top of cans.

Firecracker Can Candles

Tin cans have never looked so good! Here's a bang-up display of firecracker candles made from a variety of cans, stacked, glued together, and painted patriotic. Flag Day, Fourth of July, Washington's Birthday, or election-day parties—they're all good excuses to spark up a table with these red, white, and blue beauties.

Materials

Firecracker containers
- Empty cans in several sizes
- Epoxy
- Paper towels
- Papier-mâché
- White glue
- Gesso

- Fine-grade sandpaper
- Acrylic paints in red, white, and blue
- White adhesive-backed paper
- Clear gloss varnish

Candles
- Commercial candle wax
- A container (can for finished candle)
- Stearic acid or plastic crystals
- Wicking
- Wick tab

Tools
- Paintbrushes
- Scissors
- Newspapers
- Pencil or dowel
- Ice pick
- Double-boiler melting pot
- Kitchen thermometer
- Hot pad
- Pot lid
- Baking soda

Directions

Firecracker containers **1.** Without removing bottoms of cans, arrange them in stacks of varying heights and diameters. (Choose a shallow can for the top one in each stack, as it will contain the wax and wick.)

2. Paint inside of each top can white. Let dry.

3. Fill top cans with wax, following candle-making instructions on page 30. Let wax harden.

4. Cement each stack of cans together with epoxy. Let dry completely.

5. Cover the outside of each stack with strips of torn paper toweling dipped into a paste of white glue and water (half and half).

6. Wind papier-mâché strips around cans between the rims until the sides are about even with rims. Wrap the last few layers from top to bottom of each stack, covering rim. Allow papier mâché to dry completely.

7. Give each stack three coats of gesso. Let dry between coats.

8. Sand between each coat to provide a smooth surface for painting and decorating.

9. Paint stacks. Let dry.

10. Cut numbers or stars from white adhesive-backed paper. Apply to painted containers.

11. Apply a coat or two of clear gloss varnish. Let dry completely before continuing.

(continued on next page)

Candle-making safety reminders

Making your own candles is easy and fun, if you heed these precautions:

Ventilate your working area. Excessively overheated wax can give off toxic fumes, so pay special attention to the temperature limits that are given in the candle-making instructions.

Keep fire-extinguishing equipment at hand. For example, never work without a pot lid handy. Should a fire break out in your melting pot, clamp the lid on tightly to suffocate it.

Baking soda is an item you should keep within easy reach. If a burner fire flares up, sprinkle the soda on it immediately.

Pour excess wax into an empty can or carton and place it in a garbage container for disposal. (Plumbing can suffer damage if you allow the melted wax to be poured down a drain. The melted wax will harden in the drain pipes.)

Remove candle-wax stains on clothing by hardening the wax with ice and scraping off excess. Then, place fabric between layers of paper towels and press with a warm iron to absorb wax. Wash garment with water that's as hot as is safe for the fibers of the fabric in question.

Candles **1.** Cover your work area with newspapers for protection.

2. To determine how much wax you need to fill the container in which you're making the candle,

• Fill the container with water and pour it into your melting pot.

• Add 25 percent more water to allow for shrinkage as wax hardens.

• Note the water level in melting pot.

• Discard the water and dry the pot thoroughly.

(**Note:** A quart container holds 2 to 2½ pounds of wax with no problem.)

3. Break wax into chunks. Add to melting pot.

4. Attach a thermometer to the rim of the pot (see sketch A).

5. Set the pot in a pan of water.

6. Melt the wax over hot water until it reaches 200-210°. Don't heat wax to more than 230°. Never let water bubble into hot wax and don't leave melting wax unattended.

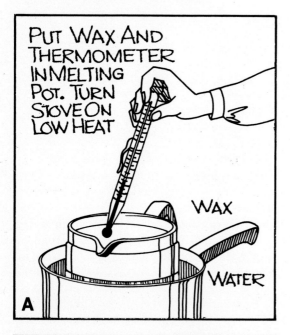

PUT WAX AND THERMOMETER IN MELTING POT. TURN STOVE ON LOW HEAT

WAX

WATER

A

SUSPEND WICK IN CANDLE MOLD. REST PENCIL ON MOLD AND CENTER WICK IN MOLD

B

POUR WAX SLOWLY DOWN SIDE OF CONTAINER TO MINIMIZE AIR BUBBLES

C

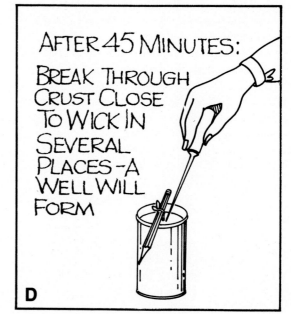

AFTER 45 MINUTES:

BREAK THROUGH CRUST CLOSE TO WICK IN SEVERAL PLACES—A WELL WILL FORM

D

7. Add the stearic acid or plastic crystals when wax reaches 200°. Use about three tablespoons of stearic acid to one pound of wax. (**Note:** Plastic crystals add gloss to the surface of wax. Use crystals according to package directions. See tip box on this page for the additional information on candle-making materials.)

8. Prepare the container and the wick while the wax melts, but continue to watch the thermometer very carefully.
- Have container clean and perfectly dry before proceeding to next step.
- Dip the wick in melted wax and let it harden. (This adds stiffness and makes setting it easier.)
- Cut off a piece of wick the depth of the container plus several inches.
- Slip one end through a wick tab.
- Hold the tab so bent corners point up. (Corners grip wax as it hardens and secures the wick at the base of the candle.)
- Knot the wick at the bottom of the tab and cut off the excess.
- Suspend the wick in the container, straighten it, and wind the excess around a pencil or a dowel that rests across the top of the container (see sketch B on page 30).
- Center the wick.

9. Pour the wax into container (see sketch C on page 30). (For metal container, pour wax at 200°.)
- Grasp the melting pot with the hot pad and wipe off water before pouring.
- Pour very slowly down side of the container to minimize air bubbles.
- Fill to within ⅛ inch of top. (Let stand 45 minutes.)

10. Poke several holes all the way to the bottom of the container near the wick, using an ice pick or a pencil (see sketch D).

11. Fill this hole with hot wax to prevent a well around the wick as the wax hardens and shrinks. Repeat as often as necessary to level the candle. (Always reheat the wax to the proper pouring temperature.)

12. Let wax harden for at least 8 hours.

13. Shine the candle surface by rubbing it with a nylon stocking or painting it with the decoupage glaze.

14. Decorate your container after the candle is made. (Hot wax can affect paints and glues of pre-decorated containers.)

The candle-making materials you will need

Hobby and crafts stores offer a wide variety of candle-making supplies. Here's a list of materials and their characteristics:

Wax is available in 3- to 4-pound chunks or 10- to 11-pound slabs. The same weight slab may carry two different prices, indicating a fine-quality wax or one of less quality. (You probably won't notice any difference in quality in the finished candle.)

Instant wax is a relatively new candle-making product. It's granulated for quicker melting and is available in colors.

Beeswax is available, but it is costly and difficult to use in molds. It's tacky and does not release well. Beeswax is usually used as an additive rather than as a candle wax.

Two types of wicks are available—braided wicking and metal-core wicking. Wicks with metal cores are more rigid and are easier to handle.

Wicks come in three sizes: small, for containers less than two inches in diameter; medium, for two- to three-inch containers; and large, for four-inch and larger candles.

Correct wick size is important. Too small a wick allows the flame to sink into the candle; too large a wick smokes.

Stearic acid and plastic crystals are additives that improve appearance and performance of candles. They make candles harder, more opaque, and slower burning.

You can add color to plain wax with various wax-soluble dyes, ranging from color crayon shavings to commercial candle color agents. Add color at 200°.

Add fluorescent colors after the wax has cooled to 175°.

Add scents to the wax just before pouring it. Use only wax-soluble chemicals designed for candle making. Perfumes, colognes, and toilet waters do not dissolve in wax. (To scent a candle after it is made, add drop or two of liquid scent to well at base of candle's burning flame.)

Metal-Trimmed Tree

Needle fallout becomes a thing of the past when you set up this contemporary Christmas tree. Even though it's green and decked with candles just like old-fashioned trees, this one is different. This updated version is made of cans, in fact, 250 of them! If you want this particular tree for the holidays, better start saving cans in earnest along about the Fourth of July.

Materials
    250 tin cans
    Epoxy
    Metal primer
    Green enamel paint
    61 red votive candles
    Florist's clay
    Green boughs

Tools
    Paintbrush

Directions
1. Remove labels and wash cans thoroughly. Allow to dry completely.
2. Glue cans together in stacks: 24 stacks of two cans each; 18 stacks of four cans each; 12 stacks of six cans each; 6 stacks of eight cans each; and 1 stack of ten cans. Let dry completely. (**Note:** Be sure top can in each stack is glued in place with solid bottom up. This provides a base for the votive candles.)
3. Paint each stack of cans with metal primer. Let dry completely.
4. Give each stack of cans two or three coats of green enamel. Let dry completely between coats and before proceeding to next step.
5. Position cans to form tree:
• Surround center stack of ten cans with the six stacks of eight cans.
• Surround eight-can stacks with the 12 stacks of six cans. Continue until final circle containing the 24 stacks of two cans is in position to complete the basic tree.
6. Top each can with a votive candle. (To make sure candles are stationary, place a small piece of florist's clay on the can top. Press the candle into it firmly to secure.)
7. Surround base of Christmas tree with fresh green boughs.

Juice Can Wreath

Traditional no, but beautiful nonetheless, this wreath features colorful balls and shimmering tin cans—all reflected to great advantage in a bow-topped mirror.

Materials
    28 juice cans with paper labels
    An 18-inch circular mirror
    28 Christmas balls (various colors)
    Epoxy
    Picture hanger for mirror back
    4 yards of 4-inch ribbon

Tools
    Can opener

Directions
1. Remove tops of juice cans. Remove labels.
2. Glue 17 cans around outer edge of mirror and glue 11 cans into circle inside outer row. Let dry completely before proceeding.
3. Glue balls into each can. Let dry completely before proceeding to next step.
4. Attach hanger to back of mirror.
5. Attach bow to top of can wreath.

1. Wash empty can thoroughly. Dry completely.
2. Pierce holes in sides of cans, using an awl or pointed object and a hammer. (Make the holes at random or work out a design on paper, mark the spots to be punched on the can, and pierce the can sides accordingly.)
3. Saw off the tips of the metal funnels, using a hacksaw. On some, saw off the tips, leaving one inch of metal at the base.
4. Cut the remaining portion of the funnel tip into strips, using tin snips.
5. To achieve the effect shown in the photo at left, curl strips back. Use long-nosed pliers.
6. Punch holes in sides of funnels using the awl or any pointed object.
7. Paint cans and funnels with metal primer. Let dry completely. (Leaving some cans and funnels unpainted will yield shiny silver lanterns.)
8. Paint cans and funnels with two or three coats of enamel paint. Let dry.
9. Place votive candles in bottoms of cans. Rest funnel tops on lanterns.

Tin Can Lanterns

Flickering candlelight adds atmosphere to most any setting. But these tin can lanterns have taken flickering candlelight one step further. Here, the candle flames dance behind intricately pierced designs to create a charm that's perfect in any room of your home. Try these quaint lanterns as tabletoppers, mantel decorations, or welcoming beacons on your windowsill. Use them singly or in clusters as shown in the colorful arrangement in the photograph above.

Materials
    Empty tin cans of various sizes
    Metal funnels in sizes needed to rest on cans
        (as shown in photo)
    Metal primer
    Enamel Paint in red, black, and gold
    Votive candles

Tools
    Awl or pointed object for piercing cans
    Hammer
    Hacksaw
    Tin snips
    Long-nosed pliers
    Paintbrush

How to use a hacksaw

Cutting most metal requires the use of a hacksaw. With the right choice of blades and a little practice, sawing metal is no problem at all.

Blades have 14, 18, 24, or 32 teeth per inch. The best blade for general use is an 18-tooth one. To cut thin materials, use a 32-tooth blade.

Use both hands to hold the saw. Apply cutting pressure on forward stroke; lift the blade off the work on the return stroke. Hacksaws cut only one way—forward. Bear down just enough to keep the saw cutting. Putting too much pressure on the forward end dulls the blade's teeth and causes the blade to skip over the metal.

Use a light, steady stroke—about 40 to 50 times a minute is best.

To start a cut, nick the surface of the metal with a file, then start the blade.

Replace blades by inserting them in the frame with the teeth pointing away from the handle. Tighten wing nut.

Juice Can Bird House

Here's a condominium that's for the birds—and the birds love it. Juice cans, wood, and wire work together to make chickadees or martins comfortable in any kind of weather.

Materials

Ten 1-quart juice cans
One piece 1x12-inch lumber, 12 inches long
One piece ¼-inch plywood, 12x12 inches
Scraps of 1-inch lumber
Four small dowel rods for perches
Heavy-gauge wire
Wood glue
White paint

Tools

Wire cutter
Saber saw
Keyhole saw
Drill

Directions

1. Stack the 10 cans in a pyramid on top of a 1x12 board and tie with wire.
2. Cut front triangle out of plywood.
3. Drill holes for birds. (1⅛ inches for chickadees; 2½ inches for martins.)
4. Glue on perch supports. Let dry.
5. Drill holes for perches and attach.
6. Paint birdhouse. Let dry.

Tea Can Lamp

About five minutes is all it takes to turn any interesting tin can into a tiny accent lamp like the one shown above. If you're looking for a one-of-a-kind gift, try this. It's quick as well as inexpensive!

Materials

One empty tea can
Lamp cord with line switch
Brass lamp socket
25-watt light bulb

Tools

Drill
Screwdriver

Directions

1. Drill a hole in the back of the can for the lamp cord.
2. Thread the cord through the hole.
3. Attach the cord to the terminals of a brass lamp socket.
4. Add a plug to the other end of the lamp cord.
(**Note:** See pages 252-253 for complete instruction on wiring lamps.)
5. Screw in a 25-watt light bulb.

Striking Candlesticks

If you ever doubted the Cinderella story, these "rags-to-riches" candle holders ought to make a believer of you. Once upon a time, these regal silvery candle holders were a collection of tin cans, gelatin molds, and metal odds and ends. Now, they're fit for a king.

Materials

(**Note:** The following materials are needed for all candle holders)
⅛-inch threaded steel rods as long as desired height of candle holder
Metal washers
Bolt nuts
Flat black paint
Paint thinner

Candlestick 1
One large can
One tuna can (both ends cut out)
One individual serving-size juice can
Eight gelatin molds
50 pull top can tab rings
50 beads
Wire

Candlestick 2
One individual serving-size juice can
Three gelatin molds

Candlestick 3
Six gelatin molds
One escutheson (plumbing hardware) attached to drain pipe
12 medium chair glides
12 small chair glides
Liquid steel

Candlestick 4
Two ring molds
Four gelatin molds
Two 1-inch wooden beads
18 pull top can tab rings
One tuna can
One large tin can
Eight large chair glides
Liquid steel

Tools
Drill
Pliers
Very fine steel wool
Large darning needle

Directions
(**Note:** Steps 1 through 7 apply to each candle holder. See specific candle holder instructions for assembling of materials and special detailing.)
1. Drill holes in the bottom of the molds and the cans. (**Note:** The holes should be large enough to accommodate ⅛-inch rod.)
2. Slide parts of candle holder onto the rod.
3. Secure individual sections with metal washers and bolt nuts.
4. Decorate candle holders according to instructions for each design.
5. Paint candle holders with flat black paint.
6. To antique, wipe off paint with a cloth dampened in paint thinner. Let dry.
7. Rub with very fine steel wool to add the highlights you desire.

Candlestick 1 **1.** Starting at the bottom, assemble pieces in the following order: one large can; one mold; one tuna can with both ends cut out; four molds; one individual juice can; and three molds.
2. Thread one pop-top ring, one bead, another ring, and another bead on fine wire.
3. With darning needle, puncture edge of mold and attach ring-bead strings to mold.
4. Paint and finish candle holder according to general instructions.

Candlestick 2 **1.** Starting at bottom, assemble pieces in the following order: one mold; one individual juice can; and two molds.
2. Finish according to general instructions.

Candlestick 3 **1.** Assemble pieces as follows: six molds and one escutheson attached to drain pipe.
2. Apply chair glides as shown in photo, using liquid steel.
3. Finish according to general instructions.

Candlestick 4 **1.** Assemble pieces as follows: one large can; one tuna can; one ring mold; one mold; one bead; two molds; one bead; and one mold.
2. Glue 18 pop-top rings to one ring mold. Let dry completely before proceeding.
3. Glue ring mold to top of candle holder with liquid steel. Let dry.
4. Finish according to general instructions.

Twisted Tin Furniture

Doll furniture is part of the magic of childhood. In this case the magic comes in cans which have been transformed into exquisite furniture with the airy look of Victorian wicker. The cans are cut into strips and curled. The furniture is destined to become an heirloom.

Materials

Empty tin cans in assorted sizes
Metal primer
Enamel paint in blue, yellow, orange, green, purple, and white
Fabric scraps
Cotton batting
Cardboard
White glue

Tools

Serrated tin snips
Needle-nose pliers
Curling tool or sardine can key-type opener from which you have snipped the end to form a small pronged tool
Metal ruler
Ice pick or sharp-pointed object
Template made from scrap tin (see directions below for how to make it)
Small level
Heavy work gloves
Paintbrush

Directions

(Note: You can make furniture pieces from various sizes of cans. Simply adjust the number of cut strips, snipping out excess strips or adding more. The patterns shown on pages 40-42 are guidelines for designs and may be changed to your specifications.)

1. To make a template to serve as a guide for marking the width of the strips to be cut (you need one template for each size and shape can you plan to use).
• Remove the top and bottom lids from a can the type and size to be used for furniture.
• Remove rims and side seam with tin snips.
• Around the top and bottom edges of the can, cut evenly spaced slits ¼ inch deep and ⅛ inch wide. (You may have to adjust these measurements, depending on circumference of can.)

2. Remove the lids from cans to be used for the doll furniture.
3. Cut rims off tops of cans, using tin snips.
4. Remove the side seams by cutting straight down each side of the seam.
5. Tape the template over the can so its edge is even with the seam line.
6. Scribe a mark at each template slit along the top and bottom edges of the can, with an ice pick.
7. Remove template.
8. Draw a line connecting the top and bottom marks on the can, using a metal ruler and an ice pick.
9. Cut with tin snips along each line down to bottom rim, making equal-width strips all the way around the can (see top photo on page 40).
10. Bend the individual strips up or down according to the pattern of the particular piece of furniture using your pliers. Twist each strip to conform to the pattern.
11. Link groups of strips together with connectors where indicated.
• Cut narrow strips about ½ inch long from an extra can.
• Bend these connectors around groups of strips to hold them in place.
12. Curl the ends of the strips as indicated in bottom photo on page 40.
• Insert the end of each strip in the prong section of the curling tool and curl tightly.
• Remove tool.
(Note: For additional curlicues, cut 4-inch-long strips from an extra can. Attach with connectors where indicated on the pattern. Curl.)
13. To adjust all furniture legs to same height,
• Place a small level on top of chair or table to gauge its levelness.
• Bend legs evenly, using the curling tool.
14. Primer completed pieces. Let dry thoroughly.
15. Give each piece two or three coats of enamel. Let dry completely.
16. To add upholstery to furniture,
• Cut cardboard to shape of chair seat or bed top.
• Lay cardboard on fabric scrap and cut fabric, allowing 1-inch extra on all sides.
• Place cotton batting on cardboard base.
• Place fabric over cotton, wrap around edges, and glue to underside of cardboard. Let dry.
17. Place cushions in chairs and on beds.

(continued on next page)

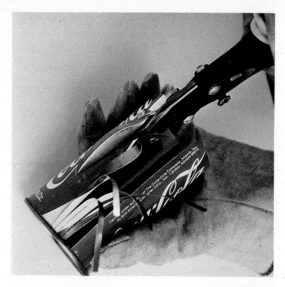

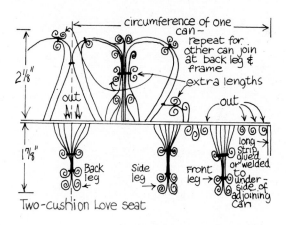

Out = strips removed
▬ = connectors
☺ ☺ = extra lengths

circumference of one can —
repeat for other can join at back leg & frame
extra lengths

2⅛"

out

1⅞"

Back leg   Side leg   Front leg →   long strip glued or welded to underside of adjoining can

out

Two-cushion Love seat

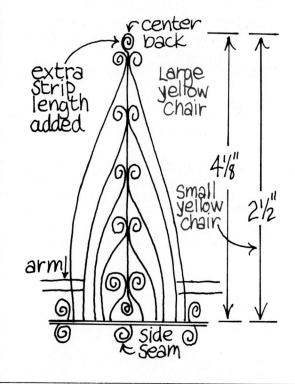

center back

extra strip length added

Large yellow chair

4⅛"

Small yellow chair

2½"

arm!

Side seam

Caution—working with metal

The raw edges of metal cans are dangerous if handled improperly. Exercise the following precautions:

Wear gloves while cutting a can into strips. If gloves are awkward, discard them while curling strips, but use care!

Cut only a portion of each can into strips so your hands come into contact with fewer edges.

Supervise older children closely. Don't allow young children to handle the tin.

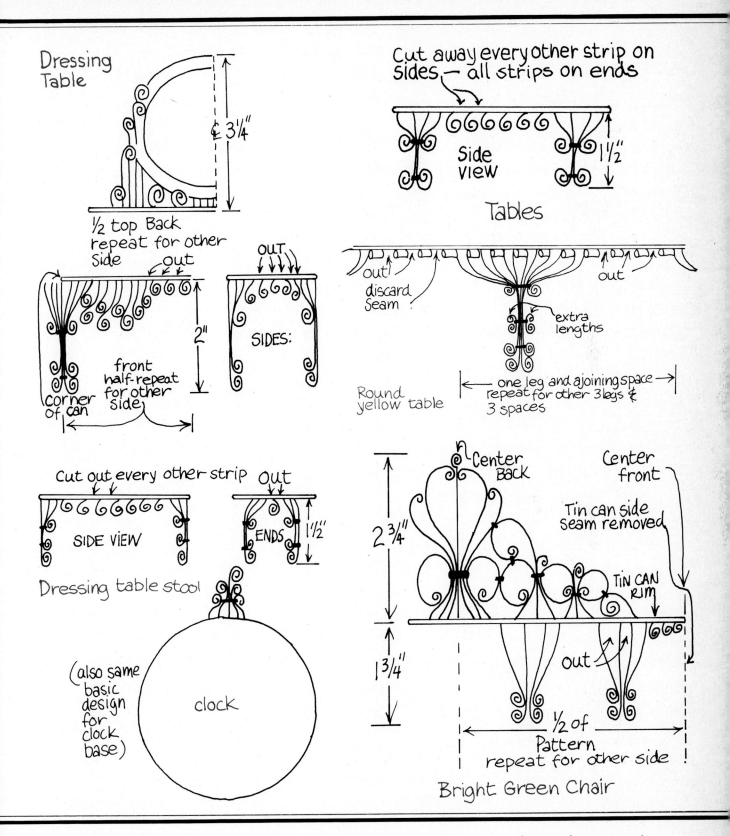

Dressing
Table

£ 3¼"

½ top Back
repeat for other
Side

OUT

front
half-repeat
for other
side)

2"

OUT

SIDES:

Corner
of can

Cut out every other strip OUT

SIDE VIEW

ENDS

1½"

Dressing table stool

(also same
basic
design
for
clock
base)

clock

Cut away every other strip on
Sides — all strips on ends

Side
VIEW

1½"

Tables

out!
discard
Seam

out

extra
lengths

Round
yellow table

one leg and a joining space
repeat for other 3 legs &
3 spaces

Center
Back

Center
front

Tin can side
seam removed

2¾"

TIN CAN
RIM

1¾"

out

½ of
Pattern
repeat for other side

Bright Green Chair

(continued on next page)

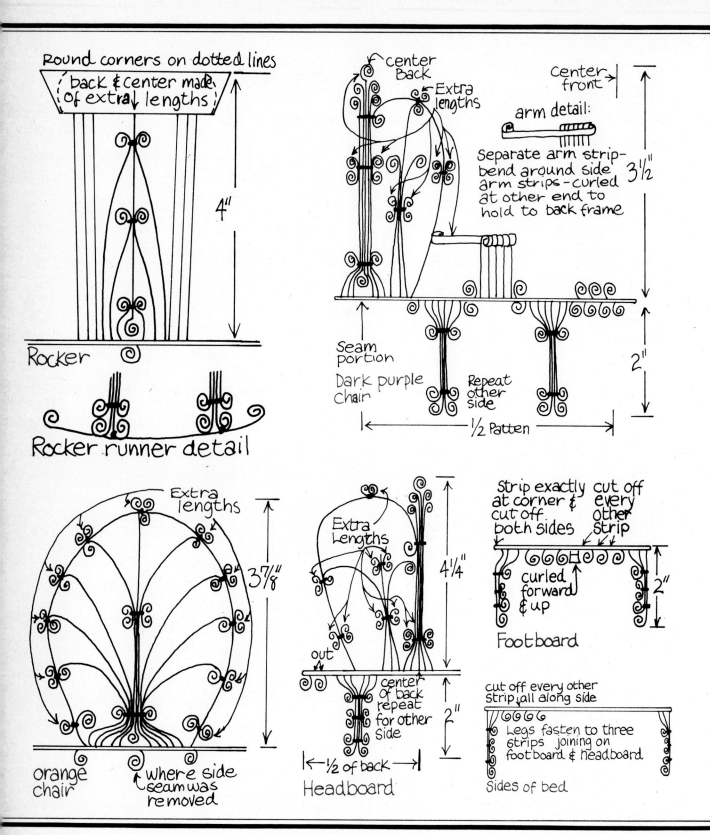

Round corners on dotted lines

back & center made of extra lengths

4"

Rocker

Rocker runner detail

center Back

Extra lengths

center front

arm detail:

Separate arm strip—
bend around side
arm strips—curled
at other end to
hold to back frame

3½"

Seam
portion

Dark purple
chair

Repeat
other
side

2"

½ Patten

Extra
lengths

3⅞"

orange
chair

where side
seam was
removed

Extra
Lengths

out

center
of back
repeat
for other
side

4¼"

2"

½ of back

Headboard

Strip exactly cut off
at corner & every
cut off. other
both sides strip

curled
forward
& up

2"

Footboard

cut off every other
strip all along side

Legs fasten to three
strips joining on
footboard & headboard

Sides of bed

Tin Can Candle Holder

When it comes right down to it, you could set a candle on just about anything. But "just about anything" couldn't possibly have the panache this candle holder has. You'd hardly guess, looking at its classic geometry, it's an old tin can that changed its spots from a vegetable label to this smart black and white ink drawing. If art's not in your bag of tricks, use this same technique with wrapping paper or magazine clippings. The result is still smashing.

Materials
One tin can
One sheet white watercolor paper
One 9x12-inch piece clear self-adhesive
    backed paper
White acrylic paint
India ink

Tools
Tape measure
Ink pen
Scissors

Directions
1. Measure the height of the can between the top and bottom rims.
2. Measure the circumference of the can. Add ¼ inch to this measurement.
3. Using these measurements, cut a piece of white watercolor paper.
4. Lay paper flat, and with pen and India ink draw design. Let ink dry.
5. Paint rims of the can with white acrylic paint to blend with design. Let dry.
6. Cut a piece of clear self-adhesive backed paper slightly larger than the paper with the inked design.
7. Lay the paper on the table with the sticky side up.
8. Carefully lay the design face down on it, smoothing out from the center to avoid air bubbles.
9. Trim away the paper from the top, bottom, and one back edge. (This will leave an overlap of paper on one side of the back; this will hold the design onto the can.)
10. Wrap the design around the can carefully.
11. Overlap margin of self-adhesive backed paper to "tape" design to can.

chapter 2

Barrel and Crate Bonanza

Packing-crate furnishings used to be politely ignored as just financial necessities. Now, they're considered "casual chic." Just search supermarkets and drug firms for sources and when you latch onto a barrel or crate in good shape, you can display it as proudly as anything else in your home. This chapter is packed with items to make barrel and crate furnishings every bit as uptown as Bauhaus.

Packing Barrel Coffee Table

The mod coffee table pictured at left is sure to become one of your most-talked-about furnishings. Pick up the packing barrels needed for the base from a drug manufacturer or a shipping firm. (Note, too, that barrels are used for the end table and the hassock.)

Materials
Three packing barrels with lids (about 30 inches high and 18 inches in diameter)
One piece of ¼-inch plate glass with polished edges (30x36 inches)
Six 3-inch stove bolts (¼-inch diameter) with six nuts and twelve washers to fit
Twelve wooden blocks (2x2x¾ inches)
Three oversized mod calendar pages
White glue
Black paint

Tools
Drill
Adjustable wrench
Nylon paintbrush

Directions
1. Paint the bottom, lid, and bottom and top rim of each barrel with black paint. Let dry.
2. Measure the circumference of each barrel, then cut the calendar pages to fit.
3. Carefully glue the calendar pages onto the packing barrels.
4. Drill holes in barrel sides to accommodate the stove bolts, spacing them five inches from each end and in the center. (**Note:** The end barrels have holes only in one side, and the center barrel has holes in both sides.)

(continued on next page)

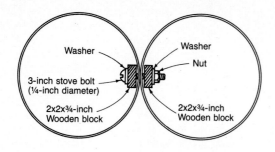

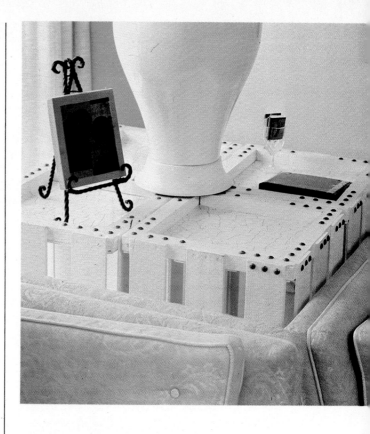

5. Drill holes in the wooden blocks for bolts.

6. To connect the packing barrels,

• Thread the stove bolts through the washers, blocks, and barrels as shown in drawing above.

• Screw nuts on bolts and tighten, using the adjustable wrench.

7. Place the glass on top of the barrels. (The weight of the glass will keep it in place.)

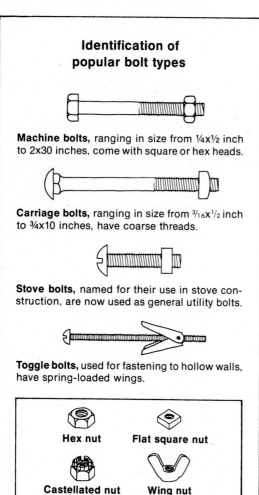

Identification of popular bolt types

Machine bolts, ranging in size from 1/4x1/2 inch to 2x30 inches, come with square or hex heads.

Carriage bolts, ranging in size from 3/16x1/2 inch to 3/4x10 inches, have coarse threads.

Stove bolts, named for their use in stove construction, are now used as general utility bolts.

Toggle bolts, used for fastening to hollow walls, have spring-loaded wings.

Hex nut	Flat square nut
Castellated nut	Wing nut

Vegetable Crate Corner Table

This versatile table is an enclosed cube or a storage unit with shelves, depending on how you arrange the crates. Directions for both versions are given below. And, as a bonus, it can be broken down and used as moving crates.

Materials

Four wooden vegetable crates
3/4-inch plywood
Two-penny nails
Varnish or shellac
Latex enamel paint
Four metal mending plates and screws
Floor vinyl (four squares)
Upholstery tacks

Tools

Saw
Screwdriver

Sandpaper
Hammer
Paintbrush

Directions

1. To add strength to the vegetable crates, make a shelf for each crate.

• Cut a piece of plywood to fit the inside width and depth of each crate.

• Center shelf in crate and nail through the slats of the crate into the edge of the shelf.

2. Give inside and outside of crates a prime coat with varnish or shellac. Let dry.

3. Sand varnished surfaces to rough up.

4. Paint crates with latex enamel. Let dry.

5. For an enclosed cube, position the crates open side in.*

6. Position the metal mending plates on the outside of crates at the shelves (see sketch A), then attach to the crates with screws.

7. If desired, paint the plates.

8. Position the four floor-vinyl insets on the tabletop, cutting to fit.

9. Trim the table with upholstery tacks, as shown in the photograph.

*****Note:** To make this table serve as a storage unit, follow the steps below. (You will need two more metal mending plates.)

1. Prepare the crates through step 4 as above.

2. Arrange the crates in pairs as shown in sketch B.

3. Use a metal mending plate, as in step 6 above, to connect the shelves of each pair.

4. To connect the pairs into the table cube,

• Place two metal mending plates through the slats at top as shown in sketch B.

• Screw on the plates from underneath the wood as shown in sketch C.

5. For the lower connection, repeat step 4, reversing the direction of the screws.

6. Finish the table as above.

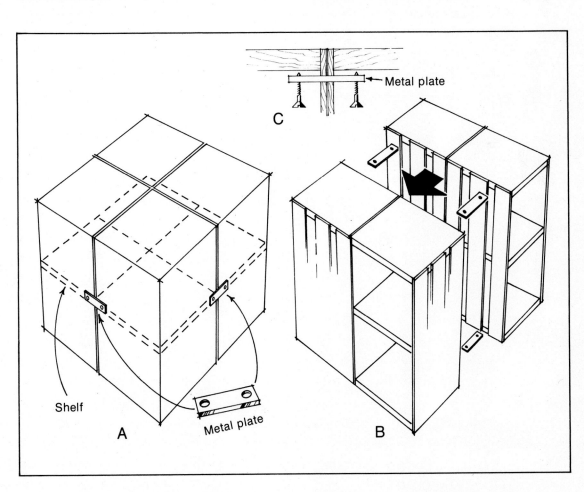

Metal plate

C

Shelf

A

Metal plate

B

Cardboard Crate Coffee Table

Cardboard boxes and crates have long been considered good for little else besides storage, but not anymore. Cardboard's taken on class. The table at left, for instance, presents a good case for cardboard as a building material—when reinforced, it's amazingly strong. It's got more going for it than just durability. It's easy to work with, easy to obtain, and if you tap the right sources—it's free! What other material can give you so much?

Materials
Several large cardboard boxes
White glue or contact cement
One sheet colored paper the size of the base
¼-inch plate glass or clear plastic (six inches larger on each side than the base)

Tools
Scissors
Utility knife

Directions
1. Select a cardboard box the size you want your table base. (**Note:** The lettering on the side of the box should be bold and simple for better design elements.)
2. Cut scraps of cardboard to form an egg-crate structure within the box. (**Note:** The structure should be two inches shorter than height of box for a recessed effect as shown in photo at left.)
3. Measure and cut a piece of cardboard to fit into the recess in the top of the structure, then rest it on the egg-crate reinforcements.
4. Measure and cut a piece of colored paper to cover positioned cardboard.
5. Glue colored paper in place. Let dry completely before proceeding.
6. Cut several 1½-inch strips of cardboard.
7. Roll up cardboard strips and arrange in design on top of colored paper.
8. Cut decorative cardboard panels to cover sides of table base.
9. Glue panels to sides of base. Let dry completely before completing project.
10. Rest glass or plastic on top of table base.

Wooden Crate Table

Whatever this packing crate's original purpose in life, it couldn't hold a candle to its job as a fashionable end table. Becoming an addition to a comfortable living room certainly beats kicking around a loading dock.

Materials
One wooden packing crate
¾-inch plywood scrap (cut one inch larger on all sides than crate top)
Wood glue
Primer
White latex paint
Polyurethane varnish
Coarse-grade sandpaper

Tools
Paintbrush

Directions
1. Glue plywood top to crate. Let dry. Sand.
2. Primer crate and top. Let dry.
3. Paint the unit white. Let dry.
4. Apply polyurethane varnish to top. Let dry.

Boxed Storage Wall

A bunch of boxes provide a whale of a lot of storage when they're wall-hung. Collect wooden shipping crates (certain fruits are still packed in wood), or build some plywood companions for a whole wallful of boxes in various sizes.

Materials

    ½-inch plywood (number of sheets depends
        on the number and size of boxes to be built)
    Wooden shipping crates
    Wood glue
    Fourpenny finishing nails
    Wood stain
    Shellac
    Wood screws (for attaching boxes to wall)

Tools

    Saber saw
    Hammer
    Paintbrush
    Drill
    Screwdriver

Directions

1. Measure and cut plywood for box sides.

2. Assemble the units and glue together. Let dry.

3. Secure with finishing nails. (**Note:** There are two ways to assemble the units—butt-joining and mitering the corners. The process of butt-joining will result in a roughhewn effect, whereas mitering yields a much more finished look.)

4. Measure the inside dimensions of each box, then cut back panels to fit.

5. Coat edges of back panels with glue and insert in box. Let dry.

6. Secure with finishing nails.

7. Stain boxes. Let dry completely.

8. Apply two coats of shellac. Let dry completely between coats.

9. Determine where wall studs are (tap on the wall and listen for a dull thud or use a magnetic stud finder). Group the units so you will have one or more studs behind each.

10. Mark back of boxes to indicate where they will attach to studs.

11. Drill holes for screws.

12. Position boxes and screw into studs.

Liquor-Box Wall

If you're faced with an unattractive basement or family room wall, try this unique wall covering. Look for old liquor boxes in antique stores, or ask a liquor store to save their wooden boxes for you. Complementing this wall are other wooden containers turned into shelves.

Materials
    Wooden liquor or wine boxes
    Wooden orange crates
    Wooden caviar boxes
    Glue (sub-grade adhesive for basement area)
    #9 wood screws
    Masonry bolts or toggle bolts

Tools
    Hammer
    Saber saw
    Drill

Directions
1. Carefully pry wooden liquor or wine boxes apart, making sure you don't split the wood.
2. Put the ends and the sides of the boxes in piles according to size.
3. To plan your paneling project,
• Study the labels to determine what patterns you want adjacent to each other on the wall.
• Do a comprehensive layout of the wall area you plan to cover. Be sure you have the exact measurements for openings such as windows, and saw the wooden pieces to fit.
4. Remove moldings, marking for reuse.
5. Repair any extensively damaged wall areas.
6. Glue wooden box ends and sides directly to the wall, following your layout. Let dry.
7. Replace the moldings.
8. To fasten small caviar box shelves to wall,
• Drill pilot hole at each corner of box.
• Attach box to wall with wood screws.
9. To fasten large orange crates to wall,
• Drill pilot hole at each corner of crate.
• Position crate where desired and mark where holes are.
• At marks, drill through the liquor boxes into the wall. (**Note:** Use masonry bit to drill concrete block walls.)
• Attach orange crate to wall with masonry bolts (for concrete walls) or toggle bolts.

Cardboard Stereo Unit

Stereo components come to rest in some highly imaginative surroundings, but none to compare with the cardboard tube pyramid shown here. The easy-on-the-budget tubes are used to stash not only the stereo unit, but records, books, plants, and other miscellany.

Materials
Cardboard packing tubes or round cartons (20, 18, 16, and 12 inches in diameter; obtain from drug firms)
White glue
Medium to heavy cotton or cotton-blend fabric (yardage according to diameter)
¾-inch stove bolts (¼ inch in diameter) with nuts and washers to fit
Floor spotlight (optional)

Tools
Utility knife
Paintbrush
Drill

Directions
1. Cut tubes to desired lengths. (If you are using cardboard cartons, remove bottoms to let light shine from behind. Remove any metal rims.)
2. To cover the tubes with fabric, measure length of tube.
• Add two inches to this measurement to determine width needed to cover the outside surface.
• Measure the circumference of the tube and add ½ inch for overlap to determine length. Cut outside cover fabric.
• Cut tube lining fabric as wide as tube is deep, front to back, and as long as the inside circumference, plus ½-inch overlap.
• Brush white glue onto outside surface of tube. Center fabric on tube, allowing 1-inch turn-under on each end. Smooth out.
• Apply glue along the edges of the inside of the tube. Turn fabric allowance under and glue in position. Let dry.
• Apply glue to interior surface of tube and smooth on lining fabric. Let dry.
3. Arrange fabric-covered tubes in a pyramid.
4. Mark spots where tubes touch.
5. Drill holes where marked.
6. Insert bolts through holes to join tubes.

Coke Case Organizer

Unlike glass milk bottles and clamp fruit jars, wooden soft drink cases are still in current use. You can still pick up these cases at bargain prices if you are willing to do a little scouting around secondhand stores, junk stores, or flea markets. And once you've got one, it's a cinch to turn it into an office organizer second to none like the one shown above.

Materials
One wooden soft drink case
Spray can lids (to hold paper clips, rubber bands, and other small items)
Adhesive-backed flowers or decals

Directions
1. Stand the soft drink case on end.
2. Apply adhesive backed flowers or decals to the spray can lids.
3. Place cans in various sections of the case.

...⊰ chapter 3 ⊱...

New Flair for Old Furniture

With today's cost of living on the rise, new furnishings created from yesterday's resources are increasingly popular. Whether you have a discarded upright piano or a variety of budget furniture long ago dispatched to the attic, you can turn these pieces into furniture treasures.

Piano Planter

Old instruments often take up valuable space long after they have served their musical function. Here's an idea for salvaging an old, almost-beyond-repair 600-pound upright piano by recycling it into a huge decorative plant holder. And the cost of this piano was only $25.00. The plants come extra.

Materials
Upright piano
Finishing nails
One 2x6-foot piece of ¼-inch
    hardboard
Contact cement
1x2s
One 2x6-foot piece of ¾-inch plywood
White enamel paint

Tools
Screwdriver
Nail-cutting nippers
Saw
Drill
Hammer
Paintbrush

Directions
(**Note:** The directions below leave the sounding board in place. Although removing the sounding board greatly reduces the weight of the planter, it is very difficult to do and may even require beating it to pieces with a sledge hammer. If you remove sounding board, make a wider top shelf and put the 1x2 support along the inside back.)
1. Remove the screws and bolts that hold the piano keys and hammers in place. Lift out the keys and hammers. (See sketch A on page 56.)
2. Fold keyboard cover back. Secure in place with finishing nails.
3. Measure dimensions of the space left at back of keyboard when the keys were removed (see sketch A on page 56).
4. Cut a piece of ¼-inch hardboard to fit vertically in this space. Nail and glue in place. Let dry.

(continued on next page)

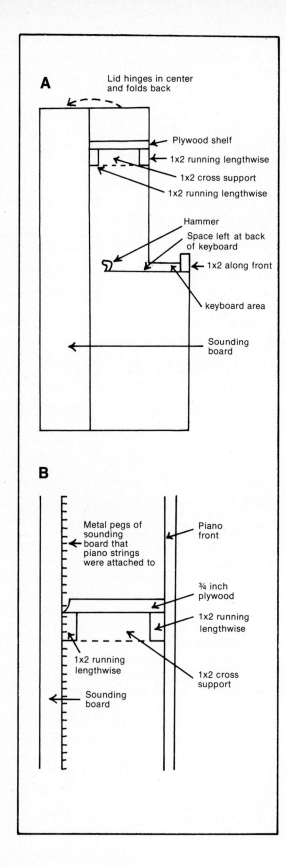

A

Lid hinges in center
and folds back

← Plywood shelf

← 1x2 running lengthwise

1x2 cross support

1x2 running lengthwise

Hammer

Space left at back
of keyboard

← 1x2 along front

keyboard area

Sounding
board

B

Metal pegs of
sounding
← board that
piano strings
were attached to

Piano
front

¾ inch
plywood

1x2 running
lengthwise

1x2 running
lengthwise

1x2 cross
support

Sounding
board

5. Measure length of front of keyboard.

6. Cut 1x2 to fit this length.

7. Nail and glue this 1x2 in place along front, as shown in sketch A. Let dry.

8. Measure length and width of bottom of keyboard area (see sketch A).

9. Cut piece of ¼-inch hardboard to fit these dimensions.

10. Nail and glue hardboard in place to form level bottom. Let dry.

11. Fold piano lid back.

12. Using nail-cutting nippers, cut piano strings and remove them.

13. Measure inside length and width of piano top.

14. Cut a piece of ¾-inch plywood to fit these dimensions.

15. Cut two pieces of 1x2 to fit inside length of piano top.

16. Position one of these 1x2s along inside of piano front eight inches below the surface of piano top. Glue and nail this 1x2 in place. Dry.

17. Position other 1x2 along sounding board eight inches below surface of piano top. (Be sure top of this 1x2 aligns with 1x2 already nailed in place so shelf will sit level.)

18. Tap board with hammer to imprint position of metal pegs on side of 1x2.

19. Remove 1x2 and drill a hole at each imprint so 1x2 will fit snugly over metal pegs.

20. Reposition this 1x2 and hammer until it fits securely over pegs (see sketch B).

21. Nail through ends of piano into ends of this 1x2 to secure it.

22. To add cross supports,

• Measure the distance between the two 1x2s running lengthwise.

• Cut five pieces of 1x2 to fit this length.

• Glue and nail one of these 1x2 pieces at each end of piano. (Be sure these 1x2s align with lengthwise 1x2s so shelf will sit level.) Dry.

• Space remaining three pieces evenly and glue and nail in place. Dry. (Again, align 1x2s.)

23. To fit shelf,

• Position the plywood piece atop the 1x2s.

• Mark position of the metal pegs and cut notches in side of plywood piece so it will fit securely over these pegs.

• Set shelf in position.

24. Paint the planter with white enamel. Let dry thoroughly. Paint with another coat if necessary to cover. Let dry.

Remodeled Dining Set

It seems unlikely that an old, clunky kitchen table would make a good match for graceful ice-cream-parlor style chairs (see photos on page 58). Yet, by redesigning table slightly and having chairs professionally chrome-plated, they are!

Materials
Table
Kitchen table with chrome legs
One 4x8-foot sheet of ¾-inch plywood
Finishing nails
Epoxy
One 4x8-foot sheet of plastic laminate
Contact cement
Chairs
Four metal frame chairs
Remainder of the plywood sheet used for the tabletop or enough ¾-inch plywood for the chair seats
1-inch-thick foam
2 yards of 54-inch-wide vinyl upholstery fabric

(continued on next page)

Tools

Drill
Saber saw
Hammer
Wooden block
Screwdriver or adjustable wrench
File
Electric router with attachment
    designed for trimming plastic laminate
    (optional)
Yardstick
Heavy-duty, industrial-type staple gun

Directions

Table **1.** Disassemble table and discard top. (**Note:** If chrome legs are chipped or rusted, send them along with chairs to be chrome-plated.)
2. Cut the ¾-inch plywood in half crosswise.
3. With a compass, draw a 36-inch circle on one of the plywood pieces. (To make maximum use of the plywood, see steps 3 and 4 of directions for Chairs and fit two chair seats on the same plywood piece as the tabletop. Then, when the two plywood pieces are nailed together, you can cut out one 1½-inch-thick tabletop and four ¾-inch-thick chair seats.) (**Note:** To improvise a compass, put a nail at the 1-inch mark of the yardstick and a pencil in a hole at the 19-inch mark. Fasten nail into plywood and swing yardstick around full circle.)
4. Epoxy and nail the two pieces of plywood together to form a 1½-inch-thick piece. (**Note:**

Since you want to use ¾-inch thickness for chair seats, put epoxy only on the portion of the plywood that's needed for the tabletop.)
5. Cut out the tabletop with a saber saw.
6. Space legs equidistant from each other on tabletop and mark position of leg screws.
7. Drill pilot holes for screws at marks.
8. Screw old table legs to new tabletop.
9. For tabletop edging,
• Cut two 1½-inch-wide strips from the long edge of the 4x8-foot sheet of plastic laminate.
• Fit strips around circumference of tabletop and cut off excess. (You'll use only part of the second plastic strip.)
• Coat the table edge and the back of the edging strips with contact cement. Let the surfaces dry to tackiness.
• Position strips and then press in place by tapping with a hammer against a wooden block. (Be sure to place the laminate in the correct position the first time, since once it touches it is firmly set.) Let dry.
• File top edge so it is flush with plywood top.
10. For tabletop,
• Cut a plastic laminate circle 1 inch larger than the plywood top.
• Apply contact cement to the plywood top and the laminated plastic circle. Let both of the surfaces dry to tackiness.
• Spread waxed paper on the tabletop surface to keep laminate and plywood from adhering before you get them positioned accurately.

A

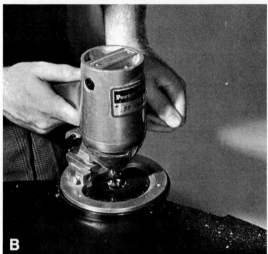

B

C

• Position laminate atop plywood.
• Ease out waxed paper, a piece at a time, and press laminate into place (see photo A).
• Trim overhanging edge of laminate by filing at an angle or, to simplify the job, rent an electric router with an attachment for trimming plastic laminate (see photo B).

Chairs **1.** Remove seats from chairs.
2. Have the metal chair frames and all bolts chrome-plated. (If the original bolts are missing, replace them with ¾-inch-long wood screws and have these chrome-plated also.) (You'll find chrome plating listed in the telephone book Yellow Pages either under "plating" or "metal finishing".)
3. Make paper pattern from old chair seats. (If seats are missing, measure diameter of chair seat space and make pattern. The average seat is about 15 inches in diameter.)
4. Cut seats from ¾-inch plywood. (If seats are average size, you should be able to cut four seats from the sheet of plywood used for tabletop—see step 3 of directions for Table. If seats won't fit on this sheet, you'll need additional ¾-inch plywood for the seats.)
• Position pattern on plywood. Trace around it.
• Reposition pattern and trace around it for remaining seats.
• Cut out seats with saber saw.
5. Upholster chair seats:
• Using pattern, cut a piece of the foam for each seat. (If chair seat rims have top flanges, fit foam into metal frame and taper foam edges so they fit under flanges better.)
• Add 8 inches to the diameter of chair seat and cut a circular paper pattern this size.
• Using larger pattern, cut a piece of vinyl upholstery fabric for each chair.
• For each seat, place foam atop plywood seat and cover with one of the vinyl pieces.
• Pull edges of vinyl to underside of seat and staple as shown in photo C.
6. Reassemble the chairs:
• Push vinyl-covered seat into position in metal seat frame. (If chair has flanges, make sure seat fits securely against flange.)
• Secure seat by replacing original bolts. (If original bolts are missing, use ¾-inch-long wood screws inserted through original holes in frame and screwed into side of plywood seat.)

Handwoven Furniture

The exotic, exquisitely woven furniture pictured here was salvaged from garage sales, second-hand shops, and an attic. You can restore old, worn-out furniture in this practical way by learning an old craft called Punjabi or Indian bed weaving. It's basically a combination of weaving and crochet in which you use the furniture frame as the loom for your work.

Materials
Rustic chair (shown at right)
    66 yards 7-ply red macramé jute
    66 yards 7-ply natural macramé jute
    Silicone fabric protector
Stool (shown at left)
    55 yards yellow cotton macramé seine cord
    43 yards red cotton macramé seine cord
    30 yards green 3-ply macramé jute
    Emerald green exterior paint
    Silicone fabric protector
Wicker rocking chair (shown at left)
    150 yards of No. 30 yellow cotton macramé cord
    150 yards red 3-ply macramé jute
    Semigloss polyurethane varnish
    Silicone fabric protector

Tools
    Two sturdy metal crochet hooks (large enough to handle your cord—H, I, and J work well)
    Fork
    Pair of scissors for cutting wicker
    Steel wool
    Wood cleaner wax
    Paintbrush

Directions
General directions (**Note:** The yardages given in the materials list are those required for the size furniture shown.)

1. To estimate the yardage needed to fit the specific furniture you choose,
- Lay jute or cord you are using side by side and measure how many cords there are in an inch.
- Measure the length and width of the furniture's frame and then add enough to these dimensions to allow for a loop under the frame.
- Multiply this figure by the number of cords you

figured per inch and then divide by 36 to give the yardage figure.

2. When tying in a new ball of cord, tie a loose overhand knot and leave long tail ends. (When weaving is completed, you'll undo the knots and weave in the tail ends.) (**Note:** Use large balls of cord in order to have fewer knots in your work.)

3. Choose tightly wrapped cords that will not fray. If you are using colors, be sure to purchase colorfast cord. (**Note:** In a two-color pattern woven on a rectangular frame, the color wrapped along the long side of the frame will appear dominant.)

4. To begin the weave, place the frame and the ball of cord in front of you. Take the strand of cord to the back left-hand corner and tie securely, leaving a tail on the knot. (You now have one strand running across the frame with the ball in front of you.)

5. Take the cord back across the frame. Pass the cord under the frame and bring up a loop on the left side of the strand running across the top. Put the crochet hook through the loop to hold it (see drawing A on page 62). (**Note:** The front of the frame appears at left side of sketch and the back of frame appears at right side.)

6. Bring the cord back under the frame and across the top. Carry a double strand of cord

(continued on next page)

to the back of the frame. (**Note:** The ball of cord remains in front of you.)

7. Take the double strand over the top of the frame and under, bringing up a loop to the left of the tied cord. Secure with the second crochet hook as shown in drawing B. (**Note:** When making this loop, pull on cord that is secured to opposite side of frame. This makes one side of loop tight while the cord coming from the ball is loose. As you continue working back across frame, pull loose cord to tighten it before you make another loop. This will keep cords firm and even in the frame.)

8. Bring the cord back over and under the front of the frame. Catch a loop of cord with the crochet hook (see drawing C). Bring this loop across the three strands of cord and through the loop already on the hook. Leave the crochet hook in the loop.

9. Bring the cord back over the top of the frame; take a double strand over and under the back of frame (see drawing D).

10. Pull up another loop and bring it across three strands and through the loop on the hook. Leave the hook in loop (see drawing E).

11. Continue in this manner, as shown in drawings E and F. Each subsequent time bring a loop across two strands. Watch to make sure the cords lie flat over the frame, as shown in drawing G. Do not twist across one another.

12. When the frame is filled, fasten off the front corner by pulling the cord through the loop and cutting, leaving a tail. (Be sure to leave the hook in the back right loop.)

Directions for weaving in pattern　**1.** Turn the frame so the crocheted edges are to your right and left, with the crochet hook that was left in place positioned at your right hand. Tie end of contrasting color of cord onto frame right in front of you, making knot beside hook as shown in photo A on page 64.

2. With your fingers separating the cords, work a double strand of cord over and under the number of cords that correspond to your pattern. (Use photo A as a guide.) (**Note:** If your pattern needs to be centered, count the cords in order to locate the middle.)

3. Think in groups of twos. If there is an uneven number of cords in your first color, work a group of three at the edge.

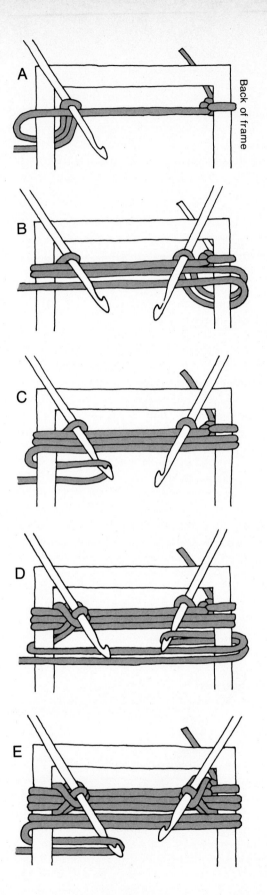

Back of frame

A

B

C

D

E

62

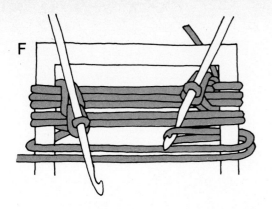

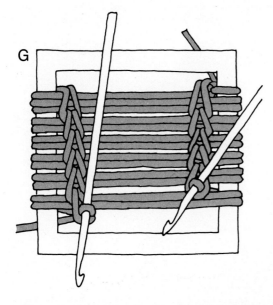

4. Insert another crochet hook in first stitch at other end of crocheted row that already has hook in it. When you have woven double strand completely across the frame, fold cord in a loop and pull it through loop on hook. Leave hook in place (see photo B on page 64).

5. Pull this loop tight and then pull up a loop in the same manner with the hook positioned just in front of you. (**Note:** Both ends of this double woven strand have now been crocheted securely onto the frame.

6. Continue looping the cord over and under the frame and crocheting the cord in place as before (see drawing H on page 64). (Keep strands tight and keep crochet loops loose enough to get through easily. This is especially important when the furniture frame is contoured.)

7. Pack tightly or loosely space the cords to get pattern to fit frame that you have selected. To save wear and tear on your fingers, use a fork for pushing cords in place against one another

(see photo C on page 64).

8. Leave ball of cord on your side of weaving and leave crochet hooks in place at either end till weaving is done (see photo D on page 64).

9. To correct a mistake, unfasten one loop at a time from the crochet hook and pull out the row or rows back to the mistake. Then, just simply reweave.

10. When only a few inches of weaving are left, it is difficult to separate the cords with your fingers, so use another crochet hook or hairpin to help get the cords through.

11. When weaving is completed, fasten off one corner by pulling the cord through the loop and cutting it, leaving a tail.

12. Pull the tail of the last loop of contrasting color through the other loop and pull till tight. Then, work all loose tails into the weaving, using a crochet hook. (Take care that these ends do not show on the right side of the weaving.)

13. To finish and strengthen the weaving, undo any knots and weave in the ends.

14. Cover the finished weaving with a heavy coating of silicone fabric protector.

Rustic chair (**Note:** This pattern is a good beginning project.) **1.** Remove the chair's seat and back, leaving frames of seat and back intact.

2. Remove any protruding nails.

3. Use steel wool on any rough spots.

4. Clean the frame of the chair with wood cleaner wax to keep the natural look.

5. For the weave of the rustic chair, follow the general directions above.

6. Consult the rustic chair pattern guide on page 65 for a guide on the weaving pattern.

Stool (see pattern guides on page 65) **1.** Clean, sand, then paint the stool with two coats of exterior paint. Let dry.

2. Wrap and crochet the yellow cord lengthwise, as instructed in general directions.

3. Start the pattern in red cord, packing tightly with fork.

4. When the red portion is completed, tie on the green cord.

5. Rather than cut the red cord, run the cord along the underside of the frame and wrap the green cord over the red strand until you are ready to begin the next sequence. (Tie red cord to leg temporarily to keep it out of the way.)

(continued on next page)

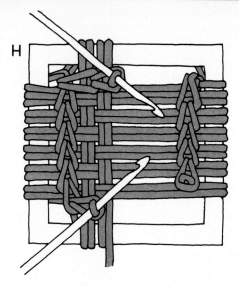

Do the same with the green cord while doing the next sequence of red pattern.

Wicker rocking chair (see pattern guides on page 65)   **1.** Carefully remove the wicker trim so that you can use it later. Remove the seat, the back, and the nails.
2. Carefully cut the wicker on the arms back to the first vertical support for weaving.
3. Wrap and crochet the cut ends with red jute to give finished appearance.
4. Clean the frame and cover with polyurethane varnish to renew and protect finish.
5. Wrap the corners of seat frame with cord to

RUSTIC CHAIR

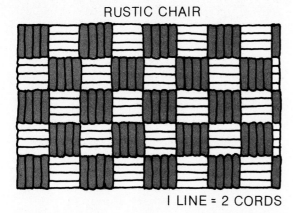

I LINE = 2 CORDS

ROCKING CHAIR

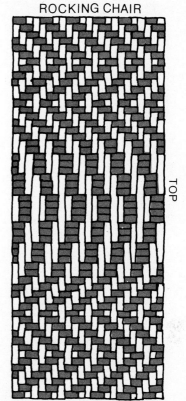

TOP

BACK

STOOL

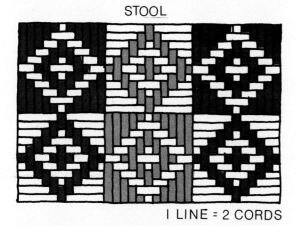

I LINE = 2 CORDS

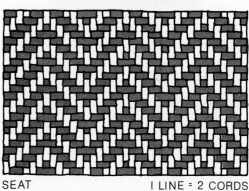

SEAT   I LINE = 2 CORDS

give a mitered effect before weaving.

6. Find the middle of your piece and count so the waves are balanced on each side.

7. Wrap and crochet the red jute from side to side, and weave the yellow cord from front to back. (This will make points of waves run from front to back; reverse for waves on their sides.)

8. When all weaving is completed, replace the wicker trim.

seating function. Combine their parts as shown here to make an attractive plant stand.

Materials
    Bentwood chair parts:
        Two chair backs (back legs included with back)
        One seat frame (with cane or wooden seat removed)
        One chair round
        Two curved wooden supports
    Paste wood filler
    12 ¾-inch wood screws (No. 6)
    Varnish
    Glass or Plexiglas (cut to fit top of seat frame)

Tools
    Drill
    Screwdriver
    Paintbrush

Directions
1. Use wood filler to fill in the screw holes on the chair backs where the original seats were located. (You'll be setting the seat up higher for the shelf.) Let dry completely.
2. Measure 6 inches above these original seat holes.
3. Drill two holes into the back of each chair at this higher location.
4. Screw the back of both chairs to the same seat frame at this higher level (see photo).
5. Screw the backs of both chairs to the same chair round, using the original holes.
6. To support the seat frame,
• Position the curved supports at opposite corners of the stand (see photo).
• Mark location of supports on chair back (here about midway between the chair round and the seat frame) and on seat frame.
• Drill a hole into the chair back at the mark and a hole into the seat frame at the mark.
• Screw on the supports at these locations.
7. Sand the assembled chair unit. Dust thoroughly before proceeding to the next step.
8. Give the plant stand two coats of varnish. Let dry after each coat. (The varnish protects the surface and brings out the wood's natural beauty as well.)
9. Position glass or Plexiglas.

Bentwood Chair Plant Stand

When you find bentwood chairs with missing parts in antique and secondhand stores, don't pass them up simply because they have lost their

Dresser Top Headboard

Often, seemingly minor changes can drastically affect the look of something. Here, an ordinary twin-size headboard takes on great importance in this child's room with the inexpensive addition of a decorative piece from an old dresser. Note how antiquing the two parts of the unit the same color unifies them.

Materials
- Bed headboard
- Dresser top with elaborate trim
- Two molly bolts
- Antiquing kit

Tools
- Liquid sander

Directions
1. Remove the trim or molding from the top of an old dresser. Discard remaining parts.
2. Antique the dresser top and the bed headboard to match, following these general steps:

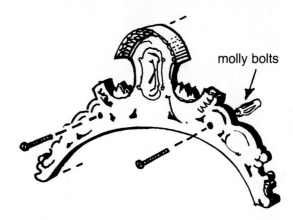

molly bolts

• Apply liquid sander. Let set number of minutes specified on the back of the container, then wipe off.
• Apply one or two coats of undercoat paint. Let dry after each coat.
• Paint on the glaze.
• Wipe off the glaze until you achieve the results you want.
3. Center the dresser trim or molding above the bed headboard and fasten to the wall with molly bolts, as shown in the drawing.

Converted Nightstand

Study all the design possibilities of your outdated furniture before discarding them. These coffee tables, for example, are actually the redesigned offspring of a golden oak-finished nightstand, which represents the popular style of the fifties. The real charm of this project is that you turn one piece of furniture into two. Look for outdated pieces such as this nightstand at secondhand stores and garage sales.

Materials
Nightstand or end table similar
    to the one illustrated in the
    photograph at right
1½ yards upholstery vinyl fabric
One quart vinyl wallpaper paste

Tools

Saber saw or circular saw
C-clamps
Stiff bristle brush
Craft knife
Straight piece of lumber

Directions

1. Cut the nightstand apart to make two pieces. (To ensure an accurate cut, clamp the lumber piece to the table as shown in photograph A.)

2. To make the two pieces the same height,

• Measure height of shorter piece and mark on taller piece. (To minimize splintering, put masking tape down, draw your line, and cut through the tape.)

• Cut off legs of taller piece at marks.

3. To cover tables with vinyl,

• Fit vinyl around tables and drawer front, cutting as necessary but keeping seams to a minimum.

• Brush the paste on one surface at a time.

• Lay on the vinyl.

• Starting at center and working toward edges, work out air bubbles as shown in photo B.

• Fold the sides under so that all the edges meet inconspicuously on the underside.

• Miter each corner by overlapping the vinyl from the side and top then cutting through both layers at a 45° angle as shown in photo C. Lift the top layer, remove cut-off piece underneath, and lay top layer back.

When to use what adhesives	
White glues	Use for general repairs and woodworking jobs when waterproof bond is not necessary.
Contact cements	Use for gluing plastic foam, hardboard, and metal to wood; not good for furniture building.
Epoxy adhesives	Use for waterproof bonds in general repairs and metal to metal bonds.

Artistic Armoire

Since it is an everlasting challenge to find a place to store everything, consider this decorative solution. At first glance, the chest may seem overpowering, but properly decorated, it becomes a good-looking piece of furniture.

Materials
Old armoire
Wood filler
White latex paint
One set of wallpaper graphic panels
Wallpaper pasting kit
Clear plastic varnish

70

Tools

Medium-grade sandpaper
Liquid sander
Wallpaper smoothing brush
Utility knife
Scissors
Pry bar
Paintbrushes

Directions

1. If armoire has split turnings at the sides of the doors, pry them off.

2. Fill in any decorative grooves on armoire with wood filler, as shown in photo A. Let dry completely before proceeding.

3. Sand the filler until smooth.

4. Apply liquid sander to entire unit. Wipe off as directed on label.

5. Apply two coats of white paint to both the inside and outside of the armoire. Let dry completely between coats.

6. Lay out wallpaper panels and decide how you want to position panels on armoire. (Wallpaper graphics include a scale drawing to help you plot out exactly where each element of the overall design will fall.)

7. Wallpaper the armoire:

• Spread out the first big panel.

• Brush plenty of wallpaper paste over the panel. (Let panel soak up paste well so that it is good and limp.)

• Fit the panel onto armoire in one piece, covering doors, moldings, and hinges, as shown in photograph B.

• Use a wallpaper smoothing brush to help work out wrinkles and bubbles.

• Use the utility knife to slice away any part of the paper that won't fit into or around a molding; let white undercoating show.

• Continue pasting on panels until entire armoire is covered. (**Note:** Seams of mural panels are designed by the manufacturers to overlap an inch or so for a smoother fit.)

8. Cut out openings for doors, moldings, and hinges with utility knife, as shown in photo C.

9. If you have extra wallpaper panels in the set, line the inside, using the same papering procedures as in step 7 above. Let stand for two days before proceeding.

10. Cover the wallpaper with a coat of clear plastic varnish. Let dry.

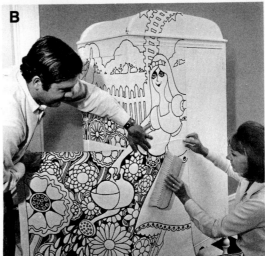

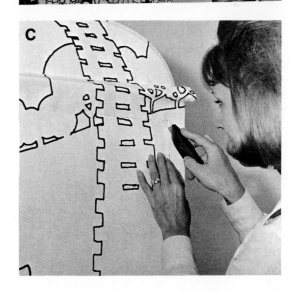

Fashionable Cushioned Chairs

Even on a limited budget, it is possible to furnish a room beautifully by just combining your imagination with some select throwaways. In this case, a dingy three-piece sectional couch, which was high style in the fifties, is updated into three chairs that reflect today's furniture tastes. As an added new touch, sunburst pillows replace the common square back cushions.

Materials
Chair frames
    Three-piece sectional couch, such as the
        one shown in photo at right
    Neutral wood filler
    Wood stain (optional)
    Varnish, shellac, or lacquer

Sunburst pillow (for each pillow)
    Round pillow form
    Two large pillow buttons
    Strong carpet or button thread
    Fabric for pillow cover (determine amount
        needed from size of pillow form—*see
        steps 1 and 3 for pillow on page 73)*
    Muslin fabric (determine amount needed

72

from size of pillow form—see steps 1 and 2 for pillow directions)

1-inch-wide white trim (length determined by pillow dimensions)

Box-edge cushion (for each cushion)

Box-edge cushion form (use the original one if it is in good condition)

Fabric for cushion cover (determine amount needed from dimensions of cushion form —see steps 1 and 4 for cushion on page 74) (lightweight fabric won't wear well)

Muslin fabric (same amount as cushion cover fabric yardage—see steps 1 and 2 for cushion on page 74)

Zipper (4 inches shorter than ½ of cushion form perimeter)

Two pieces ⅛-inch cable cord (each cut to fit around cushion form perimeter plus 2 inches for seam allowances)

Tools
Chair frames
Medium- and fine-grade sandpaper
Paint remover
Paintbrush
Screwdriver
Sunburst pillow and box-edge cushion
Crewel needle
Sewing machine with cording or zipper foot

Directions
Chair frames **1.** Unscrew the side arms of couch and discard them.

2. With paint remover, strip off the finish of couch.

3. Fill the screw holes where the arms were with neutral wood filler. Let dry.

4. Sand the entire couch with medium-grade sandpaper, then sand with fine-grade sandpaper until smooth. Dust the wood.

5. Stain wood, if desired. Let dry completely before proceeding to next step.

6. Apply one coat varnish, shellac, or lacquer. Let dry.

Sunburst pillow (for each pillow) **1.** Determine the diameter of the pillow form:

• Measure from the center of top of the pillow form to the center of side of pillow form.

• Double this measurement.

2. Cover the pillow form with a muslin casing:

• Cut two circular pieces of muslin the diameter of the pillow form plus 1 inch for seam allowances.

• With right sides together, stitch around the muslin sections, making a ½-inch seam (be sure to leave large enough opening for inserting the pillow form).

• Notch seam allowance as shown in sketch A on page 135.

• Turn casing right side out and press seam.

• Insert the pillow form.

• Turn edges of opening to inside and stitch together by hand or machine.

3. To begin the outside cover of the pillow,

• Cut two strips of fabric on the true bias. (The true bias is the diagonal of a square. To determine this, fold material as shown in sketch D on page 136. The folded edge is the true bias.) The length of each strip should be 3½ times diameter of form plus 1 inch for seam allowances; the width should be ½ the diameter plus 1 inch for seam allowances.

• Position 1-inch-wide white trim on right side of one of these strips, placing trim 2 inches from one edge.

• Pin trim in place.

• Sew trim in place by stitching as close as possible to each edge of trim. (If sewing machine has zigzag, use zigzag stitching. Use white thread to match trim.)

• Stitch the ends of each strip together by placing the right sides together and lapping the ends so that the strips form a right angle, as shown in sketch E on page 136. Stitch on the straight grain; press the seam open.

• Using machine basting stitch, sew ¼ inch from one edge on each piece (on piece with trim, sew around edge furthest from trim). Then sew another line of stitching ¼ inch from first stitching.

• To gather each piece, gently pull top threads as shown in sketch B on page 135. Continue pulling thread until material is gathered in sunburst, as shown in sketch C on page 135.

• Pull the center raw edge to the wrong side of the gathered material and secure the gathering by tying knots in the thread.

• Using heavy-duty thread, sew circle around center about ⅛ inch from the center, as shown in sketch C on page 135.

4. To join the gathered sections,

• Place them right sides together, aligning edges.

(continued on next page)

- Pin in place and notch the seam allowances as necessary to keep the seam lying flat.
- Stitch around the gathered sections, making a ½-inch seam (be sure to leave large enough opening for inserting the pillow form).

5. Turn the pillow cover right side out.

6. Insert the pillow form.

7. Turn edges of opening to inside and stitch together by hand.

8. Sew on center buttons, using a crewel needle and strong carpet or button thread. (If desired, use matching fabric-covered buttons.)
- Push the needle up through the pillow, leaving a 3-inch tail of thread hanging.
- Run the needle through the button shank on the top of the pillow, as shown in sketch J (bottom left) on page 137.
- Direct the needle back through the pillow about ⅛ inch from the thread.
- Run the needle through the shank of the second button on the bottom.
- Run the needle and thread through the shanks and pillow two or three more times.
- Draw the thread taut and tie securely to the 3-inch tail of thread so the knot is under the button. Cut off the thread ends.

Box-edge cushions (for each cushion) **1.** Determine measurements needed for cushion casing and cushion cover:
- Measure length of box-edge cushion form (measurement A).
- Measure width of form (measurement B).
- Measure depth of form (measurement C).
- Measure perimeter of cushion form (measurement D). (You can determine this measurement by adding measurement A to measurement B and then doubling this figure.)

2. Cut pieces for muslin casing:
- For casing top and bottom, cut two rectangular pieces of muslin as long as measurement A plus 1 inch for seam allowances and as wide as measurement B plus 1 inch for seam allowances.
- For boxing strip, cut piece of muslin the length of measurement D plus 1 inch for seam allowances and the width of measurement C plus 1 inch for seam allowances.

3. To make muslin cushion casing,
- With right sides together, pin muslin top to muslin boxing strip, easing boxing strip as needed to fit at corners. (**Note:** Position ends of boxing strip in center of one side of muslin top. Leave ends free to allow for seam.)
- Stitch around the pinned sections, making a ½-inch seam. Remove pins.
- With right sides together, stitch ends of boxing strip together, making a ½-inch seam. (**Note:** Seam may be slightly wider or narrower as needed to fit boxing strip to muslin top.)
- With right sides together, pin muslin bottom to boxing strip.
- Stitch around pinned sections, making ½-inch seam (be sure to leave large enough opening for inserting cushion form). Remove pins.
- Turn the muslin cushion casing right side out and press the seams.
- Insert the cushion form.
- Turn edges of opening to inside and stitch together by hand or machine.

4. Cut pieces for outside cushion cover:
- For the cushion cover top and bottom, cut two rectangular pieces of cushion cover fabric as long as measurement A plus 1 inch for seam allowances and as wide as measurement B plus 1 inch for seam allowances.
- For boxing strip, cut three pieces, each measuring as long as ½ measurement D plus 4 inches for seam allowances and as wide as measurement C plus 1 inch for seam allowances.

5. Cover the cable cord with a bias strip of cushion cover fabric. (Continuous bias is the best method to use when you need several yards of bias strips—see tip box on page 137.)
- Cut two 1½-inch-wide bias strips of fabric. Length of strips should be measurement D plus 2 inches for seam allowance. (If not using continuous bias, sew bias pieces together to give desired length—see sketch E on page 136.)
- Fold bias strip around one length of cable cord (cut to same length as bias strip), right side out, encasing it completely. Align raw edges of bias strip.
- Using an adjustable cording or zipper foot, stitch close to cable cord, without crowding it. (Stretch the bias slightly as you are stitching it over the cord.)
- Repeat with remaining bias strip and length of cord.

6. Insert zipper in boxing strip:
- Fold two of the three boxing strip pieces in half lengthwise, right sides out. Align raw edges. Press at fold.
- Unfold the two pieces and place them right

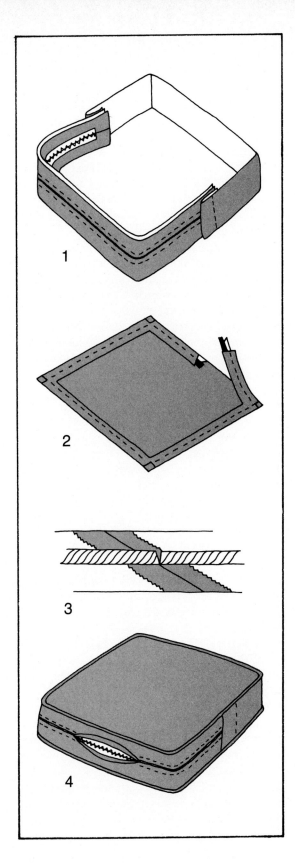

1

2

3

4

sides together, matching fold lines.
• Stitch the two pieces together along fold line, using machine basting stitch.
• Press seam open.
• Insert zipper following directions given on zipper package.
• Remove basting stitches.
7. Complete boxing strip (see sketch 1):
• Turn under 2 inches on ends of remaining boxing strip piece.
• Lap these ends over the ends of the zippered piece of boxing strip.
• Stitch 1½ inches from fold, sewing through all four thicknesses.
8. Sew cording in place:
• Position one length of the fabric-covered cable cord on right side of cushion cover top, aligning raw edge of fabric-covered cord with edge of cushion cover top (see sketch 2).
• Pin in place and clip at corners to fit.
• Stitch along seam line of cording. Leave several inches of cording free at either end so you can join it. Remove pins.
• Join ends of bias strip with seam on straight grain of fabric, as shown in sketch 3.
• Cut cord so ends just meet. Fold the bias strip over the cord and finish sewing to the edge of cushion cover top.
• Repeat with the other length of fabric-covered cord and the cushion cover bottom.
9. To complete cushion cover (see sketch 4),
• Place boxing strip and cushion cover top right sides together, aligning edges.
• Pin in place and clip at corners to fit.
• Stitch together, following seam line of cording. Remove pins.
• With right sides together, stitch ends of boxing strip together, making ½-inch seam. (**Note:** Seam may be slightly wider or narrower as needed to fit boxing strip to cover top.)
• Turn right side out and press.
• Open zipper.
• Place other edge of the boxing strip and the cushion cover bottom right sides together, aligning edges.
• Pin in place and clip at corners to fit.
• Stitch together following seam line of cording. Remove pins.
• Turn cover right side out and press.
10. Insert cushion form in cushion cover and close zipper.

Customized Lawn Chair

Before sending "outdated" outdoor furniture to the dump, analyze the design features of the pieces. Think of a way to put these furnishings to other uses. Here, a metal lawn chair was converted for comfortable indoor use through padding and vinyl upholstery.

Materials
Metal lawn chair
Brown paper (to make pattern)
2 yards 54-inch-wide crushed vinyl fabric
1-inch-thick foam padding
⅛-inch cable cord
1x2s
One 3x3-foot piece of ¼-inch plywood
1-inch-long flathead wood screws
Finishing nails
Chrome-head upholstery tacks

Tools
Hammer
Screwdriver
Sewing machine with cording
  or zipper foot attachment.
Electric drill with countersinking drill bit
Heavy-duty industrial-type stapler
Saber saw

Directions
1. Disassemble chair.
2. Have tubular leg unit and heads of bolts used to fasten legs to chair rechromed at chrome-plating works. (You'll find chrome-plating service listed the in telephone book Yellow Pages under "plating" or "metal finishing.")
3. To make patterns,
• Lay chair seat upside down on brown paper and trace around seat. Cut out. (Pattern 1)
• Trace around chair back. Cut out. (Pattern 2)
4. Measure for boxing strips:
• Measure perimeter of chair seat and add 2 inches for seam allowance (measurement 1).
• Measure perimeter of chair back and add 2 inches for seam allowance (measurement 2).
5. Cut vinyl pieces:
• Cut one seat cover piece, using pattern 1 and adding ¾ inch for seam allowances.
• Cut three back cover pieces, using pattern 2 and adding ¾ inch for seam allowances.
• Cut one seat boxing strip 8 inches wide and the length of measurement 1.
• Cut one boxing strip 8 inches wide and the length of measurement 2.
6. Cut two pieces of cable cord—one the length of measurement 1 and one the length of measurement 2.
7. Cover both lengths of cable cord with a bias strip of vinyl according to the directions given in step 5 of Box-edge cushions on page 74.
8. To sew cording in place,
• Position the measurement one length of vinyl-covered cord on the right side of the seat cover vinyl piece. Align raw edges (see sketch 2 on page 75).
• Paper clip in place and clip at corners to fit. (Do not use pins, since they leave holes.)
• Stitch along seam line of cording. Leave several inches of cording free at either end so you can join it. Remove paper clips.
• Join ends of bias strip with seam on straight grain of fabric, as shown in sketch 3 on page 75.
• Cut cord so ends just meet. Fold the bias strip over the cord and finish sewing.

• Repeat with the other length of vinyl-covered cord and one of the back cover vinyl pieces.

9. Sew on boxing strips:

• Place seat boxing strip and seat cover right sides together, aligning edges.

• Paper clip to hold in place and clip at corners to fit.

• Stitch together, following seam line of cording. Remove paper clips.

• Right sides together, stitch ends of boxing strip together, making a 1-inch seam. (**Note:** Seam may be slightly wider or narrower as needed to fit boxing strip to seat cover.)

• Turn right side out.

• Repeat with remaining boxing strip and the corded back cover piece.

10. Position remaining two back cover pieces right sides together, aligning edges. Paper clip to hold in place.

11. Stitch around these pieces, making ½-inch seam. Leave bottom edge open. Turn the vinyl cover right side out.

12. Fit back side of chair seat and chair back with 1x2 frame:

• Measure dimensions of inside of seat and back rims.

• Use the saber saw to contour-cut the 1x2 pieces to fit inside rims, as shown in photograph A. (Leave spaces where leg unit bolts onto chair seat and back.)

13. To attach 1x2s to chair,

• Drill holes through side of chair rim and into 1x2 at both ends of each 1x2 piece. (Use countersinking drill bit so screw head will fit flush with surface and thus avoid poking through the vinyl.)

• Secure 1x2s in place with wood screws.

14. To cut the foam padding,

• Cut seat padding piece, using pattern 1.

• Cut back padding piece using pattern 2.

15. To cover seat,

• Place seat padding atop seat.

• Fit seat cover over padding and seat.

• Staple boxing strip to 1x2 frame as shown in photograph B. (While stapling, gently tug and stretch cover to eliminate wrinkles.)

16. To cover back,

• Position back padding on chair back.

• Position back as it attaches to seat and trim back padding so there's no padding where chair pieces overlap. (**Note:** For neater fit, taper back padding at bottom.)

• Fit back cover over padding and back.

• Staple boxing strip to 1x2 frame.

17. Bolt the chair seat and back together.

18. Reattach the rechromed leg unit.

19. To finish the chair back,

• With saber saw cut piece of ¼-inch plywood, using pattern 2.

• Fit the remaining vinyl cover over plywood.

• Turn bottom raw edges to inside and hand-stitch closed.

• Position vinyl-covered plywood on back of chair back.

• Nail around edge, nailing through plywood and into 1x2s.

• Cover nail heads with chrome tacks. (Offset tacks slightly to avoid nails.)

Macramé Sling Chair

Although sling chairs have provided comfortable seating for many years, they have not always had a strong decorating role. Now, combine both function and beauty by using your macramé skill to fashion a sturdy and decorative sling seat for an old chair like the one shown here.

Materials
    Sling chair
    Paint (optional)
    8 spools of number 72 nylon seine twine
        (63 yards per spool)

Tools
    Paintbrush (optional)
    Scissors
    Rubber bands
    Long-nosed pliers
    Needle with large eye (candlewick needle
        or tufting needle)
    Awl

Directions
(**Note:** The cord lengths given are for an average-size chair frame such as the one shown in the photograph at left.)

1. Remove chair's original sling seat and discard it before starting the macramé.

2. If desired, paint the chair frame. Let dry before proceeding.

3. Cut twine (a total of 40 cords):
- Cut two pieces of twine 51 feet long.
- Cut 38 pieces of twine 36 feet long.

4. Fold the 51-foot cords so one side is 33 feet long and the other 18 feet long.

5. Attach these cords to the far left and right ends of the chair frame's top bar:
- Position the 33-foot lengths on outer edges.
- Tie cords onto bar with lark's head knots (see sketch of lark's head knot on page 80).

6. Fold the remaining 38 cords in half (each half will be 18 feet in length) and use lark's head knots to mount them between the two cords already on top bar of chair.

7. To make cord easier to work with, roll each cord about halfway up and secure with a rubber band. (Unroll cord as length is needed.)

8. Using the left-hand 33-foot-long cord as knot-bearing cord for double half hitches, work one row of horizontal double half hitches across the chair (see sketch of horizontal double half hitch on page 80).

9. Work another row of horizontal double half hitches back across the chair, using the right-hand 33-foot cord as knot-bearing cord.

10. Starting from left side, use the first four cords to make a sinnet consisting of four square knots with filler cords (see sketch of square knot with two filler cords on page 80). (**Note:** A sinnet is a series of knots tied to form a vertical column.) Repeat to form sinnets all across chair.

11. Knot three rows of alternating square knots (see sketch of alternating square knot on page 80). (**Note:** The outer two cords on each side will be loose on the first and third rows but worked into second row.)

12. Repeat step 10.

13. Repeat pattern as detailed in steps 8 through 12 until overall length is long enough to fit chair frame (45 inches was needed for the chair shown here). (See page 80 for detailed pattern layout.)

14. End work with two rows of horizontal double half hitches as directed in steps 8 and 9.

15. Cut off cord ends to length of 18 inches.

16. Remove lower seat bar from chair frame. Then, turn the work upside down and place the lower seat bar over all the cord ends.

17. To attach sling to this seat bar,
- Starting at left edge, bring two cords up over the seat bar.
- Using right cord of these two cords, pass cord over bar, bring it back around the two cords on front of work, and then pass it out on the left side to the back of the work.
- Repeat with left cord over bar, around two cords on front, and out right side to back.
- Tie these two cords together at the back with a square knot.
- Repeat with remaining cords until all are attached to lower seat bar.

18. Run cord ends well back into work to be sure the seat will hold:
- Thread cord into the large eye of either a candlewick or tufting needle.
- Use an awl to make a path for the needle, and a pair of long-nosed pliers to help pull the needle through. Pull tight.
- Repeat with remaining cords.
- Cut off excess cord.

19. Reposition lower seat bar in chair frame.

(continued on next page)

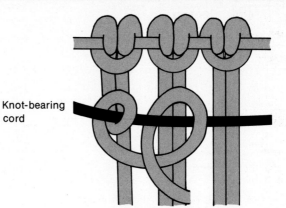

Knot-bearing
cord

Lark's head knot

Horizontal double half hitch

Square knot with two filler cords

Alternating square knot

PATTERN FOR MACRAMÉ CHAIR SEAT

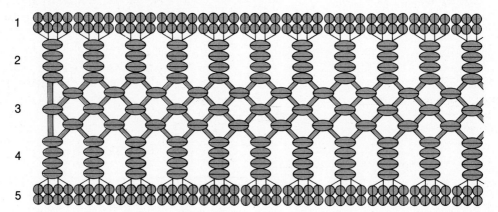

1
2
3
4
5

1 Two rows—Horizontal double half hitch
2 Four rows—Square knot sinnets
3 Three rows—Alternating square knots
4 Four rows—Square knot sinnets
5 Two rows—Horizontal double half hitch

Hospital Bed Sofa

Here's definitive evidence that it is possible to convert a bed once used for strictly practical purposes into attractive as well as comfortable seating without altering any of the basic lines of the bed. The transformation was accomplished with the aid of bold fabrics, paint, and bolster pillows.

Materials
Old metal hospital bed
Eight ⅜-inch machine bolts (length
   determined by bed used)
Enamel paint
Primer for metal
¾-inch plywood
1x2s

(continued on next page)

Finishing nails
Foam mattress to fit bed
Two rectangular bolster pillow forms
Two round bolster pillow forms
Patterned upholstery fabric (measurements
   of mattress and pillow forms determine
   the amount needed)
Muslin for mattress casing
Five zippers (one for mattress and one for
   each pillow—use zippers that are 2 inches
   shorter than the side they are being
   inserted in)
⅛-inch cable cord
Solid color upholstery material (optional)

Tools
Hacksaw
Cold chisel
Heavy hammer
Electric drill
Adjustable wrench
Coarse- and fine-grade sandpaper
Sewing machine with cording or zipper foot

Directions
1. To convert bed frame to sofa frame,
• Use cold chisel and hammer to break brackets off legs of headboard. (These brackets are used to hold side rails of bed frame.) Save brackets for reuse.
• Cut the legs of headboard off with hacksaw so height of headboard matches height of footboard (see photograph at right).
• Measure the distance from the side-rail brackets on the footboard to the floor.
• Mark headboard legs to correspond to this measurement.
• Drill holes through legs at these marks to accommodate machine bolts.
• Fasten brackets to legs with machine bolts. Place side rails in position.
2. Sand all the rough spots on the sofa frame by first using the coarse-grade sandpaper, then sand the entire area with fine-grade sandpaper feathering the chipped areas so they blend smoothly. Dust thoroughly.
3. To paint the sofa frame,
• Primer the frame. Let dry.
• Paint frame with two coats of enamel. Let dry after each coat.
4. Make plywood platform:

• Cut piece of ¼-inch plywood to fit frame.
• Cut four 1x2 pieces to fit across width of plywood piece.
• Nail one of the 1x2 pieces across each end of the plywood piece.
• Space the remaining two 1x2 pieces evenly between the end 1x2s and nail in place.
• Position platform on sofa frame.
5. Cover the foam mattress with patterned box-edge cushion cover, following directions for Box-edge cushions on page 74. (Use zipper that's 2 inches shorter than width of mattress, so in step 6, sew the part of seam not occupied by zipper with regular stitches instead of basting stitches.)
(**Note:** If desired, match effect shown in photo by using solid color fabric to cover cable cord, as directed in step 5 of Box-edge cushions.)
6. Determine measurements needed for cover for the rectangular bolsters:
• Measure length of rectangular form and add 1 inch for seam allowances (measurement A).
• Measure width of form and add 1¼ inches for seam allowances (measurement B).
• Measure depth of form and add 1¼ inches for seam allowances (measurement C).
• Add measurement B and measurement C and then double this figure (measurement D).
7. Cut pieces of patterned upholstery fabric for rectangular bolster covers:
• Cut two rectangular pieces of fabric the length of measurement D and the width of measurement A.
• Cut four rectangular end pieces of fabric the

length of measurement B and the width of measurement C.

8. Cut four pieces of cable cord the length of measurement D.

9. To sew cover for rectangular bolster,

• Using one of the large rectangular pieces, cut a 5-inch-wide piece from the side corresponding to measurement A.

• Position this piece along edge you just cut it from with right sides together.

• Using a machine basting stitch, sew these pieces together, making a ¾-inch seam.

• Press seam open and insert zipper, following directions on zipper package.

• Remove basting stitches and open zipper.

• With right sides together, align raw edges parallel to zipper.

• Stitch these edges together, making ½-inch seam. (This will make a tube.)

• Press seam open.

• Cover two lengths of cable cord with bias strips of fabric, as directed in step 5 of Box-edge cushions on page 74.

• Sew cording in place on two of the end pieces, following directions given in step 8 of Box-edge cushions on page 75.

• Position an end piece in each end of zippered piece with right sides together. Pin in place and clip at corners to fit.

• Sew end pieces to zippered piece, stitching along seam line of cording. (Hold tube upright and turn it as you stitch.) Remove pins.

• Turn cover right side out and press.

• For other rectangular cover, repeat with remaining cut pieces of fabric and cable cord.

10. Determine measurements needed for round bolster cover:

• Measure length of bolster form and add 1 inch for seam allowances (measurement E).

• Measure circumference of form and add 2½ inches for seam allowances (measurement F).

• Measure diameter of form end and add 1 inch for seam allowances (measurement G).

11. Cut pieces for bolster cover from patterned upholstery fabric:

• Cut two circular end pieces with a diameter equal to measurement G.

• Cut one rectangular piece the length of measurement E and the width of measurement F.

12. To sew cover for round bolster,

• Cut a 7-inch-wide piece from the long side of one of the rectangular pieces cut above.

• Position this piece along edge you just cut it from with right sides together.

• Using a machine basting stitch, sew these pieces together, making a ¾-inch seam.

• Press seam open and insert zipper according to directions on zipper package.

• Remove basting stitches.

• Open zipper.

• With right sides together, align raw edges parallel to zipper.

• Stitch these edges together making ½-inch seam. (This will form a tube.)

• Press seam open.

• Cut two lengths of cable cord the length of measurement F.

• Cover cord with bias fabric strips as directed in step 5 of Box-edge cushions on page 74.

• Sew cording in place on circular end pieces following directions in step 8 of Box-edge cushions on page 75.

• Using machine basting stitch, sew line of stitching around end of tube, sewing ¼-inch from edge. Clip back to stitching line, as shown in sketch below.

• With right sides together, position end pieces in ends of bolster cover tube. Pin in place, as shown in the sketch.

• Sew end pieces to tube, stitching along seam line of cording. (Hold tube upright and turn it as you stitch.)

• Remove pins and turn cover right side out.

• For cover for other round bolster, repeat with remaining cut pieces of fabric.

13. Place covers on bolster forms.

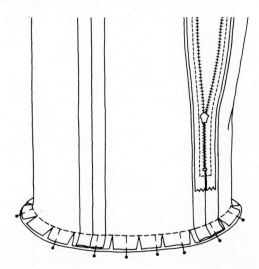

83

Wall-Hung Vanity

Here's a charming way to turn a dressing table into an attractive vanity and bench. You hang the tabletop from the wall and use the table legs for the bench. The addition of a mirror completes this space-saving project.

Materials

Dressing table
Mirror from small dresser or wall mirror
Stain (optional)
Varnish, shellac, or lacquer (optional)
Lag bolts
¾-inch plywood (about 15x25 inches)
1x2 (if table has stretcher, use it instead)
10 wood screws for bench legs
1-inch-thick foam (cut to fit bench top)
Velveteen material to cover bench
1-inch-wide trim for bench
Fabric glue
Four big velveteen-covered buttons
Four small buttons
Strong carpet or button thread
Braided picture wire for hanging mirror
Two screw eyes to support mirror weight
Heavy-duty mirror or picture hanger
Nails

Tools

Paint or varnish remover (optional)
Long needle
Craft knife
Saber saw
Drill
Fine-grade sandpaper (optional)
Paintbrush (optional)
Adjustable wrench
Heavy-duty staple gun

Directions

1. If desired, refinish table and mirror frame,
• Strip off finish as directed on remover.
• Sand wood until smooth. Dust.
• Stain wood, if desired.
• Cover with two coats of varnish, shellac, or lacquer. Let dry after each coat.
2. Cut legs off dressing table and set aside.
3. To hang vanity on wall,
• Locate wall studs at height you want to hang vanity and drill pilot holes for lag bolts.
• Make marks on table back corresponding to space between pilot holes.
• Drill holes for lag bolts at these marks.
• Secure table to wall studs with lag bolts.
4. To make bench,
• Cut plywood to desired dimensions for top.
• Shorten table legs to desired height for bench (about 18 inches).
• Cut three 1x2 pieces for stretchers (or shorten original stretcher). Make pieces to fit between legs.
• Stain and varnish stretchers to match legs.
• Attach the two short stretchers to legs with wood screws.
• Attach long stretcher with wood screws.
• Attach legs to bench top with wood screws.
5. To cover bench with velveteen,
• Cut piece of velveteen 4 inches longer and 4 inches wider than dimensions of bench top.
• Position the four big buttons on plywood bench top, spacing them in rectangle as shown in photo. Mark button position on plywood.
• Drill tiny hole through wood at each mark.
• Position foam atop plywood and mark position of the holes.
• Cut a small X-slit in foam at each mark.
• Cover foam with the velveteen, pulling edges to underside of bench and stapling to secure.
• Glue 1-inch-wide trim around seat edge.
6. To sew the buttons to the bench seat,
• With a long needle, run the thread up through the holes in plywood.
• Continue needle up through slits in foam and through velveteen, leaving 3-inch tail of thread hanging on underside of bench.
• Run needle through shank of big button on top.
• Direct needle back through the cushion about ⅛ inch from the thread.
• Run needle through small button under bench.
• Run the needle and thread through the buttons and cushion two or three more times.
• Draw thread taut. Tie tightly to thread tail.
• Cut off the thread ends.
• Repeat with remaining buttons.
7. To hang the mirror above the vanity,
• Nail hanger to the wall.
• Screw a screw eye into center of each side of the back of the mirror.
• Run ends of braided picture wire through screw eyes and twist tightly to secure.
• Hang the mirror on the hanger.

Dresser Corner Desk

With the price of furniture what it is today, it would cost quite a lot to purchase a good work desk. Even then, the desk might not be as sturdy or provide as much storage space as you'd like. Here's a low-cost alternative that starts with a dresser or commode. Check secondhand stores for suitable dresser units.

Materials

Old dresser or commode
One 4x8-foot sheet of ¾-inch plywood
White glue
4 inside corner braces with screws to fit
Metal tracks, brackets, and screws for adjustable shelves
Primer
Paint (flat, semigloss, or gloss)
Wood-edging tape
Contact cement
Sealer
Wood putty

Tools

Paintbrushes
Saber saw or circular saw
Sanding block
Medium- and coarse-grade sandpaper
Drill

Directions

1. Unscrew the mirror from the dresser unit and remove any molding that extends above the top level; discard these. (Desk height should be about 29 inches, so if necessary cut the dresser or commode down to that height.)
2. Remove any drawer pulls and set them aside.
3. Sand unit with medium-grade sandpaper. Dust.
4. Primer the unit. Let dry completely.
5. Give the unit and drawer pulls two coats of paint. Let dry after each coat.
6. Replace the pulls on the drawers.
7. Measure the width of the dresser unit. Figure the length you want the desk top to be.
8. Cut a rectangle of plywood according to these measurements. (To avoid chipping and splintering, lay a piece of masking tape down, draw cutting line, and cut through tape.) (Save the remaining plywood to make the shelves.)

9. Use wood-edging tape to cover the edges of the plywood rectangle. Apply the tape with contact cement.
10. Fill any nail holes and blemishes with wood putty. Let harden completely.
11. Sand the plywood smooth with coarse-grade sandpaper wrapped around the sanding block.
12. To keep the wood grain from raising, apply sealer as directed on container. Let dry.
13. Sand the plywood lightly with medium-grade sandpaper until smooth. Dust.
14. Position dresser topped with plywood desk top against wall and mark on wall where corner braces need to be placed to hold desk top level. (Use two braces on end and two along back side; position braces so they will screw into studs.)
15. Drill holes at marks and screw in braces.
16. Attach metal tracks for adjustable shelves to wall under end braces. (Make sure the tracks screw into studs.)
17. Glue desk top to dresser. Let dry.
18. Attach desk top to braces with screws.
19. Primer the plywood desk top. Let dry.
20. Paint the desk top to match the rest of the desk. Let dry.
21. Cut shelves from rest of plywood sheet.
22. Sand shelves and apply sealer as in steps 11, 12, and 13 above.
23. Primer the shelves. Let dry.
24. Paint shelves to match desk. Let dry.
25. Position brackets in track; add shelves.

How to paint over wood that has been stained

Although you can paint directly over many wood stains, some types of stains tend to bleed through the paint, causing it to discolor. To guard against this happening to one of your projects, do a test area by applying the paint you plan to use to a small spot of the stained piece. After several days, check to see if the paint has discolored. If there is any discoloration, cover the entire piece with two coats of thin white shellac. Let the shellac dry completely, then sand lightly with fine-grade sandpaper to prepare the surface for the paint.

Updated Chest

The old cedar chest that stored bridal silverware and linens in the thirties is just as useful for storage today. And, with this bold treatment, it becomes a memorable piece.

Materials
    Cedar-lined chest
    Roll of vinyl-faced wallpaper
    Paint for lid molding
    Vinyl adhesive

Tools
    Liquid sander
    Coarse-grade sandpaper
    Brush for spreading adhesive
    Wallpaper smoothing brush

Directions
1. Remove the body moldings and the legs from the chest. Save the lid moldings for reuse.
2. Apply liquid sander to the outside of the chest. Wipe off as directed on the product.
3. To wallpaper the chest,
• Wrap one width of wallpaper around lid. (To give the chest a more professional-looking finish, wrap the paper around the edges to the inside of the chest.)
• Trim off the paper on the inside of chest.
• Thin the vinyl adhesive with a little water and spread on chest and/or wallpaper as directed on container.
• Fit the wallpaper strip onto chest and smooth out wrinkles with smoothing brush.
• Wrap lid with another width of wallpaper, carefully matching the pattern as shown in photograph A. (This will involve some waste, but one roll of wallpaper will more than cover the chest.) Trim and paste as above.
• Cover rest of chest in the same manner.
4. Wipe wallpapered chest with damp sponge to remove excess adhesive. Let dry completely before proceeding.
5. Paint the lid molding. Let dry.
6. Replace the lid molding on chest.
7. Sand the chest's interior with coarse-grade sandpaper, as shown in photograph B. (**Note:** A cedar surface oxidizes with time. By sanding the old surface of the chest, you renew the nostalgic cedar aroma.)

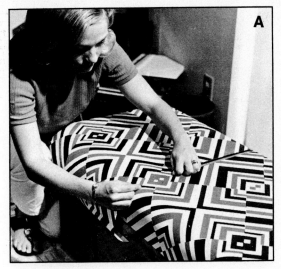

What sandpaper should you use

Sandpaper type	Usage
Very fine-grade	Between coats of paint or varnish
Fine-grade	Final sanding before primer
Medium-grade	To smooth light nicks or scratches
Coarse-grade	To smooth deep nicks or scratches
Very coarse-grade	To remove heavy coats of finish

Victrola Teen Bar

An old Victrola will never replace stereo or TV as entertainment, but as a teen-age party center it's still "the cat's pajamas." Or, in latter day linguistics, it's really cool!

Materials

    Floor-model Victrola
    Enamel paint
    White fabric glue
    Two yards patterned cotton fabric
    One 4x4-foot sheet of hardboard (cut to size
        of speaker grill)
    Six brads
    Four L-shaped metal braces
    Length of chain (cut to size)
    Two screw eyes

Tools

    Liquid sander
    Hammer
    Paintbrush
    Stiff brush
    Sharp utility knife

Directions

1. Remove turntable deck, inside parts, and record partitions.
2. Support wobbly legs or interior corners by screwing on L-shaped metal braces.
3. Paint the inside of top, the turntable area, and the piece of hardboard for grill. Let dry.
4. Fasten the hardboard behind the speaker grill, using brads.
5. Remove the doors of the unit.
6. Apply liquid sander to entire outside of cabinet. Use according to directions.
7. Apply white glue on the Victrola with brush.
8. Lay the fabric on the wet surface.
9. Use a stiff brush to tamp fabric into corners and around moldings. Let dry.
10. Apply the fabric to the doors by repeating steps 6 through 9. Reattach.
11. Use small strips and circles of fabric on moldings and other curved or hard-to-cover areas. Apply as before.
12. On the covered grill, cut out the pattern with a sharp utility knife.
13. With screw eyes, attach chain to Victrola, as shown in the photo.

Recycled Sewing Machine

Don't relinquish that old treadle sewing machine. It might be just the addition you need for your kitchen. The model above is still going strong—its drawers for utensils and its new butcher block top as a work table.

Materials

    Treadle sewing machine
    Latex paint
    One 36x25-inch piece of 1½-inch-thick maple
        cutting board or butcher block
    Four number 10 wood screws
    Coarse-grade sandpaper

Tools

    Band saw or saber saw
    Drill
    Paintbrush

Directions

1. Remove the lid and sewing machine parts.
2. Paint wooden machine frame. Let dry.
3. Draw a paper pattern of machine top.
4. Transfer pattern to the cutting board.
5. Cut out wood to conform to machine top.
6. Sand down edges until curves are smooth.
7. Position cutting board on top of machine.
8. Drill through each corner of machine from below.
9. Screw the cutting board to the machine top.

chapter 4

Sparkling Spools and Spindles

Utilize the unusual. Borrow the flair of such odd-shaped wood pieces as spools, spindles, Tinkertoys, and blocks to design such creative items as chessmen, toy soldiers, door decorations, and puppets. Use the even larger wooden spindles to accent windows and to serve as novel room dividers.

Spool Chess Set

Anyone with moxie to play chess certainly has all it takes to assemble this eye-catching, one-of-a-kind chess set. It's made of empty thread spools and wooden doorknobs. If your game is weak, it's a delight to sit and study the beauty of the chess pieces while your opponent thinks you're studying your next move.

Materials
Wooden thread spools in various sizes
Wooden doorknobs
White glue
Cardboard scraps
Gesso
Model paint (red, black, and white)
Adhesive-backed felt paper

Tools
Paper punch
Paintbrush
Scissors

Directions
1. Stack the spools and doorknobs in such a way that they resemble the playing pieces shown in the photograph. (**Note:** You'll need two kings, two queens, four bishops, four knights, four rooks or castles, and 16 pawns in order to make a complete set.)
2. With a paper punch, punch out cardboard circles to use as levelers for any doorknobs that are not perfectly flat.
3. Glue wood pieces together with cardboard spacers where needed. Let dry completely before proceeding.
4. Coat all pieces with gesso to seal wood. Let dry completely.
5. Paint with several coats of model paint. Make half the chessmen red; the other half black. Let dry completely.
6. Paint simple geometric forms to decorate chessmen, using photo as a guide. Let dry completely before proceeding to final step.
7. Cut adhesive-backed paper to fit bottoms of each chess piece. Apply to chessmen.

Clothespin Soldiers and Spool Cannon

This "changing of the guard" was preceded by the changing of the guardsmen from clothespins and corks to the miniature militia you see here. Issue the troops a wood spool cannon and your tabletop ought to be safe from any invasion.

Materials
Toy soldiers
  Clothespins
  Corks
  Black enamel paint
  6-inch pieces of chenille stems
  Red map tacks
  1½-inch red chenille stems
  Small nails
  Glue
  1-inch dowel rod
  Red, black, and white felt pieces
Guardhouse
  Scraps of ¼-inch plywood
  Small headless nails
  Wood glue
  Primer

Black and white paint
Red felt
Small hinges
One gimp tack
Cannon
  Block of wood 1½x1¼x1¾ inches
  Three whole thread spools
  One large spool center
  Two large spool ends
  One round clothespin end
  Two wooden beads
  Black and red paint
  ⅛-inch dowel rods

Tools
  Saw
  Hammer
  Scissors
  Side-cutting pliers
  Coping saw
  Sandpaper
  Router
  Paintbrush

Directions
Toy soldiers **1.** Saw off rounded bottom tips of clothespins.

2. Saw in half a ½-inch slice of the 1-inch dowel rod and glue halves to bottom of clothespin to form feet. Let dry.

3. Dip the bottom of the clothespin into black enamel up to the "waist." Dip corks in black enamel and let pins and corks dry.

4. Push the piece of chenille stem through the "armhole" of clothespin and bend the ends to form hands.

5. Push red map tacks in heads to form noses.

6. Using pattern below, cut a visor from black felt.

7. Glue visor to the bottom of the cork. Dry.

8. Bend a 1½-inch red chenille stem in half, and put wire ends into top of cork for plume.

9. Lightly tap a small nail into the hole in the top of the clothespin.

10. With side-cutting pliers, cut off most of it.

11. Push cork hat down on nail.

12. Cut a chin strap of black felt and glue in place. Let dry.

13. Cut coat and sleeve from red felt, using the pattern below.

14. Glue on the sleeves. Let dry.

15. Slide the coat over the arms, bending arms as necessary.

16. Glue sparsely at center front. Let dry.

17. Cut a strap from white felt and glue one end to the right front shoulder, cross it over the chest, around the waist, and glue the other end at the center front to the diagonal felt strip. Let dry completely.

Guardhouse 1. From ¼-inch plywood scraps, cut one piece 4⅜x6¾ for back, two pieces 3½x6¾ inches for sides, one piece 4⅜x3¾ inches for bottom, one piece 4⅜x3½ inches for top, and one piece 4⅛x6½ inches for front.

2. Make a ⅛-inch deep groove ⅛ inch in from the edge on the long edge of each of the sides.

3. Make a ⅛-inch deep notch on both long edges of the front piece. Notch should be ⅛ inch wide. (This allows front to slide into sides.)

4. Cut out guardhouse door with a coping saw.

5. Butt-joint the sides to the back with the grooved side edges to the front.

6. Glue and nail with small headless nails. Dry.

7. Glue and nail on the bottom piece. Let dry.

8. Position top piece ¼ inch in from the front edge. Glue and nail in place. Let dry.

9. Also from plywood, cut two triangles with 4¼-inch bases and two rectangles 2⅝x3½ inches for the roof.

10. Nail the triangular eaves to the front and back of the top piece. (Front triangle will sit back ¼ inch from edge of top.)

11. Glue the side roof pieces in place. Let dry.

12. Sand and coat house with primer. Let dry.

13. Paint roof black; and sides and door white. Dry.

14. Cut 1-inch strips of red felt.

15. Glue strips on guardhouse diagonally. Let dry completely before proceeding.

16. Attach door with small hinges.

17. Push in gimp tack for door handle.

Cannon 1. Cut wood block into the L-shape shown in the sketch below. (Notch measures ⅜x⅜ inch.)

2. Drill a hole through block for the axle.

3. Glue tne spools together, following the sketch.

4. Attach the spools to the base with a dowel rod inserted through the spool and into base.

5. Paint all parts with primer. Let dry.

6. Paint with black enamel. Let dry.

7. Paint bead (hub cap) red. Let dry.

8. Assemble parts. (See drawing.)

9. Put the axle through the holes.

10. Add the wheels and the dowels.

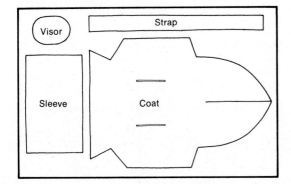

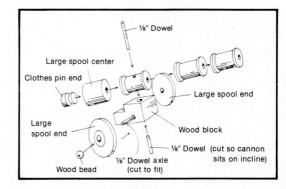

Ornate Window Treatment

Give emphasis to any window by adding a Victorian fan scroll. Comb junk shops for such a scroll, then enlarge it to fit the desired area by adding a plywood frame.

Materials
Victorian fan scroll
Latex enamel paint
Plywood (buy thickness that matches scroll)
No. 10 wood screws
White glue
Five brace bars with 10 screws to fit

Tools
Drill
Paintbrush
Saber saw

Directions
1. Choose a window area at least as large as the scroll, and measure the area.
2. To fit the scroll to the area,
• Measure the scroll, then figure the length and width the plywood strips must be to fit the chosen area.
• Cut three pieces of plywood (one top and two side pieces) according to these measurements.
• Cut side pieces to fit curve of scroll.
• Glue side pieces to top piece. Let dry.
• Attach brace bars as shown in drawing.
3. Paint the fan scroll. Let dry.
4. To hang fan scroll,
• Drill a hole at each corner of scroll to accept wood screw.
• Secure scroll to wall with wood screws.

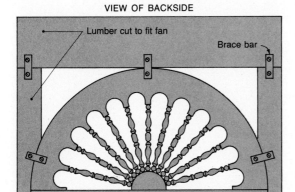

VIEW OF BACKSIDE

Lumber cut to fit fan

Brace bar

Newel-Post Clothes Tree

Looking for a solution to that never-ending problem of getting children to hang up their clothes? Try this child-size clothes tree. Place the free-standing post near a bed or closet.

Materials
One newel post
Four ceramic clothes hooks with colorful
    enamel coating
One round wooden base turned on a lathe
    or any heavy flat-surfaced object suitable
    for use as a base
White glue
High-gloss enamel in several bold colors

Tools
Stain or varnish remover
Masking tape
Medium-grade sandpaper

Directions
1. Strip down the old newel post to the natural wood with stain or varnish remover.
2. Sand the post to a smooth finish.
3. Paint one section of the post, masking off remaining sections. Let dry. Repeat with the remaining sections.
4. Paint the base. Let dry completely.
5. Screw a hook into each side of post.
6. Glue the post to center of base. Let dry.

Tools
Scissors
Large darning needle
Paintbrush
Hammer

Directions
1. Assemble wood "stars" by inserting different length spokes in round wood Tinkertoy centers.
2. Coat "stars" with gesso. Let dry.
3. Paint "stars" white. Let dry completely.
4. Weave red yarn over and under spokes to form center design.
5. Use slots in tips of some spokes to hold thread, creating points on the stars.
6. Cut black felt panel as long as the door is high, plus two inches, and as wide as the door, minus 10 inches.
7. Lay felt panel on flat surface and position the stars where desired.
8. With black yarn and darning needle "sew" stars onto felt panel. (Bring needle up through center hole and down between spokes.) (**Note:** For larger stars, secure the tips of the points by bringing the needle up on one side of the spoke, running the yarn through the slot at the tip of the spoke, then inserting the needle on the other side.)
9. Hang panel on door:
• Overlap two inches at top of door and tack felt to top edge of door.
• Use double-sided tape to secure the bottom of the panel to the bottom surface of the door.

Tinkertoy Decoration

When the youngsters tire of their Tinkertoys, it's your turn to have fun. Use the wheels and spokes to put together this door-hung galaxy of stars, wrapped with yarn and backed by a winter sky of black felt.

Materials
2½ yards black felt
Odd pieces of Tinkertoys
Spool of heavy white cotton thread
Lightweight yarn in red and black
Gesso
White paint
Double-sided tape
Tacks

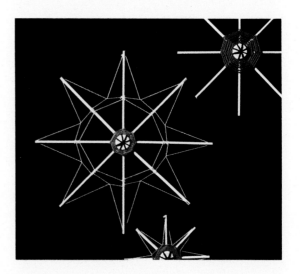

Spool Top Coffee Table

Cultivating some friends at utility companies is the best way to acquire the wire spool top and conduit sections needed for coffee table.

Materials
One top of a big wire spool
Four sections of concrete underground wiring conduit
Black and white paint
Varnish

Tools
Paintbrush

Directions
1. Paint interiors and front edges of conduit with black paint. Let dry.
2. Paint exteriors of conduit white. Let dry completely before proceeding.
3. Clean top of spool. Varnish it. Let dry completely before proceeding.
4. Arrange conduit sections to form table base.
5. Rest spool top on base.

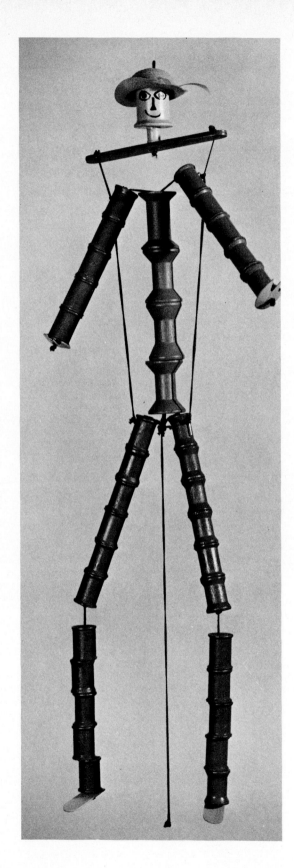

Cowboy Spool Puppet

This cowboy is hardly what you'd call a big, bad hombre. Instead, he's an easy-going cowpoke puppet whose wooden spools will delight little mavericks for hours on end.

Materials
One large spool for head
One very small spool for neck
Four large spools for body
32 spools for arms and legs
Four tongue depressors
Small hat (doll's hat or party favor)
Glue
Paint in desired colors
Two wooden spoons
Screw eyes, brads, or staples
Green soutache for stringing

Tools
Craft knife
Drill
Paintbrush

Directions
1. Glue head and neck spools together. Let dry completely before proceeding.
2. Cut off three tongue depressors to 6-inch lengths, rounding off cut ends.
3. Stack and glue the three depressors together for added strength. Let dry.
4. Drill a hole ½ inch in from each end.
5. Glue two groups of five spools together for arms. Let dry.
6. Glue two groups of six spools together for thighs. Allow to dry. (**Note:** Lower leg spools and body spools are not glued, but are strung separately in this project.)
7. Paint spools. Let dry.
8. Glue on hat. Let dry.
9. Cut off two 2-inch lengths of tongue depressor for feet.
10. Cut off bowl part of spoon for hands.
11. Drill holes in center of feet and hands.
12. Paint feet and hands and let dry completely before proceeding.
13. Place screw eyes, brads, or staples at upper arm and thigh. (See photo.)
14. Following sketch, string parts together. (**Note:** Leave a space between thighs and legs.)

Spool Soldiers

A band of soldiers like this could march from childhood play to decorating a bookshelf—and end up commissioned as family heirlooms. Make them out of wooden spools and door pulls.

Materials
Short soldier
Two large wooden spools
One medium spool
One small spool
One wooden door pull
Two tongue depressors
Glue
Gesso
Paints

Medium soldier
Three large spools
Two medium spools
One small spool
One wooden door pull
Two tongue depressors
Glue
Gesso
Paints

Tall soldier
Six small spools for legs
One large spool
One short fat spool for head
One wooden door pull
Glue
Gesso
Two tongue depressors
Paint

Drum
2-inch section of mailing tube
2 lightweight cardboard circles
Scraps of fabric braid
Glue
Two toothpicks
Gold foil
Two small wooden beads

Tools
Scissors
Craft knife
Paintbrush

Directions
Soldiers **1.** Glue spools together according to arrangements in photo. Let dry.
2. To make arms,
• With craft knife, cut tongue depressors off at "cuffs."
• Use short cut-off section as hands. Glue to underside of sleeve section. (**Note:** Position hand so it's slanted forward.)
3. Glue knobs on top spools to form hats. Let dry.
4. Coat soldiers with gesso. Let dry.
5. Using photo as guide, paint uniforms on soldiers. Let dry.

Drum **1.** Glue cardboard circles to section of mailing tube. Let dry.
2. Paint end circles black. Let dry.
3. Cut fabric scrap to cover sides of drum.
4. Glue fabric in place. Let dry.
5. Cut strips of black felt. Glue in place to form lacing on drum sides. Let dry.
6. Glue on bands of gold braid on top and bottom edges of drum. Let dry.
7. Cover toothpicks with foil. Glue in place. Let dry completely.
8. Insert and glue into wooden beads for drumsticks. Let dry completely.

Novel Breakfast Nook

Rescue lengths of old stair railing from an about-to-be-dismantled building and build a unique unit like this one. Adapt the railing to any bench shape you want. See instructions for box-edge cushions for bench on page 74.

Materials
Stairway railings (straight lengths only)
1x4 lumber
2¼-inch window casing molding
Long wood screws (length and number determined by railing you use)
Primer enamel paint
Varnish
One 4x8-foot sheet of ¾-inch plywood
1x2 lumber
1-inch molding for bench trim
2-inch molding
Finishing nails
Wood putty
White glue

Tools
Saber saw
Miter box
Furniture clamps
Medium-grade sandpaper
Countersink
Paint and varnish remover

Directions
Bench **1.** Determine measurements for shape and size bench you want to build. (Bench shown here is 14 inches high and 16 inches deep.)

2. Cut out plywood pieces for side legs, tops, and front of the bench according to these measurements. (**Note:** If making semi-U-shaped bench as shown, you'll need to miter the top and front pieces to form semi-U, and you'll need two center legs to fit inside bench at these mitered junctions.)

3. Glue and nail the pieces together to form bench. (Bench will be three-sided, with bottom and back left open.) Clamp joints. Let dry.

4. Cut 1x2 pieces to fit back edge of bench top and side legs as shown in sketch. Miter corners of 1x2 pieces.

5. Glue and nail the 1x2 pieces to the plywood, as shown in the sketch. Let dry.

6. Countersink the nails. Fill the holes with wood putty. Let dry.

7. For trim on side legs,
● Cut 1-inch molding to lengths needed.
● Miter the corners of molding.
● Glue and nail the molding to the side legs of the bench. Let dry.

8. To give the bottom edge of bench a finished look,
● Cut 2-inch molding to fit around bottom edge of side legs and bench front.
● Miter corners of molding.
● Glue and nail molding in place.

9. Sand the bench until smooth. Dust.

10. Primer the bench. Let dry.

11. Paint the bench with a coat of enamel. Let dry completely.

Railing **1.** Strip the paint or varnish off the railing. (**Note:** If the railing is ornate, you may want to have it stripped by a professional paint stripping firm.)

2. Repair or replace any areas of the railing that are in poor condition.

3. To build the bench back,
● Measure bottom edge of bench back.
● Cut 2x4s according to these measurements.
● Cut stairway railing to fit around back of bench. (**Note:** If bench is semi-U-shaped, miter corners and nail and glue pieces together. Dry.)
● Glue and screw 1x4 to the bottom of the railing turnings with long wood screws. Let dry.
● Nail 2x4s to the floor.
● Nail 1x4 with attached railing to 2x4s.

4. Cut the 2¼-inch casing molding to fit around sides and back of railing platform, as shown. Miter corners.

5. Glue and nail molding to the 2x4 base. Dry.

6. Countersink the nails. Fill the holes with wood putty. Let dry.

7. Sand the railing until smooth. Dust.

8. Primer the turnings and base of railing. Dry.

9. Paint turnings and base with enamel. Let dry completely before proceeding.

10. Varnish the top of railing. Let dry.

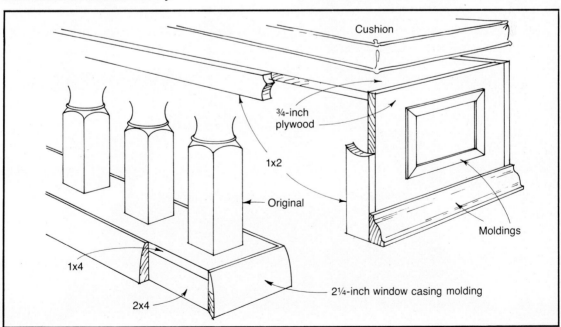

Cushion

¾-inch plywood

1x2

Original

Moldings

1x4

2x4

2¼-inch window casing molding

Tinkertoy Chess Set

What do you think of wooden spools and Tinkertoys for an opening gambit? Pretty pedestrian for an intellectual game like chess? Not at all! The chess pieces shown here have as much style and sophistication as any that ever moved across a board, yet these pieces are easy and inexpensive to create.

Materials
Kings (make two)
    Four large Tinkertoy wheels
    Two small Tinkertoy wheels
    Two large wooden spools
    Assorted wooden beads
Queens (make two)
    Two 1½-inch squares of ¼-inch wood
    Two large Tinkertoy wheels
    Two small Tinkertoy wheels
    Two small wooden spools
    Assorted wooden beads
Bishops (make four)
    Four 1½-inch squares of ¼-inch wood
    Four 1¼-inch-diameter circles of ¼-inch wood
    Four 2-inch sections of ¾-inch dowel rod
    Four small Tinkertoy wheels
    Four square wooden beads
    Assorted wooden beads
Knights (make four)
    Four 1½-inch squares of ¼-inch wood
    Four large wooden spools
    Four Tinkertoy cylinders
    Four short Tinkertoy sticks
Rooks (make four)
    Four 1½-inch squares of ¼-inch wood
    Four large Tinkertoy wheels
    Four wooden spools
    Assorted wooden beads
Pawns (make 16)
    16 large wooden spools
    16 large round beads
    16 small round wooden beads
All pieces
    Glue
    Gesso
    Paint (orange and yellow high-gloss enamel)
    Adhesive-backed felt paper

Tools
    Paintbrush
    Scissors

Directions
1. Assemble spools, Tinkertoys, and bases as shown in drawing and photograph.
2. Glue together and let dry completely.
3. Glue wood beads in holes of Tinkertoy wheels as shown. Let dry.
4. Glue beads to tops of chess pieces. Let dry completely.
5. Coat each piece with gesso. Let dry.
6. Paint half the chess pieces bright orange; the other half bright yellow. Apply several coats and allow to dry completely between coats.
7. Cut pieces of adhesive-backed felt to fit bottoms of each chessman.
8. Peel off backing and apply felt to bottoms of pieces. Smooth in place.

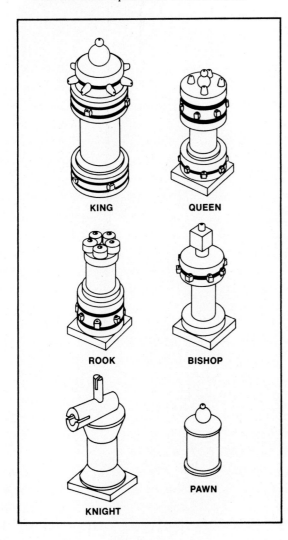

KING   QUEEN

ROOK   BISHOP

KNIGHT   PAWN

chapter 5

Riches from Old Clothes and Rags

Few things come and go in a family the way clothes do. Every season usually brings a purging of the closets and a fattening of the ragbag or Salvation Army pickup box. Rather than toss the misfits, it's time to give your old clothes and rags a second chance. Use them for the imaginative craft projects that are presented in this chapter.

Necktie Wreath

You won't have to part with those old favorite neckties that suddenly seem either too wide or too narrow or else too wild or conservative. They'll fit just perfectly into this elegant patchwork wreath in the Victorian crazy quilt design as shown in the photo.

Materials

Approximately 24 colorful old ties (shop garage sales, thrift shops, and Salvation Army stores, or use scraps of any medium-weight fabric)

One yard acetate tie silk for bow

⅔ yard lining fabric

¾ yard lightweight muslin

24-inch square of cardboard

Two spools of #5 pearl cotton in gold

One package of quilt batting

Sewing thread

Tools

Scissors

Needle

Sewing machine

Pins

Iron

Stapler

Directions

1. Cut off 6 inches from both ends of each tie.

2. Remove backing and lining fabric.

3. Iron pieces flat (leave edges turned under at points and along sides).

4. Cut a circle of muslin 25 inches in diameter.

5. From center, clip out a 9-inch circle.

6. Arrange tie pieces on muslin:

• Begin at the top of wreath and work counterclockwise.

• Lay tie points out on muslin, alternating colors and pattern.

• Overlap points of ties.

(continued on next page)

7. Pin and baste all pieces in place, clipping away excess where ties overlap.

8. Leave about 1 inch unstitched at center of wreath to allow for give when wreath is stretched over cardboard frame.

9. Cut a cardboard circle 22 inches in diameter.

10. To make wreath frame, cut out a 10-inch circle from center of 22-inch cardboard circle.

11. Cut three layers of batting slightly larger than the cardboard frame.

12. Stretch batting over the frame and staple raw edges around on the back of the frame.

13. Lay pieced tie wreath over padded frame.

14. Clip inside edges to ease. Adjust edges where necessary to make wreath fit well.

16. Remove wreath and machine-stitch ties down.

17. Remove basting.

18. Using #5 pearl cotton, work a row of feather-stitching along seams. See diagram below.

19. Gently iron patched wreath from backside.

20. Stretch over frame and staple raw edges to back of cardboard.

21. Cut lining fabric to fit and slipstitch to the back of the wreath.

22. Make bow:
- Cut a piece of tie silk 14 inches wide and 1½ yards long. (Piece if necessary.)
- With right side together, fold tie silk piece in half lengthwise and sew along the long raw edge with ½-inch seam allowance.
- Turn right side out and press.
- Tie into bow.
- Clip ends on the diagonal, turn under raw edges and slipstitch closed.

23. Hand-tack bow to wreath.

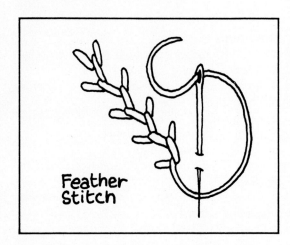

Feather Stitch

Slipper Wall Hanging

When your dancer outgrows that first pair of ballet slippers, don't throw away the fond memories. Duplicate this project and you'll have a visual reminder of those recital days.

As a decorative touch, add a blue china bird or small bouquet of strawflowers.

Materials
One pair ballet slippers
White paint (flat finish)
1 yard 1-inch-wide white satin ribbon
Fabric glue
Decorative screw hook

Tools
Paintbrush
Drill

Directions
1. Clean the ballet slippers with a damp cloth and soap. Let dry.

2. Paint slippers inside and out with at least two coats of paint. Let dry between coats.

3. Tie ribbon into big bow as shown in photo.

4. Glue one end of the ribbon to the inside of each slipper. Let dry.

5. Drill a hole in the wall for screw hook.

6. Screw hook into wall.

7. Hang slippers by ribbon from hook.

1. Cut a 7-inch cardboard square for template.
2. Lay template on wrong side of lining fabric and trace around edges, leaving ½-inch seam allowance on all four sides.
3. Trace and cut out six squares.
4. Repeat steps 2 and 3 using fabric for outside of box.
5. With right sides together, pin and sew the six lining squares together as shown in diagram. (Use ½-inch seams.)
6. Repeat with the outer fabric squares.
7. Press all seams open.
8. Decorate satin box by appliquéing lace. Decorate floral box by sewing on ribbons.
9. Pin right sides of lining and outer fabric together, matching seams and corners carefully.
10. Sew ½-inch seams around sides of squares, leaving opening on bottom of front square.
11. Trim all seam allowances, except at opening. Trim outer corners and clip inner corners of squares. Turn fabric right side out and press.
12. Cut ¼ inch off two adjacent sides of cardboard template.
13. Using this for a pattern, cut 6 squares from mat board.
14. Slip a mat board square into open end of front section; slide it up to top section of box.
15. Stuff the space between mat board and outer fabric with small pieces of batting. Stuff between board and lining. Stuff corners snugly.
16. Using zipper foot, stitch along seam line between top and back sections.
17. Slide a mat board square into back section and repeat steps 14 through 16.
18. Repeat for remaining sections.
19. Turn raw edges under and blindstitch closed.
20. Pin open edges together to form box.
21. Pull thread through beeswax several times.
22. Slipstitch box together along its sides.

Fabric Boxes

Sometimes the box is better than the gift that's in it, —and sometimes the box is meant to be the gift. That's the case with these luxurious fabric boxes. They're priceless catches!

Materials
Both boxes
  Mat board
  Dacron batting or quilt stuffing
  Thread
  Beeswax
  Cardboard for pattern
Green box
  ⅔ yard green satin
  ⅔ yard lining fabric
  Lace for appliques
Ribbon box
  ⅔ yard floral cotton sateen
  ⅔ yard lining fabric
  4 yards green velvet ribbon
  2 yards pink velvet ribbon

Tools
  Scissors
  Sewing machine
  Sewing needle

Directions
(**Note:** Instructions given are for 7-inch boxes.)

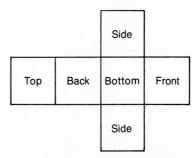

7 inch square box pattern

Braided Panty Hose Rug

It could be mind-boggling to hear how much money a woman invests in hose each year—only to discard them after a snag or a run. The sensible thing to do is not toss them. Braid them into a winsome, washable rug instead, like the one in progress shown here.

Materials

Used stockings (all sizes, colors, styles; with or without runs)
Thread (either brown or neutral tones to match the stockings)

Tools

Scissors
Needle
One safety pin
Crochet hook

Directions

1. Prepare stockings for braiding. (Cut off feet and reinforced tops of stockings. With regular panty hose, cut just below the panty part. For sheer to the waist panty hose, divide in two along center seams and remove the waistband before proceeding.)

2. Join pieces of stocking by stitching along the diagonal. (See sketch A.)

3. Make one strand 10 feet long; another 5 feet long.

4. Fold the longest strand in two to form three strands for braiding.

5. Tack the end of the shorter strand to the middle of the folded longer one with a few backhand stitches.

6. Use a safety pin to anchor the strands to the back of a chair. (Sketch A.)

7. Roll stocking strips tightly and braid. (See Drawing B. To form braid, turn outer two strands toward the center alternately.)

8. Lay completed length of braid flat on a table and coil. Slipstitch coils together.

9. Add more stockings to each strand of the braid as needed.

10. Finish off rug at desired size by stitching raw edges to the edge of the rug.

11. Weave the ends into the outer round with a crochet hook.

12. Press flat, using a steam iron.

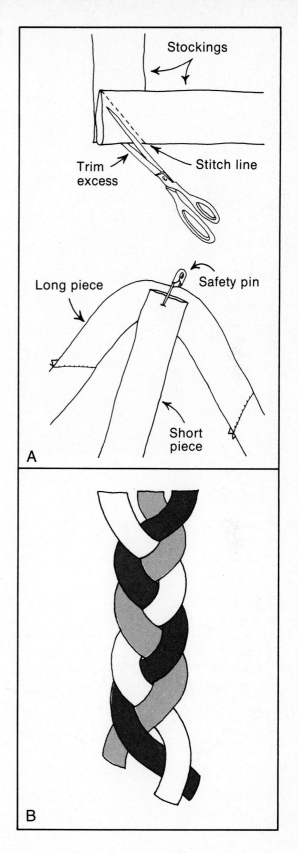

2. Fold strips in half lengthwise with the right sides together.

3. Machine stitch along long edge to form tube.

4. Turn tube right side out.

5. Braid three tube strips together tightly. (**Note:** When you come to the end of a strip, add another strip by tucking raw edges inside and hand-stitching the tubes together.)

6. Braid until length reaches 12 feet.

7. Using strong thread and large needle, coil the braid into a spiral, sewing tightly as you go. (See black and white photograph.)

8. Make the spiral the size desired for purse.

9. Cut out two lining pieces and two body pieces (front and back) 1 inch larger than braid.

10. Pin lining pieces right sides together and stitch around, leaving an 8-inch opening.

11. Clip curves and turn.

12. Repeat for body front and back.

13. Make an 8-inch button loop from velvet.

14. Stitch to inside top of velvet backing.

15. Insert lining into purse; turn under raw edges along opening and tack to purse, making sure loop extends out between lining and backing.

16. Tack coiled braid to front of purse.

17. Make a 65-inch-long strap of a velvet tube, a braid, or both. Position around bottom and sides of purse and stitch in place.

18. Attach button on front of purse.

Braided Shoulder Bag

If you're looking for a way to bag compliments, this breezy braided purse will do it for you. Make it easily with fabric scraps braided into a coil a la the old rag rug technique.

Materials
Fabric scraps for braid
1 yard velvet or other heavy fabric
1 yard lining fabric
Carpet or button thread
Large button

Tools
Scissors
Sewing machine
Darning needle

Directions
1. Tear or cut fabric scraps into 36-inch-long strips 4 inches wide.

Button Necklace

Here's a great idea for all those buttons you find at garage sales and in Grandma's attic. Make stunning, primitive-looking necklaces out of them. For no more than the cost of a few accent beads, you'll turn those shirt buttons into a string of pseudo puka shells to make even the Islanders envious of you.

Materials

Shirt, collar, or coat buttons
Accent beads (ceramic, wood, or cork)
Heavy thread

Directions

1. Lay out different styles and colors of buttons. Work out the pattern, placing accent beads if desired.
2. Tie ends of two strings together, leaving a 4-inch "tail".
3. Thread buttons through both holes so they'll stack against one another. Knot between buttons.
4. Tie the two threads together when desired length is reached, then tie both ends of the necklace together to finish.

Stuffed Shirt Pillows

Kids have a funny way of developing sentimental attachments to everyday things like their outgrown or worn T-shirts. Don't play the villain by getting rid of those tattered tops. Just simply stuff them! Kids will get even more attached to these cuddly T-shirt pillows which will undoubtedly add punch to any good pillow fight.

Materials

Worn T-shirts and sweat shirts
Polyester filling
Matching thread

Tools

Needle

Directions

1. Patch rips or holes in shirts. Wash.
2. With matching thread, slipstitch neck and sleeve openings closed.
3. Stuff with polyester filling, making sure tips of sleeves are completely stuffed.
4. With matching thread, slipstitch the bottom opening closed.

Old Clothes Quilt

Since kids' clothes generally end up thrown on the bed, make the practice official and use left-over garments as "patches" for this unusual, quilted coverlet shown at right.

Materials
    Two twin-size sheets
    Variety of old garments
    Polyester batting
    Border fabric (about 4 yards)
    Thread
    Cotton rug yarn for tufting
    Embroidery floss for decorating garments

Tools
    T-pins
    Scissors
    Needles (various sizes)
    Pins

Directions
1. Cut pieces of clothing into "fronts" and "backs".
2. Pin the garments to a twin-size sheet.
3. Stitch garments securely to sheet. (**Note:** Work out a random design by placing garments so they overlap. Position clothing in all directions—up, down, and sideways.)
4. Spread second sheet on large work surface.
5. Spread polyester batting over sheet.
6. Position "patched" sheet on top of batting.
7. Pin the layers together using T-pins.
8. Quilt the layers together using the tufted method:
• Cut a long strand of yarn and thread the needle with it, pulling the ends even.
• Force the needle down through the various layers of material and pull it through to the wrong side.
• Force it up to the right side again, about ¼ inch away from where it went down.
• Pull yarn through and tie a firm double knot.
• Cut off, leaving ½ inch at the ends.
9. Cut 13-inch wide strips of border fabric.
10. Fold in half to make 6-inch border with two ½-inch seam allowances.
11. Sew strips together to form fabric "frame" for quilt. Sew to quilt.
12. Add fancy embroidery to desired clothing.

Embroidery Tray

Frequently, secondhand stores are stocked with old trays featuring art atrocities under glass. Next time you see one, pick it up, and replace the old design with your needlework.

Materials
    One old glass-topped tray
    One piece of embroidery or lace
    Red enamel
    Red felt
    Cardboard the size of the tray
    Brads
    Glue

Tools
    Paintbrush
    Coarse-grade sandpaper
    Scissors
    Tack hammer

Directions
1. Remove backing from tray. Sand wood frame.
2. Paint with red enamel. Let dry.
3. Center embroidery or lace on cardboard.
4. Insert in frame. Tack brads in place to hold cardboard.
5. Cut felt to cover back. Glue in place. Dry.

Fabric Scrap Valance

The patchwork that for years was bedridden in the form of spreads has now taken to the windows. Here, fabric scraps make a striking valance.

Materials
Fabric scraps
Matching thread

Strip of molding as long as width of window
Interlining (1 yard for every eight flaps)
Cardboard
Nails

Tools
Sewing machine
Staple gun
Scissors

116

Iron
Hammer

Directions

1. Calculate the width and depth of flaps, adding ½-inch seam allowance on all sides and an extra inch at the top for mounting. (**Note:** Flaps shown in the photo at left measure 9 inches wide and 14 inches deep at the point.)
2. For each flap, cut two pieces of fabric, plus a piece of interlining.
3. Using diamond pattern (A) below, make a cardboard template. (Plan ¼ inch seam allowance on all sides.)
4. For each flap, cut four diamonds from print fabric, four from another.
5. Assemble to form eight-pointed star (B).
6. Appliqué star to front flap.
7. Stitch front and back pieces of flaps together. Turn and press.
8. Trim interlining to fit and insert.
9. Topstitch around star and also ⅜ inch in from the edges of the flap.
10. Staple flaps to a strip of molding.
11. Nail molding to the ceiling about 1½ inches in front of the curtain.

A

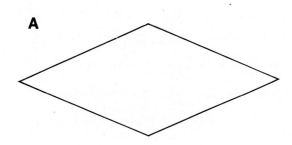

B

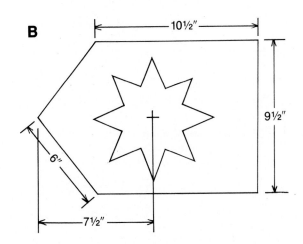

Lace Window Hanging

The "lace curtain" Irish could take a lesson from this delicate window hanging—or maybe it was the Irish who invented this unique way to display a lacy panel. The hanging is simply sandwiched between glass and hung from its frame.

Materials
One panel of lace
Two sheets of window glass slightly larger than the lace to be framed
One aluminum frame to fit glass
Two screw eyes
Two metal S hooks
Thin wire

Tools
Drill
Wire cutters

Directions
1. Center lace on one sheet of glass.
2. Place second sheet of glass on top.
3. Assemble aluminum frame around glass according to package instructions.
4. Drill holes in window frame to start screw eyes. Install screw eyes.
5. Cut lengths of wire. Fasten to S hooks.
6. Tie wire to screw eyes in window frame.
7. Attach S hooks to back of aluminum frame.

Woven Necktie Hanging

Here's an inventive way to handle that surplus of outdated neckties that clutter most closets and are forever slipping off their hangers onto the floor. Simply weave them into a striking wall hanging, using a simple-to-make nail frame loom. In fact, you use the loom as a natural frame for the finished weaving. If you don't have enough ties to complete the project, pick up more at a second-hand store, the Salvation Army, Goodwill Industries store, or else rummage sales.

Materials
A variety of old neckties
    (use any color and any pattern)
Finishing nails (use 10d nails for hanging;
    6d for loom)
Two 20-inch-long pieces 1x4
Two 39-inch-long pieces 1x4
Cord, twine, or rug yarn

Tools
Hammer
Wooden yardstick

Directions

1. To prepare the ties for weaving, remove the lining and fold each one lengthwise.

2. Build a nail loom (see sketch):

- Nail the 20-inch ends on top of the 39-inch side pieces, as shown in sketch.
- For loom pegs, nail 6d finishing nails ½ inch apart the whole length of each end (leave about 1 inch of nail protruding to act as peg).
- Position the frame with one end facing you. Then, tie a length of cord, twine, or yarn around the lower right corner nail.
- Bring the cord up and around two top right nails, then, down and under the next two bottom nails, and so on across the loom.
- Tie off at end. (This cord will serve as the warp through which you weave the ties.)

3. Starting in the lower right corner of the loom, weave the yardstick alternately over and under each succeeding warp cord. (See sketch.)

4. Turn the yardstick on its side to separate the warp threads.

5. Draw a folded tie through the space opened by the yardstick (the end of tie should extend several inches).

6. Use the yardstick to gently beat the tie flat against the end of the loom.

7. Remove the yardstick and reweave it through the warp threads of the second row, reversing the order of over and under.

8. Bring the remaining end of the first tie as far through the open space as it will go.

9. Draw the next tie through, using it to cover the end of the first tie.

10. Beat the tie into place with yardstick.

11. Repeat weaving procedure until loom is full.

12. Tuck the ends of the first and last ties into the back of the weaving.

13. Nail 10d finishing nails into the wall and hang the loom-framed work.

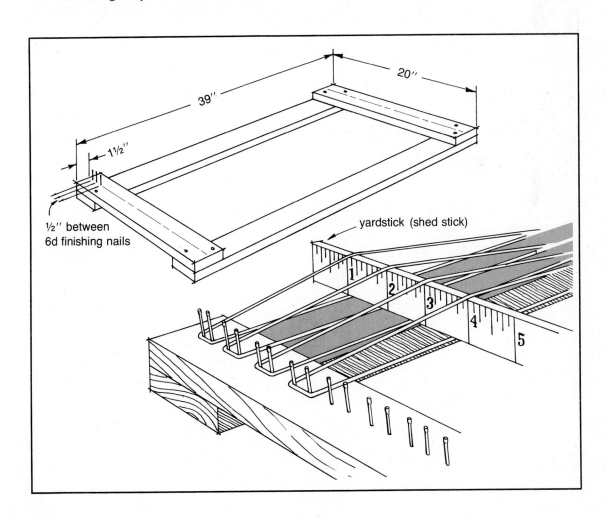

Crochet Rag Rug

When it comes to rag rugs, Granny may have held the family title until now. But no more. There's a whole new generation of rug-makers and a whole new interest in old-fashioned crochet rugs. All it takes to create the classic blue and white circle shown here is the ability to learn one easy stitch and a few simple techniques. For materials, you'll need strips of salvageable fabrics from your ragbag.

Materials

Assorted all-cotton or cotton-blend fabrics
(You'll need the equivalent of 9 yards of 45-inch fabric to make a circle rug 3 to 4 feet in diameter. The rug shown here is 8 feet in diameter.)
Thread
Soil repellent

Tools

Large (size J) crochet hook
Scissors
Sewing machine
Needle

Directions

1. Cut or tear fabric into strips. (**Note:** To keep all strips uniform in thickness, cut heavy fabrics in ¾-inch-wide strips; mediumweight fabric into 1-inch-wide strips; and lightweight cotton into 1½-inch-wide strips.)
2. Join strips into a workable longer length by machine stitching on the diagonal as shown in diagram 1, page 122.
3. Trim seam allowances.
4. Roll long strings of fabric strips into balls as shown in bottom photo.
5. Using crochet hook, chain six stitches. See diagram 2 on page 122.
6. Join stitches into a ring using a slipstitch. See diagram 3, page 122.
7. Do a single crochet stitch in the first stitch of the ring. See Diagram 4, steps A through E on page 122.
8. When completed, do another single crochet in same stitch (an increase). See Diagram 5 on page 122.
9. Repeat in all six stitches of the ring.
10. Continue single crocheting (Diagram 4),

increasing in every other stitch for the second row of the rug.
11. Increase after that as often as necessary to maintain the rug's circular shape and its flatness.
12. To change colors or add new strips, join a new strip to the preceding one by handstitching the two pieces together along the diagonal, as before. Clip the seam.
13. Continue single crocheting, increasing occasionally and changing colors as you choose, until the rug is the desired size.
14. To finish the rug, cut the last three or four yards of fabric strips narrower (decreasing to about ⅜ inch wide at the end) so the last round of the rug will decrease in width and allow you to end smoothly.
15. Coat the rug with a soil repellent.

(continued on next page)

1. Join strips of fabric together on the diagonal. Trim seam.

2. Crochet a chain of six stitches.

3. Join chain into a ring with a slip stitch.

4. Work entire rug using a single crochet stitch, steps below:

   A. Insert hook into second chain from hook, under the upper two strands.

   B. and **C.** Draw up fabric.

   D. Loop fabric over hook.

   E. Draw fabric through the two loops. Insert hook into the next stitch, and repeat from Step A.

5. To increase, do two stitches (Diagram 4, A-E) in one loop.

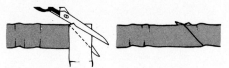

Yarn Scrap Wall Hanging

Get the entire family to yarn-paint this delightful project. This impressive wall hanging rivals stained glass for brilliance, yet it's done with bits of leftover yarn and household glue. If you lack inspiration or the ability to draw, adopt your designs from other sources. Trace them from coloring books, wallpaper, or fabric patterns, greeting cards, or anyplace you find appealing designs, then "yarn" your findings to create a wall-hung masterpiece for your home.

Materials
Two 3x3-foot pieces of ¼-inch plywood
White glue
Yarn scraps in different colors

Tools
Saw
Coarse-grade sandpaper
Pencil
Scissors

Directions
1. Cut one of the pieces of plywood into 36 small 6x6-inch squares.
2. Sand all rough edges, but be careful not to round off the corners.
3. Draw or trace a design onto each square.
4. Squeeze a fine to medium line of glue onto the outer edge of the square.
5. Place a line of yarn onto the glue and press lightly. Let dry.
6. Make the border of each square three yarn lines wide. Glue each strand of yarn as close to the previous one as possible. Let dry.
7. Outline the penciled design with glue.
8. Place a line of yarn on design. Fill rest of design with yarn. Work carefully, cutting edges straight and close. Let dry.
9. Spread glue on background. Fill with yarn. (**Note:** Be sure to use enough glue to hold down the edges, but not too much. Excess glue will cause the yarn to dry hard.) Let all squares dry completely before proceeding.
10. Assemble squares in desired sequence.
11. Spread a thin coat of glue onto the large plywood sheet.
12. Place the small squares onto the plywood.
13. Weight down and let dry overnight.

ABC Cross-Stitch Rug

The patriotic remnant rug shown above is as easy as ABC. It is a needlepoint project with a neat new twist. Strips of fabric are used instead of yarn. If you can sew on a button, you've got enough expertise to create this sturdy and washable alphabet floor covering.

Materials

    #4 penelope canvas (4-mesh-to-the-inch
        rug canvas) measuring 4x6 feet
        (may be pieced)
    Twenty-six ½- to ¾-yard remnants of
        45-inch fabric for the letters
    Four double-size white sheets for the
        background of rug
    9 yards 45-inch blue print fabric for the
        border of rug
    2 yards washable burlap or canvas for backing
    Carpet thread

Tools

    Waterproof marker
    Large-eye yarn needle
    Scissors
    Iron

Directions

1. Prepare canvas to proper size. (**Note:** If available canvas is only 36 inches wide, purchase 3½ yards; cut the piece in half and piece together. To piece, cut off one selvage edge on each half; overlap two sets of mesh, and whip-stitch the mesh together. Cross-stitches over this seam will hold the halves firmly together.)

2. Preshrink all fabric.

3. Tear fabric into 2-inch-wide strips, each approximately 45 inches long.

4. Turn raw edges under by folding each strip in thirds lengthwise and pressing down.

5. Using waterproof marker, place an "X" on the center horizontal and vertical axes of canvas.

6. Follow graph pattern (sketch B) on page 125. Carefully outline each letter on rug canvas. (**Note:** Each square on the diagram represents one cross-stitch. For this rug, each cross-stitch covers three sets of horizontal and three sets of vertical threads. To center design, mark off center letters first, then work out toward borders.)

7. Thread a strip of folded fabric through the needle. Work, following instructions for cross-stitch given on opposite page. (Do not make knots on back of rug. Slip loose ends of strips through a few stitches of the preceding row. Clip.)

8. Work all the letters of the rug first and then do the background. Finish by doing the borders of the rug last.

9. When rug is completed, fold raw edges of canvas under and press.

10. Trim the excess canvas to 1-inch. Blindstitch the raw edges to the back of the rug with the carpet thread.

11. To form back for rug, turn under raw edges of backing fabric.

12. Whipstitch to border stitches of rug.

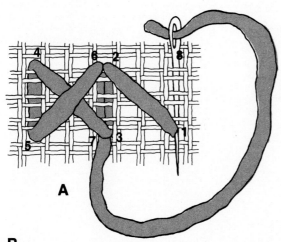

A

How to work cross-stitch

(**Note:** Each cross-stitch in this rug is worked over three pairs of horizontal and three pairs of vertical threads.)

1. Work the first half of a row of stitches moving from right to left. (See sketch A for a numbered directional guide.)
- Bring needle up through canvas at 1.
- Insert needle at 2.
- Bring needle out at 3.
- Insert needle at 4.

(**Note:** Work the first stitch of the cross completely across a row before returning.)

2. Work stitches back across row, working from left to right.
- Bring the needle out at 5.
- Insert the needle at 6 (same as 2.)
- Bring needle out again at 7 (same hole as for 3).
- Insert needle at 8.

(**Note:** Always keep the final stitch of the cross slanting in the same direction across the whole rug.)

B

3'9"

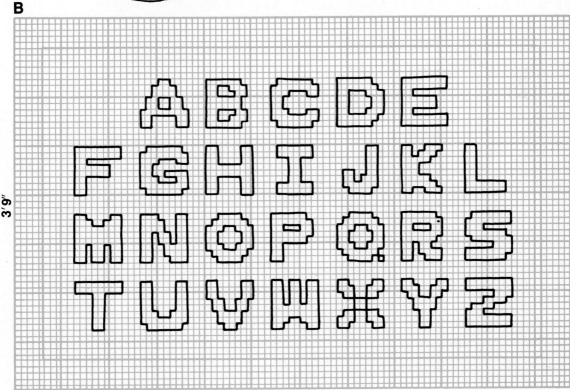

5'10"   1 square = 1 stitch

·∴⟨ chapter 6 ⟩∴·

Gems from Junked Metal

*Until recently, no one would ever have thought of rescuing
an old washing machine agitator, a boat propeller,
or beat-up tire rim. They were junk metal—pure and simple!
Today, they are the basis of imaginative designs.*

Wheel Rim Table

It takes the ability to visualize uncommon uses
for common materials before you can look at
something as ordinary as a couple of old wheel
rims and imagine them as a fashionable table.
That's what you see here—two metal wheel
rims, straight from the auto graveyard—given a
brand-new luster and a brand-new responsibility.

Materials
    Two wheel rims
    One 30x30-inch piece of ¾-inch
       interior AC plywood
    Epoxy
    Enamel paint
    Wood putty
    Polyurethane varnish

Tools
    Saber saw
    Coarse-grade sandpaper
    Fine-grade sandpaper
    Paintbrush

Directions
1. Clean up wheel rims. (If they are badly rusted, have them sandblasted. If they are in fairly
good shape, give them a thorough sanding. Pay
particular attention to sanding the edges where
the rims will be attached—epoxy will not adhere
to rusty metal.)
2. Fasten the two rims together by running a
bead of epoxy around the edge of the bottom one
and placing the other rim on top. Allow the glue
to dry overnight.
3. Cut the plywood into a circle.
4. Slightly round edges of the plywood with
coarse sandpaper.
5. Fill in the edges of plywood with wood putty.
Let dry before proceeding.
6. Sand until smooth with fine sandpaper.
7. Attach circle to top of rims with epoxy. Let dry
completely.
8. Give the base and top several coats of enamel.
Let dry, then sand between coats. (Use contrasting colors on wheel rim edges.)
9. Coat tabletop with polyurethane varnish. Let
dry completely.

Stovepipe Lamp

Lighting is a mood-maker. And the mood is one of relaxed informality with an up-tempo lamp like the one at left. What started out as a drab sheet metal stovepipe T has turned into a real conversation starter—or stopper—depending on the crowd. You'll find a variety of interestingly shaped pipes at your hardware or lumber store. With just a little work, any one of them can be a first-class turn-on.

Materials

One 6-inch sheet metal stovepipe T
Yellow enamel
White heatproof paint
One 6x6-inch piece of 1-inch plywood
One porcelain light socket
One lamp cord
One plug
One line switch
Several short nails
One 6x6-inch square of translucent plastic
One low-wattage light bulb

Tools

Coping saw
Screwdriver
Drill
Hammer
Paintbrush

Directions

1. Paint outside of stovepipe T with bright enamel paint. Let dry completely.
2. Paint inside of T with heatproof white paint. Let dry.
3. Cut a disc of plywood to fit inside the base of the stovepipe T.
4. Screw the socket to the center of the disc.
5. Drill a hole in the back of the T for the lamp cord.
6. Fasten the disc in place with nails.
7. Cut a circle of plastic to pressure-fit inside the front opening of the T to diffuse light.
8. Attach the lamp cord to the socket.
9. Add plug to the other end of cord.
10. Install a line switch at convenient place.
(Note: See page 252-253 for complete instructions on wiring lamps.)
11. Use a low-wattage bulb. (See chart—p. 252.)

Agitator Sculpture

A trip to the junkyard could turn up the old washing machine part you need to produce this "arty" agitator sculpture. And as if art for art's sake isn't good enough—this juntique also doubles as an oversized candle holder.

Materials

One washing machine agitator
Black gloss enamel
Acrylic paint in bright accent colors
One scrap of ornamental ironwork
One bolt fitted with nut
One oversized candle

Tools

Coarse-grade sandpaper
Paintbrush
Pliers

Directions

1. Sand agitator well.
2. Paint with black gloss enamel. Let dry.
3. Accent certain areas with acrylics. Let dry.
4. Bolt the scrap of ornamental ironwork to the top of the agitator to serve as candle holder.

Metal-Cardboard Lamps

Each one of these colorful stovepipe or cardboard creations will light the way for the traveller to your front door, inside your porch, or if weather permits, on the patio.

Choose different metals and select the boldest and brightest colors for lamplighters that will call out welcome to any visitor.

Materials
Red-white-blue lamp
Two 2-pound coffee cans (tops removed)
One 3½-inch tuna can (top removed)
One 6-inch glass globe (the neck must fit inside the tuna can)
Three thumbscrews
Red and blue 1½-inch-wide vinyl tape ⅛-inch IPS all-thread lamp pipe (cut to fit length of lamp)
Two nuts and two washers to fit lamp pipe
White paint
Electrical parts (cord with line switch, plug, and socket)
Epoxy
Standard bulb

Orange lamp
Roof vent cap
Stovepipe to fit roof vent cap
Water heater vent cap to fit stovepipe
Primer
Orange paint
Electrical parts (cord with line switch, plug, and socket)
⅛-inch IPS all-thread lamp pipe (just over ½ the length of the stovepipe)
Two washers and two nuts
to fit all-thread lamp pipe
Standard light bulb

Black stovepipe lamp
One adjustable stovepipe elbow (3½ inches in diameter)
One 6-inch-long stovepipe (3½ inches in diameter)
Water heater vent cap to fit stovepipe
⅛-inch IPS all-thread lamp pipe (cut to fit length of lamp)
Two washers and two nuts to fit IPS pipe
Oversized bulb
Electrical parts (cord with line switch, plug, and socket)

One brace bar to fit inside stovepipe (center hole fits over lamp pipe)
Primer
Black paint

Streetlamp
54-inch-long heavy cardboard tube (4-inch carpet roll tube)
Two 2- to 3-inch-deep cans (about 4-inch diameter to fit over carpet roll tube), tops removed
One 11½-inch-diameter glass globe (the neck must fit inside the cans you use)
One gelatin ring mold with center opening approximately the size of the carpet roll tube's diameter
1-inch IPS all-thread lamp pipe (cut to fit length of lamp)
Two brace bars to fit over lamp pipe and inside cans
Epoxy
Primer
Yellow latex house paint
Electrical parts (cord, plug, one screw-in socket with side turn-on switch, and one 1½-inch extension turn-on arm)
Standard light bulb
Three thumbscrews
Five pounds plaster of paris or mortar mix

Tools
Drill
Paintbrushes
Conduit bender
Steel wool
Adjustable wrench

Directions
Red-white-blue lamp (see sketch A on page 132)   **1.** Drill holes through the centers of all cans to accommodate the lamp pipe.
2. Rub steel wool on the coffee can rims, the tuna can rim, and the bottom of the coffee cans.
3. Thread one coffee can (bottom down) on the lamp pipe. Thread on the other coffee can (bottom up) and then the tuna can (bottom down).
4. Adjust the coffee cans so seams are aligned.
5. Epoxy the coffee cans together at the rims.
6. Epoxy the tuna can to the top coffee can.
7. Add washer and nut to the top and bottom of the lamp pipe and tighten.
8. Wire lamp (see pages 252-253).

(continued on next page)

9. Give the lamp two coats of white paint (cover the cord and plug while painting). Let dry thoroughly after each coat.

10. Alternate rows of red and blue vinyl tape, with 1 inch of white paint showing between each strip of tape (see photo). Start and end each row at the back seam of the cans.

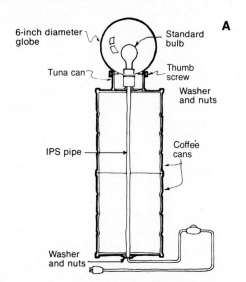

11. Drill three holes equidistant from each other just below the rim of the tuna can.

12. Screw the standard bulb into socket.

13. Put on the globe and screw in the thumb-screws to secure the globe.

Orange lamp (see sketch B) **1.** Drill a hole in the bottom of the water heater vent cap that is large enough to accommodate the lamp pipe.

2. Screw on nut, then washer about ½ inch up from bottom of lamp pipe.

3. Slide the lamp pipe through the hole in the bottom of the water heater vent cap and push vent cap securely against washer.

4. Screw washer and nut onto lamp pipe and tighten against bottom of vent cap.

5. Position stovepipe in water heater vent cap.

6. Wire the lamp according to the instructions on pages 252-253.

7. Screw in the standard light bulb.

8. Slip roof vent cap on top of stovepipe.

9. To paint the lamp,
- Cover cord and plug.
- Wash the metal with vinegar. Let dry.
- Primer the metal parts. Let dry.
- Paint the lamp orange. Let dry.

Black stovepipe lamp (see sketch C) **1.** Push the straight stovepipe on the adjustable stovepipe elbow and turn to the desired angle.

2. Drill a hole for the lamp pipe in the center of the water heater vent cap.

3. Bend the lamp pipe to approximately the shape of the stovepipe with the conduit bender.

4. Insert the lamp pipe into the stovepipe.

5. Screw on the brace bar to hold the lamp pipe in the center of the stovepipe.

6. Screw on nut, then washer about ½ inch up from bottom of lamp pipe.

7. Fit the lamp pipe through the hole in the bottom of the vent cap.

8. Push the vent cap securely onto the stovepipe and up against the washer.

9. Screw washer and nut onto lamp pipe and tighten against bottom of vent cap.

10. Wire the lamp according to the instructions on pages 252-253.

11. To paint the lamp,
- Cover cord and plug.
- Wash the metal with vinegar. Let dry.
- Primer the metal parts. Let dry.
- Paint the lamp black. Let dry.

12. Screw the oversized bulb into socket.

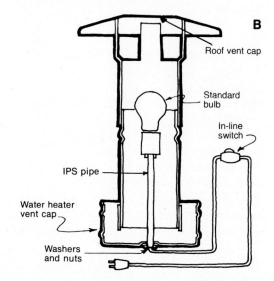

Streetlamp (see sketch D) **1.** Drill holes in the center of the can bottoms to accommodate the 1-inch lamp pipe.

2. Put the two cans together (bottom to bottom) and fit the lamp pipe through the center hole; screw one brace bar tightly against bottom of each can.

3. Position the socket on the lamp pipe and measure from the extension turn-on switch to the side of the top can.

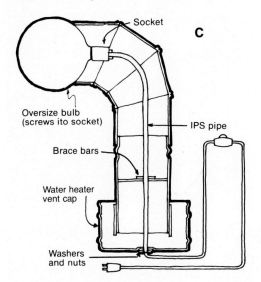

C

Socket

Oversize bulb (screws ito socket)

IPS pipe

Brace bars

Water heater vent cap

Washers and nuts

4. Mark the spot for extension switch and drill a hole in the can side to fit the extension switch. (Remove the socket while you continue working on the lamp.)

5. Drill three equally spaced holes at the top edge of the can for the thumbscrews (these keep the glass globe in place).

6. Fit the bottom can over the top of the cardboard tube **(Note:** If the can is too large, cut strips of thin cardboard the depth of the can and glue them around the top of the tube until you achieve a tight fit. Let dry.)

7. Fit the cardboard tube into the center of the inverted ring mold. **(Note:** If the tube is slightly large, remove enough of the top layer of cardboard to make a snug fit. If the tube is a little smaller than the hole in the center of the ring mold, adjust it as you did the top of the tube, gluing on cardboard strips as needed. Let dry completely.)

8. Stand the lamp up and check to make sure the lamp post and the base are level.

9. Remove the ring mold.

10. Mix plaster of paris or mortar mix according to directions on the container.

11. Fill ring mold to within ½ inch of top with plaster of paris or mortar mix. Let harden.

12. Drill a hole in the top rim of the mold so the electrical cord can come out.

13. Assemble the lamp for painting:

• Glue the bottom can to the top of the carpet roll tube with epoxy. Let dry thoroughly.
• Invert plaster of paris-filled ring mold.
• Insert the carpet roll tube in center of inverted mold and glue in place with epoxy.

14. Primer the assembled lamp. Let dry.

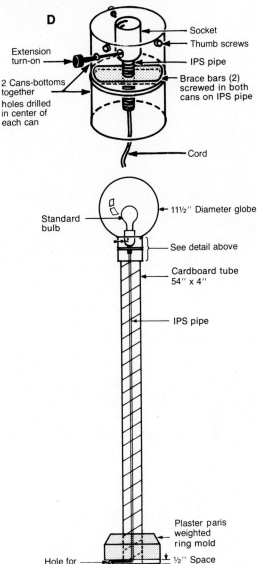

D

Extension turn-on

2 Cans-bottoms together holes drilled in center of each can

Socket

Thumb screws

IPS pipe

Brace bars (2) screwed in both cans on IPS pipe

Cord

Standard bulb

11½" Diameter globe

See detail above

Cardboard tube 54" x 4"

IPS pipe

Plaster paris weighted ring mold

½" Space

Hole for cord

15. Paint the lamp yellow (use latex house paint to slow down weather deterioration). Let dry completely.

16. Wire the lamp according to the instructions on pages 252-253.

17. Screw the bulb into the socket.

18. Put on the globe and screw in the thumbscrews to hold the globe in place.

Wheel Rim Stools

If you are spinning your wheels trying to find sturdy, inexpensive, yet decorative seating, stop and consider these sunburst-cushioned stools fashioned from steel wheel rims. Since the average wheel rim is only 15 inches in diameter, these stools are an excellent seating solution for small-space areas.

Materials (for each stool)
Stool
    Two small wheel rims
    Epoxy
    Metal primer
    Latex enamel paint (three colors)
Sunburst cushion
    1¼ yards fabric for 15-inch wheel rim
        (lightweight fabric won't wear well)
    ¾ yard muslin
    One round pillow form (to fit wheel rim)
    2 yards 1-inch cording
    Two large pillow buttons
    Strong carpet or button thread

Tools
Stool
    Medium-grade sandpaper
Sunburst cushion
    Crewel needle
    Sewing machine with cording or zipper foot

Directions
Stool **1.** Clean the wheel rim edges. (Be sure they are free of paint and grease—to bond properly, the glue requires a clean surface.)
2. Glue wheel rims together by placing a thin line of epoxy around edge of bottom rim and setting top rim on this. Let sit for several hours or as instructed on epoxy.
3. Sand the wheel rims until they are smooth enough to accept the primer.
4. Primer the wheel rims. Let dry completely.
5. Paint the rims. Let dry completely.
6. Paint the rim edges contrasting colors. Let dry completely.

Sunburst cushion   **1.** Determine the diameter of the pillow form:

- Measure from the center of top of the pillow form to the center of side of pillow form.
- Double this measurement.

2. Cover the pillow form with a muslin casing:
- Cut two circular pieces of muslin the diameter of the pillow form plus 1 inch for seam allowances.
- With right sides together, stitch around the muslin sections, making a ½-inch seam (be sure to leave large enough opening for inserting the pillow form).
- Notch seam allowance, as shown in sketch A.
- Turn casing right side out and press seam.
- Insert the pillow form.
- Turn edges of opening to inside and stitch together by hand or machine.

3. To begin the outside cover of the pillow.
- Cut two strips of fabric on the true bias. (The true bias is the diagonal of a square. To determine this, fold material as shown in sketch D on page 136. The folded edge is the true bias.) The length of each strip should be 3½ times the diameter of the form plus 1 inch for seam allowances, and the width should be ½ the diameter plus 1 inch for seam allowances.
- Stitch the ends of each strip together by placing the right sides together and lapping the ends so that the strips form a right angle, as shown in sketch E on page 136. Stitch on the straight grain; press the seam open.
- Using machine basting stitch, sew ¼ inch from one edge on each piece. Then, sew another line of stitching ¼ inch from first stitching.
- To gather each piece, gently pull top threads,

as shown in sketch B. Continue pulling thread until material is gathered in sunburst, as shown in sketch C.
- Pull center raw edge to wrong side of material and secure gathering by tying knots in the thread.
- Using heavy-duty thread, sew circle around center about ⅛ inch from the center, as shown in sketch C.

4. Cover a length of 1-inch-wide cording with a bias strip of matching fabric. (Continuous bias is the best method to use when you need several yards of bias strips—see tip box on page 137.)
- Cut a 4-inch-wide bias strip of fabric. Length of strip should be 3½ times the pillow diameter. (If not using continuous bias, sew bias pieces together as shown in sketch E on page 136 to give desired length.)

(continued on next page)

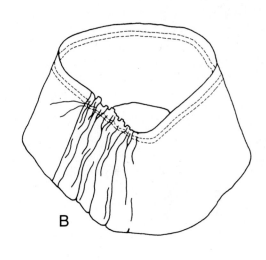

B

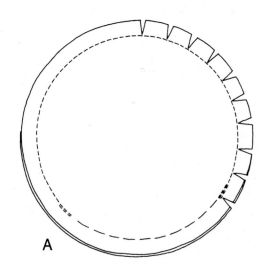

A

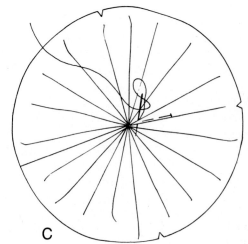

C

- Fold the bias strip around the cord, right side out, encasing it completely. Align raw edges of bias strip.
- Using an adjustable cording or zipper foot, (sketch F) stitch close to cord. (Stretch bias slightly as you are stitching it over cord.)

5. Join the gathered sections with a corded seam finish:

- Pin the fabric-covered cording to the right side of one gathered section, placing the cording's stitching ½ inch from raw edge of gathered section. (To ensure a smooth fit around the outside curves, pin the cording in place, stretching the seam allowance around the outside curve and easing the cord. Clip the seam allowances where necessary to keep the seams lying flat—see sketch G.)
- Stitch along seam line, using a cording foot as shown in sketch H.
- Pin corded edge over the other gathered section, with right sides together. Carefully match edges at the curves and clip as necessary.
- Stitch between the cord and previous stitching, crowding the cording or zipper foot against the cording. Leave large enough opening to insert the pillow form.
- To reduce the bulk in the seam, trim the seam allowance of the cording to ⅛ inch. Trim the seam allowances of gathered sections to ¼ inch (see sketch I). Trim only the cording seam allowance of opening.

6. Turn the pillow cover right side out.

7. Insert the pillow form.

8. Turn edges of opening to inside and stitch together by hand.

9. Sew on center buttons, using a crewel needle and strong carpet or button thread. (If desired, use matching fabric-covered button.)

- Push the needle up through the pillow, leaving a 3-inch tail of thread hanging.
- Run the needle through the button shank on the top, as shown in sketch J.
- Direct the needle back through the pillow about ⅛ inch from the thread.
- Run the needle through the shank of the second button on the bottom.
- Run the needle and thread through the shanks and pillow two or three times.
- Draw the thread taut and tie securely to the 3-inch tail of thread so the knot is under the button. Cut off the thread ends.

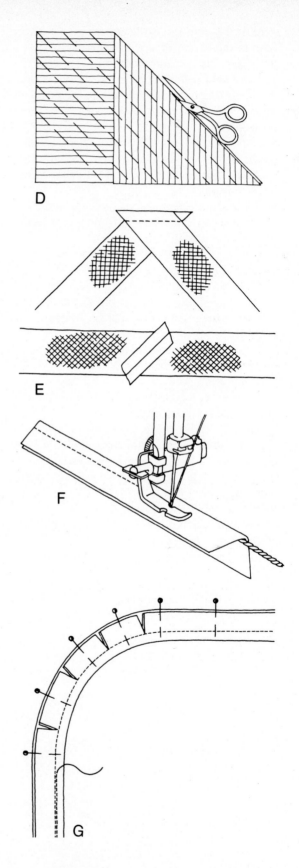

D

E

F

G

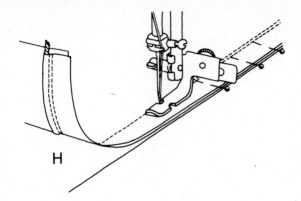

H

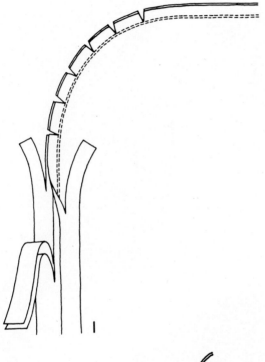

I

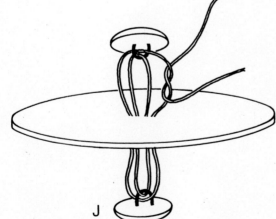

J

Continuous bias strips

When you need several yards of bias strips, cut a continuous bias as follows:

1. Cut a rectangle of fabric on the straight grain.

2. Lay fabric flat, wrong side up, and mark the true bias on the wrong side, starting at the top right-hand corner.

3. Measuring from the starting line, mark the width of the bias strip. Continue to measure and mark until you have marked sufficient length (see sketch K).

4. Cut off excess fabric.

5. Form a tube by bringing side edges together, matching lines. (The first line extends above others; see sketch L.)

6. Pin and stitch a ¼-inch seam.

7. Press seam open. Then, start cutting on the first line and continue cutting around the tube on the marked lines.

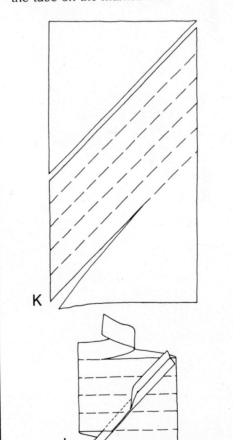

K

L

Heating Pipe Floor Lamp

By using your imagination, often you can recycle things meant for one purpose into a new useful role. For example, this unusual floor lamp incorporates heating duct pipe for the body of the lamp and an elbow boot as a shade. The use of adjustable elbows makes it possible to turn the light in various directions.

Materials

Sections of 6-inch galvanized steel pipe (total length about 6 feet)
One section 6-inch galvanized steel pipe with 45° branch
Three 6-inch adjustable elbows
One 6-inch elbow boot with standard diffuser to fit
Metal floor lamp stand
3 yards patterned fabric
Fabric glue
Flat gray paint
Flat black paint
Gravel
Electrical parts (socket with bottom switch and nut to fit, as shown in sketch; and cord with molded end plug—length depends on total length of lamp)
Electrical tape
One 60-watt showcase bulb
½-inch plastic insert
Rivets or sheet metal screws

Tools

Drill with metal bit
Paintbrush
Riveting gun (optional)

Directions

1. Take straight section of the pipe to a welder and have this section welded to the metal floor lamp stand.
2. Pour several inches of gravel into the bottom of the straight section of pipe to stabilize the lamp.
3. Drill a ½-inch hole near the bottom of the straight section of pipe.
4. Put the ½-inch plastic insert in this hole to protect the cord from the sharp edge of the drilled hole.
5. Thread lamp cord through plastic insert.
6. To assemble the lamp,

• Position the branched pipe section atop straight pipe.
• Position two of the adjustable elbows atop branched section.
• Position the remaining adjustable elbow on branched section.
• Position elbow boot on end of this adjustable elbow.
7. Thread cord up through pipe and through branch to elbow boot. Then, attach cord to the inside of the pipe with electrical tape (tape several places).
8. Secure pipe at joints by riveting with riveting gun or by drilling holes and screwing pipe together with sheet metal screws.
9. Wire the cord to the socket according to directions on pages 252-253.
10. Drill hole for socket switch in side of elbow boot, as shown in the sketch.
11. Insert socket switch through hole and secure with nut.
12. Insert 60-watt showcase bulb into socket.
13. Insert diffuser in opening of elbow boot. (**Note:** If desired, have a plastic cover made to use instead of the diffuser.)
14. Paint all the extending sections of the lamp flat gray. Let dry.
15. Paint the metal floor lamp stand black. Let dry completely.
16. Glue the fabric onto the straight section of the lamp. Let dry.

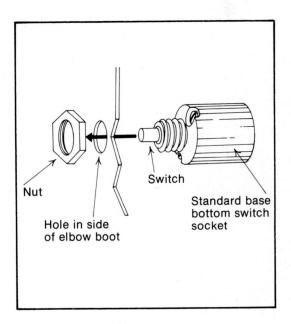

Nut

Switch

Hole in side of elbow boot

Standard base bottom switch socket

Boat Prop Sculpture

Stumbling across an old boat propeller in the junk heap isn't exactly like owning your own yacht. But give it a quick face-lift, put it to work as a handsome piece of sculpture, and even without the boat attached, you'll look like you're part of the yachting set. And, if you want to give this patriotic piece a function, use it as a paperweight.

Materials
One boat propeller
One 2¼x2¼x4-inch precut wood post (to be used as base)
One 2¼-inch precut wood ball
Enamel paint (white, red, and blue)
One dowel rod to fit through propeller
Wood glue

Tools
Coarse-grade sandpaper
Paintbrush
Drill

Directions
1. Clean up and sand boat propeller.
2. Drill hole in both wood post base and wood ball to accept the dowel rod.
3. Sand wood block base and wood ball.
4. Paint base and ball with two coats of white enamel. Let dry between coats. This will yield a smooth lacquer-like finish. Sand between coats.
5. Paint boat propeller with red, white, and blue enamel. Allow to dry completely.
6. Glue one end of dowel into base. Let dry.
7. Slide propeller over dowel rod.
8. Glue ball to top of dowel rod. Let dry.

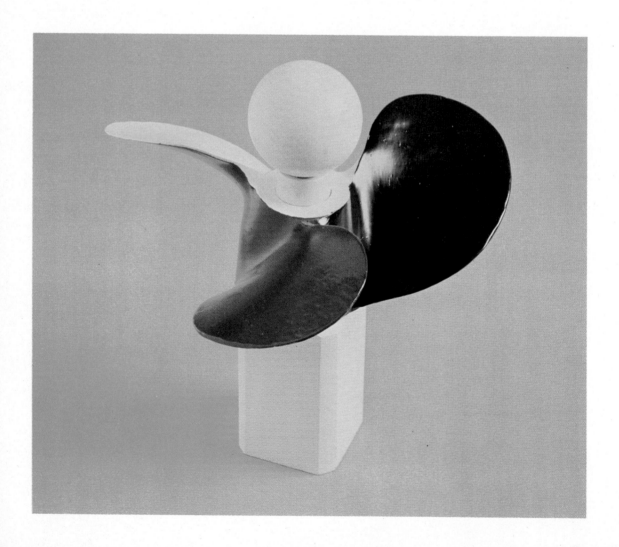

Metal Elbow Mirror

Stovepipes are, for the most part, unnoticed and unappreciated. But not these. Here, four elbows and four lengths of pipe have gone together to frame m'lady's mirror—elegantly.

Materials

Four 3-inch-diameter sheet metal elbows
Four lengths of 3-inch aluminum duct pipe
Red enamel
Mirror
Six sheet metal screws
Length of wire for hanging mirror

Tools

Metal cutter
Paintbrush
Glass cutter
Wire cutter
Punch

Directions

1. With metal cutter, cut lengths of aluminum duct pipe to desired length—these fit between elbows, which act as the mirror frame's corners. **(Note:** Pipe lengths usually come disconnected, with one end of each length crimped to fit into plain end of each elbow. Cut on plain end.)
2. Push the open lengthwise joints of the cut duct pipes together.
3. Assemble mirror frame by inserting duct pipes into elbow corners.
4. Paint with red enamel. Let dry completely.
5. With glass cutter, cut off the corners of the mirror so they won't show beyond the frame. Punch pilot holes in each corner of the frame, then fasten mirror to frame with sheet metal screws. (Heads of the sheet metal screws secure the mirror to the frame.)
6. Put two sheet metal screws into the top back of the frame, with a length of wire attached to the screws. (Use this as a hanger.)

···⁊ chapter 7 ⁊···

Decorative Paper Projects

When the Egyptians pounded out papyrus, they couldn't possibly have imagined a day when too much paper could be a problem. But the Egyptians didn't have newspapers thrown on their doorsteps every morning, or supermarket sacks accumulating each week. We do! And because we live in a big "papered" world, we're able to enjoy some of these recyclables they would have given their faience beads to have.

Newspaper Gift Wraps

If you've blown your budget on gifts, and there's little money left for wrappings, here's a solution. The Sunday comics are colorful, inexpensive, and imaginative gift wraps. More gift wrap substitutes are listed below.

Materials
Newspapers (comics or classified ads
    section, or foreign-language papers),
    wallpaper, road maps, catalog pages
    (general merchandise or seed catalogs),
    magazine pages, blueprints, brown paper
    bags, decorated sacks, posters, children's
    drawings, and/or shelf paper
Clear acrylic or varnish
Tying material (plaid ribbon, twine, yarn,
    colored plastic sacks cut in strips, or
    paper cut in strips with pinking shears)

Tools
Scissors
Paintbrush
Cellophane tape

Directions
1. Put a coat of acrylic or varnish on newspapers or any other printed papers that tend to smear. Let dry completely before proceeding with the wrapping.
2. Wrap the packages with the paper and secure with cellophane tape.
3. Tie bows. Use plaid ribbon, as shown, or any of the ribbon alternatives listed.
(**Note:** Make a package-display Christmas tree from a stepladder. Give the ladder a fresh coat of red paint and place boards across the rungs.) Place gifts on the boards. To add decoration to your ladder tree, place apothecary jars filled with Christmas candies among the packages.)

Decoupage Gifts

A few years ago "decoupage" was a French word the average American didn't know. But recently, the term has become a household word, and the craft technique has taken America by storm. Decoupage is easy, fun, and certainly one of the nicest things to happen to paper since the discovery of the printing press.

Materials
Three wooden plaques
    Three ready-made wooden plaques
    Glue
    Old greeting cards
    Three ring-type hangers
    Acrylic sealer
    Enamel (semigloss)
    Varnish—high-gloss and satin finishes

Mirror

Two-part frame or a regular frame with a cross partition
Acrylic paint (black, white, and yellow)
Flat-finish varnish
Glass and mirror (cut to fit upper and lower sections of frame)
Flat-finish acrylic coating
Mucilage or a mixture of half decoupage paste and half resoluble white glue
Transfer emulsion
Crackling liquid
Oil-base aging compound
Varnish
Design print
Paper to cover back of mirror
Mirror hanger

Wedding invitation plate

6-inch embroidery hoop
Glass plate
Circular flower print
Acrylic coating
White tack
Wedding invitation
Gold leaf size
Gold metal leaf
Gold leaf sealer
White glue
Cardboard
Heavy, silky fabric
Narrow, velvet ribbon

Yellow match box

One scrap piece of 1/8 or 1/4-inch plywood
Bright yellow paint
Silicone
Four match boxes (made of thin wood)
Four identical prints or greeting cards with bird design
Acrylic coating
Glue
Instant lacquer finish
Ribbon

Tools
(needed for each project)
Paintbrush
Scissors
Coarse-grade and, fine-grade sandpaper
Fine steel wool

Mirror
Paste wax

Wedding Invitation Plate
Glass marker
Soft brush
Cotton

Yellow match box
Saw

Directions

Three wooden plaques **1.** Sand wood plaques. Wipe.
2. Give each two coats of enamel. Dry.
3. Sand lightly.
4. Cut the greeting-card print:
• Cut around outline of design to silhouette print on background color of plaque. Or,
• Cut print to fill entire surface of plaque.
5. Seal print on both sides, using two or three light coats of acrylic sealer. Let dry.
6. Coat back of print evenly with white glue.
7. Apply the glued print to the plaque. Smooth down, working out toward the edges. Wipe excess glue with a damp cloth. Dry.
8. Finish with three or more coats of high-gloss varnish. Let each coat dry 24 hours. Rub down lightly between coats with steel wool.
9. Apply a final coat of satin varnish. Let dry.
10. Screw in a ring-type hanger at top of each.

Mirror **1.** Paint the frame with acrylics. (Use a mixture of black and yellow. Lighten some with white to make a second lighter shade.) Let dry.
2. Apply three coats of varnish at 24-hour intervals.
3. Remove dust on varnished frame with fine-grade sandpaper (used wet).
4. Polish with fine steel wool.
5. Polish surface with the palm of your hand.
6. Polish the frame with paste wax.
7. Lightly coat the print with acrylic coating. Let dry, then cut.
8. Glue the print to the underside of the glass, one section at a time, with mucilage or a mixture of half decoupage paste and half resoluble white glue. Let dry.
9. With the right side facing you, press out excess glue and air bubbles. Clean each section as you glue it. Let dry.
10. Apply two thin coats of transfer emulsion at half-hour intervals. Let dry between coats.
11. Apply one coat of crackling liquid and allow to crackle for 24 hours.

(continued on next page)

12. Pat on two coats of white acrylic paint, using a brush. Let dry between coats.

13. Paint one coat of varnish. Let dry.

14. Glue mirror and glass into frame. Let dry completely before finishing.

15. Cover the back with paper.

16. Nail hanger on the back of the frame.

Wedding Invitation Plate **1.** Lightly seal the front of a large, circular flower print, using acrylic coating. Let the print dry completely before proceeding to the next step.

2. Cut out the print in sections—single flowers and a few flowers and leaves together.

3. Hold a 6-inch wooden embroidery hoop in the center of the glass plate.

4. Draw the circle around the inner edge with a glass marker. Mark on the top of the plate.

5. Arrange flower design on the rim of the plate, with leaves, petals, and stems overlapping to form a continuous garland. The design should cover the drawn circle. Temporarily, secure elements with white tack. (**Note:** Make sure that the design extends beyond the drawn circle and provides a stopping place for gold leafing to be applied later.)

Basic tools and materials for decoupage

Decoupage projects are usually done with materials you have lying around your house. You can make stunning decoupage plaques from small boards and varnish from the workshop and from pictures taken from old magazines.

Most decoupage projects require the following basic materials and tools: designs painted on paper, white glue, sponge applicator, sable brush (several sizes), sharp scissors, tacking putty, craft knife, burnisher, rubber roller (optional), fine-grade sandpaper, tack cloth, acrylic sealer, gesso, fast-drying acrylic paint, varnish, or lacquer, fine paste wax, steel wool, and lint-free cloth.

If you need additional help, take a trip to your local art and craft shops.

---

6. Place the invitation behind this garland.

7. Adjust the arrangement:

• Leave the garland in place on the upper side of the plate.

• Move one section at a time to the underside.

8. Glue garland permanently in place with the white glue. Let dry completely.

9. Looking at it from the right side, press out excess glue. Let dry.

10. Add portions of print around the outside edge of the plate to enhance the design.

11. Apply gold size to indented rim on front outside edge of plate if there is one.

12. Turn the plate over on a can; apply size with brush over area to be gold leafed.

13. With proper tack developed, apply gold metal leaf, patting it around to front of plate at the edges.

14. Look at it from the right side, press around every portion of print to adhere leaf securely at print edges. Allow to dry.

15. With soft brush, remove excess leaf in direction of overlaps.

16. Polish gently with cotton.

17. Apply two coats of special gold leaf sealer; let dry between coats.

18. For the hoop, cut a circle of stiff cardboard to fit the outer edge of the hoop.

19. Mark match-up points on hoop and cardboard.

20. Seal invitation on the back side. Let dry completely before proceeding.

21. Cut the invitation to fit the cardboard, also with match-up points. (Add portion of back of invitation if needed to complete circle.)

22. Glue the invitation to the cardboard (glue all over if flat, but glue only around the edges if rippled by engraving.) Let dry.

23. Glue a band of narrow, velvet ribbon around the inside of the hoop. Let dry.

24. Glue the invitation and cardboard to the hoop. Weight while drying.

25. Turn the hoop over; glue heavy, silky fabric to the back of the cardboard, extending beyond the sides. Let dry.

26. Notch excess fabric and glue it to the sides of the hoop. Trim off excess. Let dry.

27. Glue the hoop to the plate with undiluted white glue. Weight while drying.

28. Glue narrow velvet ribbon over notched fabric on the outside of the hoop. Let dry.

(**Note:** Do not put hanger on the hoop. The hoop will stay in place but it will not support the weight of the plate if hung on a wall. Display on a small easel as an alternative.)

Yellow match box **1.** Cut two 3¾-inch squares from ⅛- or ¼-inch plywood.
2. Paint bright yellow on both sides. Let dry.
3. Paint the ends and the interiors of four boxes of matches. Let dry.
4. Seal four identical prints or greeting cards with acrylic coating. Let dry.
5. From the first print, cut the basic bird.
6. From the second print, cut eye, wing, beak, and as many flowers as possible.
7. From the third print, cut tail, leaves, and more flowers.
8. Cut more flowers from last print.
9. Shape the head of the bird, attached to the body, with your fingers.
10. Glue the body flat, but not on the head. Let dry.
11. Put dab of silicone behind the head to prop it up. Let dry.
12. Glue tail to the body with white glue. Let dry. (Let rest of tail stand free.)
13. Shape wing with fingers.
14. Add silicone under place where wing connects with the body. Let the end of the wing stand free. Allow to dry.
15. Shape the eye and the beak.
16. Attach with glue. Let dry.
17. Apply glue to one end of shaped leaves so they will be freestanding. Let dry.
18. Shape individual flowers.
19. Glue only the centers. Let dry.
20. Paint the finished elevation twice with acrylic. Let dry between coats.
21. Apply eight coats of instant lacquer finish to both pieces of wood. Let dry between coats. (Coat lightly at first, then more heavily until heavy porcelain finish develops.)
22. Slit bottom end of match boxes and insert the ribbon.
23. Glue ribbon across the bottom of the boxes. Leave an inch hanging out. Let dry.
24. Glue four match boxes to the wrong side of plain panel in such a way that striking surface and box ends face in all directions. Dry.
25. Glue the elevation on top of the plywood square. Let dry.

Surfaces you can and cannot decoupage

- **Wood objects:** Sand well; wipe with a tack cloth; seal with a coat of gesso, acrylic, or liquid sealer
- **Varnished or waxed furniture:** Wash surface with mineral spirits
- **New tinware:** Rinse object in solution of one part water and one part vinegar; let dry completely before proceeding; paint on two coats of rust-resistant paint; dry completely before proceeding; sand; wipe with a tack cloth
- **Old tinware:** Use heavy-duty steel wool; follow same instructions for the old tinware as used with the new tinware (*Note:* Decoupage won't adhere to tinware with a baked enamel finish.)
- **Stone:** Scrub with soap and water; dry; apply paint directly to stone; varnish, paint, or lacquer
- **Ceramic—glazed or unglazed:** No special preparation; keep surface free of dust

How to prepare prints for use in decoupage

There are some prints that are thin enough for immediate use. They are gift wrapping paper, magazine art, greeting cards, and foil trimming.

Thick prints such as postcards and photographs need to be thinned. In order to thin-out the thick prints,
- Seal front of print
- Coat wrong side with white glue; dry
- Peel up a corner of the wrong side
- Place a pencil across peeled corner
- Roll corner around pencil until tight
- Keep rolling until full layer of backing is removed
- Rub wrong side with sandpaper to smooth surface and eliminate any thick spots

Gold foil letters (spell out Joy and Merry
   Christmas)
Matte varnish
½ yard red yarn

Tools
   One 6d finishing nail
   Paintbrush
   Scissors
   Saber saw

Directions
1. Paint the 14x18-inch pressboard plaque with
a coat of gesso. Let dry.
2. Paint the front and back of the plaque with
two coats of lavender acrylic paint (or any color
that goes well with both your decor and your
selection of cards.) Let dry.
3. Lay out your collection of cards. (Select cards
with simple designs to make viewing them on a
wall easier. Plan different sizes and shapes to
make the arrangement interesting.)
4. Cut 1-inch-thick pine scraps to desired sizes.
Arrange them on the wood plaque.
5. Number each wood block on the back and put
the corresponding number on the plaque to indicate the placement.
6. Paint the front of the blocks red. Let them dry
completely.
7. Paint the sides of the blocks green. Let dry
completely before proceeding.
8. Glue the blocks in place on the plaque. Let
dry completely.
9. Cut the Christmas cards to fit. Silhouette
some designs to be backed by the red block. Trim
some cards to cover the entire front surface of
the block. Trim others slightly smaller than the
block so they appear "framed" in red. Leave
some blocks plain for gold letters.
10. Glue cards on blocks. Let dry.
11. Glue gold foil letters on top of the plain
blocks. (In this project the foil letters were used to
spell out the words JOY and MERRY CHRIST-
MAS). Let dry.
12. Give the entire unit two coats of matte
varnish. Let dry between coats.
13. Cut the desired length of yarn.
14. Glue yarn to the back of the plaque for a
wall hanger. Let dry.
15. Hang the plaque on a finishing nail on the
wall for display.

Christmas Card Mosaic

Memories of Christmas last long after the tree and
tinsel are put away, but one sure way to preserve
the beauty of Christmas is to display your holiday
cards in this charming Christmas card mosaic.
Let each member of the family choose his or her
favorite card. Or be selective and use only cards
of a particular Christmas symbol such as stars,
trees, angels, or Santas. Then add gold letter
"greetings" of your own.

Materials
   Christmas cards of all shapes, themes, sizes,
      and designs (20 used here)
   One 14x18-inch pressboard plaque
   Gesso
   Paint (lavender, red, and green acrylic)
   Twenty 1-inch-thick scraps (wood blocks)
   Glue

Magazine Cover
Christmas Card

Christmas covers on magazines often feature a design that makes a natural picture frame. Those covers are also "naturals" for personalized Christmas cards. Here's how to make cover models of your children, and solve your holiday card problem at the same time.

Materials
One magazine cover (Christmas issue—use cover with a natural opening such as circle, oval, or square—keep the design simple.)
One photograph (8x10 for magazines of 9½ x12½-inch format and 5x7 for magazines of 8x10 ¾-inch format)
Cellophane tape

Tools
Sharp pair of scissors
Camera (with normal or telephoto lens)
Color film (size and type determined by camera and lighting)
Two photoflood lights (for copy work)

Directions
1. Photograph a close-up of the face or faces of your subjects. (Have the photos processed commercially. Use school photos as alternatives.)
2. Cut out the wreath opening with a sharp pair of scissors.
3. Frame the photo so that just the face shows through the opening of the wreath.
4. Tape the photo behind the opening. (The size of the photo is determined by the size of the magazine opening.)
5. Write your own greeting somewhere on the cover and in an area that will blend with the established magazine format.
6. Frame the personalized cover behind glass and hang it on a wall.
7. Photocopy the framed cover:
• Place photoflood lights on each side of the frame to balance lighting and avoid reflections from the glass.
• Photograph the cover with your camera on a tripod. (Use a telephoto lens if you have one.)
• Or, have the framed cover photocopied by a professional photo dealer.
8. Use the negative to have cards printed to the desired Christmas card sizes.

149

Tissue-Covered Window

After most birthday parties or bridal showers, you inevitably have some tissue paper to toss. Next time, why not save it and use it in the imaginative way shown in the above photograph? This simple, striking window treatment features a large plaid design, but feel free to apply your own spontaneous and creative design.

Materials
Wrapping tissue paper (assorted colors for plaid design)
Masking tape
White glue

Tools
Paintbrush (an inexpensive one for application of glue)
Craft knife

Directions
1. Cut paper into strips of assorted sizes.
2. Mask window frame with tape.
3. Mix one part glue to four parts water.
4. Brush the glue mixture onto the glass where you intend to place the tissue strips.
5. Put the tissue on the glass and brush some glue mixture over the tissue.
6. Keep adding tissue strips while area is wet until the design is completed as desired. Let dry. (Let strips lap over edges of glass to allow for shrinkage during drying.)
7. Cut tape along edges with knife and remove.
8. Coat tissue-covered area with glue mixture. Let dry. (If you decide to change the design, simply dampen tissue-covered area and scrape off tissue with single-edged razor blade.)

Closet Door Collage

This dramatic closet door is a giant assemblage of clippings and calendar art. Save the various types of letters and clippings from magazines, catalogs, calendars, and advertisements.

Materials
Black and white clippings
Wallpaper paste
White enamel paint
Clear varnish

Tools
Seam or ink roller
Clean cloth
Paintbrush

Directions
1. Remove closet door knobs.
2. Paint door and knobs. Let dry.
3. Assemble clippings into desirable groupings.
4. Affix clippings to door:
- Brush paste over small area at top of door.
- Working across and down, apply clippings to paste-covered area, overlaying each cutout about ¼ inch.
- Smooth each with a clean cloth.
- Continue pasting small areas until door is covered as desired.
- Use a seam or ink roller to remove wrinkles.
- Wipe off excess paste.
- Let dry completely.
5. Cover clippings with a coat of clear varnish. Let dry completely.
6. Attach knobs to the door.

Grout for tile
Ceramic tile adhesive
¼x½-inch pine strips for framing tiles
Stain (optional)
Finishing nails

Tools
Brush for varnish or decoupage liquid
Notched adhesive spreader
Saber saw
Medium-grade sandpaper
Miter box

Directions
1. Carefully cut pictures from seed packets.
2. Coat the glazed tiles with varnish or decoupage liquid.
3. Lay one picture on each tile, smoothing down the picture to remove the wrinkles and bubbles. Allow to dry completely.
4. Cover tiles with three more coats varnish or decoupage liquid. Let dry between coats.
5. To make grouping shown,
• Place tiles side by side on a flat surface and measure the area the tiles will cover.
• Sand an equivalent area on the wall where tile grouping will hang. (This prepares the surface to accept the adhesive.)
• Apply adhesive to the wall with the spreader. (Do not spread more area than you can tile before the adhesive dries. Drying time of the adhesive will vary according to temperature and humidity in the room.)
• Spread adhesive to back of tile, covering about 80 percent of the back.
• Apply tiles, one at a time, using a slight twisting and sliding motion while pressing firmly into position.
• Remove excess adhesive with water while adhesive is soft.
• Grout between the tiles. (**Note:** Start the grouting immediately after the tiles set.)
6. To make frame for grouping,
• Measure the length and the depth of the tile-covered area.
• From these measurements, cut the pine strips to the correct lengths.
• Stain wood, if desired. Let dry.
• Miter the corners of the strips.
• Glue and nail the pine strips to the wall around the tile grouping. Let dry.

Tile Vegetable Garden

Bring your garden into your kitchen. Save colorful seed packets and use them to make enchanting tiles like these. Use the decoupaged tiles as shown to brighten up a kitchen splash board, or use them to outline a planter, or to decorate a bathroom wall.

Also, hang individual tiles as pictures, arranging them to highlight the decor.

Materials
Empty seed packets
Varnish or decoupage liquid
4½-inch square glazed ceramic tiles (¼-inch thick)

Sack Santa

In all the years the Santa legend has been thrilling youngsters, the jolly old bearer of gifts and goodies has been depicted in every conceivable art medium. This paper sack Santa, however, may be the first of its kind. This time around, Mr. Claus is heading the recycling parade—with three grocery sacks, and some cardboard comprising most of his make-up. Paint will bring him to life.

Materials

Two No. 12 grocery bags
One No. 6 grocery bag
Cardboard
Paper (newspaper for stuffing)
Paint
  (acrylics in white, bright red, and black)
Glue
2-inch white foam ball (for Santa's nose)
Pins

152

Tools
Scissors
Stapler
Paintbrush
Pencil

Directions
1. Cut a No. 12 grocery bag on its side folds, down 8 inches from the top edge.
2. Cut cardboard the same size as the bottom of the bag.
3. Glue cardboard in place. Let dry.

Arms **1.** Bend the front of the bag forward.
2. Bring cut side section forward with the folded edge parallel to the bottom of the bag and at right angles with the bag side. (See sketch A.)
3. Open bag sides and fold straight across at ends of cuts. (See sketch B.)
4. Fold up cuffs.
5. Reverse the center folds on the bag's sides.
6. Crease folds made in the step above, then fold the top of the bag 4 inches down from top.
7. Cut mittens from cardboard.
8. Glue mittens to sleeve. (See sketch C.) Dry.
9. Stuff bag with paper.
10. Staple the bag closed at shoulders and below the fold.
11. Paint with red, black, and white paint, using the photo on page 152 as a guide. Let dry completely before proceeding. (**Note:** The top of the bag above the fold is painted white, the rest of the bag red.)

Face **1.** Cut a face from cardboard, using the pattern below. (For help in enlarging a pattern from a grid, see page 209.)
2. Open the seam and remove the bottom of another large grocery bag.
3. Draw an outline of the beard on the bag, using the grid pattern shown here.
4. Cut the beard out.
5. Paint the beard white, and let dry. Paint the reverse side. Allow to dry.
6. Cover the cardboard face with brown paper.
7. Glue the face to the beard. Let dry completely before proceeding.
8. Slash the beard up to the face, making whiskers about an inch wide.
9. Cut a moustache from excess paper, about 1-inch wide, 4-inches long (for each side).

10. Flatten the foam ball on one side.
11. Paint the foam ball red. Let dry.
12. Glue the moustache to the face. Let dry.
13. Glue red ball nose to moustache. Let dry.
14. Secure the nose by pinning it through the back of the face.
15. Roll the beard, moustache, and hair by curling it around a pencil.

Hat **1.** Fold up a cuff on the bottom edge of a No. 6 bag, about 1½ inches.
2. Put your hand in the bag and push up the center bottom.
3. With the other hand, push outside bottom of bag to the inside.
4. Shape into a triangle.
5. Staple to hold.
6. Paint the hat red, the cuff white. Let dry.
7. Add a white circle tip cut from paper.
8. Attach face to body:
• Fold the white top of the body bag to the back.
• Slash the white portion in one-inch strips and curl with a pencil.
• Staple the face to the bag front at fold.
9. Cut belt buckle of cardboard.
10. Paint belt buckle black. Let dry.
11. Glue buckle to Santa's suit. Let dry.
12. Staple the hat on at sides and back.

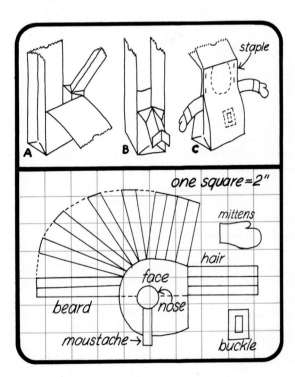

one square=2"

staple

mittens

hair

face

nose

beard

moustache→

buckle

Magazine Wall Covering

Your favorite magazine is probably great for decorating purposes. Look how these covers and pages from fashion magazines have found a permanent place on the walls of this dressing room. Preserve your "cover" job with a clear protective finish, or leave the magazine pages as they are for quick patch-ups—adding new pages to fit your fancy and to maintain the fanciful wallscape. (With this creative variety you'll never tire of staring at the walls!)

Materials

    Covers and pages from magazines
    Wallpaper paste
    Clear polyurethane varnish

Tools

    Scissors
    Brush for wallpaper paste
    Paintbrush

Directions

1. Select covers and magazine pages with the boldest images for use as wall covering.
2. Cut some of the subjects away from the page background to be used as silhouettes.
3. Plan arrangement of pages (**Note:** If using photos of people, plan for the models in the pages decorating the top of the wall to be looking down, those in the middle looking straight ahead, and those at the bottom of the wall looking up.)
4. One by one, apply wallpaper paste to the back of each page.
5. Position pasted page on the wall and smooth down, working from the center out toward the edges to avoid air bubbles. Let dry. (**Note:** To create the montage look shown here, let the edges of the pages overlap. Cut some pages in irregular sizes or shapes.)
6. Carefully wipe off any excess glue. (Magazine print may not take well to moisture, so apply only as much paste as is needed and try not to smear the paste around on the face of the pages.)
7. Position any silhouetted figures by coating the back sides with paste and placing the figures on top of the already installed pages. Allow to dry completely.
8. Coat with a clear protective finish. Let the wall covering dry completely.

Paper Bag Place Mats

With today's food prices, you can't afford to waste anything—including grocery sacks. You can cut those heavy-duty sacks in strips, then fold and weave them to make the trim, tailored place mats shown in the photo above.

Materials

    Heavy-duty grocery bags
    Brown matching thread
    Clear protective finish

Tools

    Scissors
    Sewing machine

Directions

1. Cut bags into 3½-inch-wide strips (15 strips 14 inches; 12 strips 18 inches long).
2. Fold in half lengthwise.
3. Fold again so cut edges meet at center fold.
4. Line up the 15 shorter strips, side by side. Machine stitch across strips, 1 inch from the edge.
5. Weave the longer strips over and under these, alternating the order every other strip. After each row, push strips together for firm weave.
6. Straighten and tighten mat.
7. Double machine stitch around edges close to weaving.
8. Coat the mats with clear protective finish. Let dry completely.

Colossal Papier-Mâché Christmas Balls

You can't wait forever for the Boy Scout paper drives to relieve you of a growing stack of newspapers. So why not recycle some of that old "news" into outdoor Christmas decorations that will broadcast holiday spirit throughout your neighborhood. For extra pizzazz, these gigantic globes are lighted inside their shimmery silver interiors. Despite their spectacular appearance, the Christmas balls shown here aren't as difficult to make as you think.

Materials
One weather balloon (per ornament)
Newspapers
White glue
Varnish
Aluminum foil

16 yards of outdoor velvet ribbon
Felt-tip marker
Wire
One string of large outdoor Christmas lights
Tape
Paint
Glitter
Instant papier mâché
Artificial snow
Miniature figures

Tools
Stapler
Plastic dishpan
Coping saw
Drill
Paintbrush

Directions
1. Inflate the weather balloon to the desired dimensions.

156

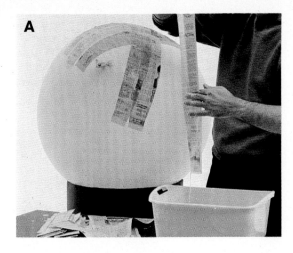

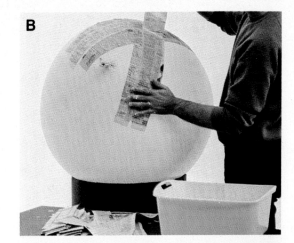

2. Tear newspaper into 2-inch strips.

3. Dilute white glue in a plastic dishpan (one part glue to six parts water).

4. Dip newspaper strips into the glue, removing any excess by pulling the paper through your fingers. (See photo A.)

5. Apply the paper strips to the balloon in a criss-cross design and smooth with fingers. (See photograph B.) Apply several coats of paper. Allow to dry thoroughly.

6. Give the entire surface a coat of varnish. Let dry. (This waterproofs the newspaper.)

7. As shown in photograph C, apply a coat of instant papier-mâché to the entire ball surface except where the opening will be. Let dry.

8. Draw the opening with a felt-tip marking pen.

9. Cut out the opening with a coping saw. (See Photograph D.)

10. Hook a wire into the top of the ball.

11. Apply instant papier-mâché around the wire. Let it dry.

12. Wire a strand of large Christmas lights and staple or tape them to the inside of the ball near the opening.

13. Drill a hole in the top of the ball.

14. Pull the light wire through the hole.

15. Paint the outside of the ball and add glitter. Let dry.

16. Crinkle aluminum foil and staple to the inside of the ball ornament.

17. Glue on the outdoor velvet ribbon to form the stripes. Let dry.

18. Add artificial snow and your own miniature figures to complete the wintry scenes. (Be sure

your choice of figures will withstand the seasonal cold temperatures.)

19. Tie ornaments to tree limbs using wire. Place near a convenient electrical source.

157

Road Map Wallpaper

Enjoy last year's vacation this year. During your travels, pick up local maps from travel agencies or service stations, then use them to paper a single wall—or a large area. That special vacation will be alive year-round.

Materials
    Road maps (number depends on size of area
        to be covered)
    Wallpaper paste

Tools
    Bucket
    Wallpaper paste brush
    Smoothing brush

Directions
1. Mix wallpaper paste according to package directions.
2. Place maps, printed side down, on worktable.
3. Apply wallpaper paste.
4. Position maps on wall, overlapping if desired.
5. Smooth maps out with smoothing brush to eliminate wrinkles and bubbles. Let dry.

Paper Bag Lanterns

Everyone knows where the Halloween party is when you mark your driveway with these eerie black cat lanterns. They're decorated paper bags with a base of sand to add stability and fire protection for the candles inside. But just to be on the safe side, keep the cats outdoors.

Materials
    Brown paper bags
    Black construction paper
    Glue
    Votive candles or candles in jars
    Sand

Tools
    Scissors

Directions
1. Make a pattern of cat outline.
2. Trace around pattern and cut cats out of black construction paper.
3. Glue cats to brown paper sacks. Let dry.
4. Pour two inches of sand in the bottom of each paper sack. (This adds weight so the wind won't blow the lanterns over.)
5. Place votive candles in the sand.

Paper Bag Animals

For pets that don't demand grooming, cage cleaning, or even feeding, create some of these "friends-of-the-family", using brown paper sacks and liquid wallpaper paste. They may not purr on your lap, but you'll love them just the same especially for gifts and decorating.

Materials
Five No. 6 sacks for each large animal
Five No. 3 sacks for each small animal
Liquid wallpaper paste
Poster paints

Tools
Scissors
2-inch paintbrush
Small paintbrush for finishing

Directions
1. Cut down a paper bag to half its size and open it.
2. Using 2-inch paintbrush, coat the surface of the sack with liquid wallpaper paste.
3. Force a second bag of the same size over the first one.
4. Coat with wallpaper paste.
5. Continue with two more bags in the same manner to reinforce the body.
6. Cut tails, ears, and other features from the fifth bag.
7. Attach features while the paste is tacky.
8. Cut out leg sections of each animal before the wallpaper mixture dries.
9. Let animal dry completely before proceeding to the last step.
10. Paint with poster paints using these characters for ideas. Let dry.

···❧ chapter 8 ❧···

Equipment and Utensil Conversions

This chapter offers creative answers to an often-perplexing question—"What can I do with my old, worn-out utensils (or the kids' swing set, filing cabinets, extra coat hangers, a typewriter, and more) besides toss them?"

Utensil Safari Wall Mount

Go on a hunt of the kitchen drawers and cabinets. And if your haul is not enough, move into a new field such as a local antique or secondhand store. All the while, the game is just the same—unused or broken utensils and cookware. Then use these trophies to decorate kitchen walls like the creative example shown here.

Materials
Assorted kitchen utensils
One 4x4-foot piece of ½-inch plywood
Epoxy
White paint (flat finish)
White paint (gloss finish)
Wood screws (assorted lengths)
Four flange-type wall fasteners.

Tools
Saber saw
Drill
Screwdriver
Paintbrush

Directions
1. Cut a 36-inch diameter circle from the piece of plywood.
2. Paint the plywood circle gloss white. Let dry completely.
3. Arrange objects attractively on surface.
4. Glue the lightweight items to the circle with epoxy. Let dry.
5. Drill holes through the heavier items and screw them to the board.
6. Primer utensils with a white flat paint. Dry.
7. Paint utensils and board with a white gloss finish. Let dry.
8. Position the art on wall. Then, drill holes through the top, bottom, and sides of the circle and into the wall.
9. Attach the art piece to the wall with flange-type wall nasteners.
10. Paint fasteners with white flat primer. Dry.
11. Paint fasteners with white gloss to blend with rest of piece. Let dry.

161

Retired Swing Shelf

Even swings get retired from active duty. This one is now leading the good life as a decorative shelf in its former "swinger's" bedroom. If the idea is appealing, but your swing is in play, here's how to make your shelf from scratch.

Materials
Bright yellow paint
Two large screw hooks
Galvanized steel chain (choose desired length)
One manufactured child's swing, *or* one
    1x6-inch board, 15-inches long
Two feet of rope

Tools
Paintbrush
Drill

Directions
1. To make the swing seat, drill holes in the front and back corners of each side.
2. Thread rope through hole from underside, then through link of chain, and down through hole on opposite side.
3. Knot rope ends on the underside of the swing shelf to secure.
4. Paint swing, rope and chain. Let dry completely before hanging.
5. Screw hooks in ceiling and hang swing shelf.

Roaster Planter

An old roaster may have seen better days in the oven but its best days are yet to come when you turn it into a hanging planter. Give the roaster a coat of black paint to cinch its look of antiquity; hang it from a light wire chain, and it becomes home for a collection of your favorite houseplants as shown here.

Materials

One old roaster, kettle or Dutch oven
Two pieces of light wire chain (choose desired length)
Wire
Black paint
Two screw hooks
Gravel
Potting soil
Plants

Tools

Paintbrush
Wire cutter
Drill

Directions

1. Clean container to remove grease.
2. Paint roaster and chains black (note special hole drilling instructions, below). Let the paint dry completely.
3. Attach chain to roaster:
• Slip chain down through open handle of roaster; bring it back up, and wire it securely to the hanging portion of the chain.
• If container has no open handles, drill hole in each side before painting. Insert chain in holes, securing chain with wire. (**Note:** Drill holes in roaster before painting.)
4. Position screw hooks in ceiling.
5. Plant roaster:
• Cover the bottom of the container with an inch of gravel for drainage.
• Fill container with potting soil.
• Place plants in roaster and moisten soil.
(**Note:** If planter is ceiling hung and watering is difficult, choose plants that require little water. Remember, larger containers retain moisture and therefore, do not require as much water as the smaller planters.)
6. Hang chains from screw hooks in the ceiling.

Coat Hanger Witch

For a bewitching party atmosphere, nothing comes close to this broomstick-propelled doll. Make this Halloween character out of coat hangers and nylon stockings, and use her for haunting good times.

Materials

Two wire coat hangers
Two old nylon stockings
One small bag of polyester stuffing
Thread
Felt scraps (red, black, and yellow)
Scraps of black rug yarn
Four small buttons
½ yard crinoline
4½x8½-inch piece of paper
2 yards of black satin fabric
2 yards of print fabric
One ¼-inch diameter stick for broom (cut to size)
Wire
Straw
Glue

Tools

Scissors
Wire cutters
Sewing machine
Knife
Sewing needle

Directions

Body **1.** Cut crossbar of first hanger in half.
2. Straighten the wires.
3. Close loop of the hook to form the head.
4. Cut bar off the second hanger and tape to twisted area of first hanger to form arms.
5. Tape together two straightened wires of first hanger 4 inches below arm wire (hip line).
6. Bend up end of each wire 9 inches below tape.
7. Bend remaining 4½ inches into oval foot.
8. Loop ends of wires for hands.
9. Pad hands and feet with polyester stuffing.
10. Cut nylon stocking in 2-inch wide spiral cut.
11. Wrap strip around the hands and feet.

Head **1.** Cut a 6-inch-wide section from hose.
2. Wrap wire loop with polyester stuffing.
3. Slide hose section over it.
4. Gather and fasten.
5. Slip a ball of polyester stuffing under hose and wrap thread around it to form the nose.
6. Stuff extra polyester stuffing in head.
7. Gather and tie off top edge of stocking.
8. Cut eyes and mouth from felt.
9. Glue them in place. Let dry.

Hair **1.** Wrap rug yarn around the piece of paper to form the loops.
2. Machine stitch through paper and yarn 4½ inches from the outer edge.
3. Pull the paper off and adjust the wig.
4. Sew in place.

Shoes **1.** Following the pattern, make adjustments to fit the feet.
2. Hand stitch in place on sole section.
3. Stitch side seam, turning under ¼ inch on raw edge.
4. Sew on buttons next to seam.

Pants **1.** Cut an 8½x8-inch piece of satin fabric.
2. Fold this piece in half to 8½x4 inches.
3. On the fold line, cut slit 4 inches up from the bottom edge to form pant legs.
4. Sew together 8½-inch long raw edges to within 4 inches of lower pant edge.
5. Match the leg edges and sew.
6. Gather around waist and leg bottoms.
7. Put pants on witch and draw up to fit.

Slip **1.** Cut a 1½x72-inch piece of print fabric.

2. Hem the piece.

3. For ruffle, gather a 35½-inch long piece of material.

4. Join the ruffle to a 7½x36-inch piece of printed fabric.

5. Hem the edges.

6. Run gathering thread on top edge.

7. Slip on doll and gather to fit waist; secure.

8. From the printed fabric, cut a 24x1½-inch piece for the apron ruffle, a 4½x12-inch piece for the skirt, two 1½x3-inch pieces for straps and a 3½x1½-inch piece for the waistband.

9. Hem ruffle and gather to fit skirt edge.

10. Stitch in place.

11. Hem sides of apron. Gather top edge to 3 inches.

12. Hem the ends and sides of the ties.

13. Sew the waistband to the skirt.

14. Sew on the ties to the ends of waistband.

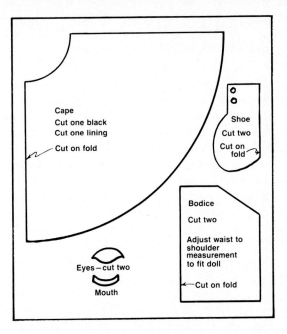

Cape
Cut one black
Cut one lining
Cut on fold

Shoe
Cut two
Cut on fold

Bodice
Cut two
Adjust waist to shoulder measurement to fit doll
Cut on fold

Eyes—cut two
Mouth

Hat brim **1.** Cut two 4½-inch diameter circles of black fabric and one of crinoline.

2. Place crinoline on wrong side of black circle.

3. Stitch right sides of black fabric together along edge, leaving a section open to turn.

4. Turn; hand stitch opening closed.

Crown of hat **1.** Cut a semicircle (4-inch radius) of crinoline and a 4½-inch radius semicircle from black fabric.

2. Turn under raw edge and blindstitch fabric.

3. Overlap edges of crinoline to form cone.

4. Baste to hold.

5. Cover the cone with black fabric, turn under raw edges and blindstitch to crinoline.

6. Turn ½-inch under at base of cone, center on brim, pin, and hand stitch.

7. Sew on ribbon ties.

8. Cut out felt flowers from the scraps.

9. Glue pieces together. Let dry.

10. Glue flowers onto hat. Let dry completely before proceeding.

11. Glue pieces of straw to hat. Let dry. (See photo for guide.)

Cape **1.** Cut one printed and one black piece of fabric to size wanted. (See drawing for shape.)

2. With the right sides together, stitch together. Stitch ½-inch seam, leaving a section open for turning. Turn and hand stitch the opening closed.

3. Sew on the ties.

Dress **1.** Cut a 7½x36-inch piece of black fabric for skirt.

2. Cut two 5x7½-inch pieces for sleeves.

3. Cut bodice according to pattern shown.

4. Hem sleeves along 5-inch measurement.

5. Stitch underarm seam.

6. Slide sleeve on arm, gather top, and sew to the doll's shoulder.

7. Cut two bodice pieces and slit back of one piece on fold line.

8. Hem both sides for back closing.

9. Sew shoulder and underarm seams, leaving armholes large enough to slide on arms.

10. Turn under hem at neck.

11. Hem the skirt and join the back seam (7½-inch edge).

12. Gather waist edge of skirt to fit waist measurement of bodice.

13. Join bodice to skirt.

14. Slip doll into dress, turn under raw edges at armholes and catch in place around armholes.

15. Dress doll in cape and apron.

Broomstick **1.** Cut out flower shapes from the felt scraps. (See photo for guide.)

2. Glue the flowers together. Let dry.

3. Glue the flowers onto the straw pieces. Dry.

4. Wire the straw to the stick of wood.

5. Wire the witch to the broomstick.

6. Suspend witch by wires attached to a light.

Filing Cabinet Coffee Table

Always look out for multifunctional throwaway items—you'll be money ahead. These old, wooden file drawers serve a twofold purpose as a spacious coffee table and as a storage unit. The money-saver and winner was the do-it-yourselfer who got these from an office that was being remodeled. Quite often the wooden files are replaced by metal ones. Keep a sharp eye out for this recurring bargain.

Materials

Two double wooden filing drawers
Four ¼-inch stove bolts with washers and nuts to fit. (**Note:** Determine the length of bolts needed by figuring the combined thickness of the backs of cabinets you're using. The bolts should be long enough to go through both cabinets with enough excess to accept washer and nut.)
Four mirrors or mirror tiles to fit top of each drawer as shown
Four 1x2s
Wood stain to match filing drawers
Finishing nails

Tools

Medium-grade sandpaper
Drill
Adjustable wrench
Hammer

Directions

1. Remove the cabinet drawers.
2. Put the units back to back. Near each corner of back, drill hole through both of the units to accept the bolts.
3. Bolt units together. Slip a washer on each bolt before tightening the nut.
4. Replace the drawers.
5. To build a wooden base for drawer unit,
• Measure length and width of drawer unit.
• Cut four pieces 1x2: two pieces 3 inches shorter than length, and two pieces 3 inches shorter than width.
• Position the 1x2s to form box frame as shown in drawing.
• Nail 1x2s together at corners.

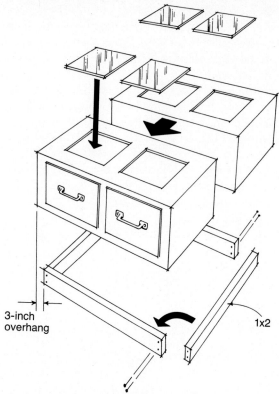

3-inch overhang

1x2

6. Sand and dust the base.
7. Stain the base. Let dry.
8. Set the drawer unit squarely on base.
9. Position mirrors on recessed panels or directly on top of drawer unit.

Guide to buying lumber

Due to the milling process, when you buy a 1x2 the board does not measure 1x2 inches. Length remains constant but width and thickness are the so-called "nominal" dimensions. The chart below shows nominal and actual lumber dimensions.

Nominal	Actual
1x2	¾x1½
1x3	¾x2½
1x4	¾x3½
1x6	¾x5½
1x8	¾x7¼
1x10	¾x9¼
1x12	¾x11¼
2x4	1½x3½

Printing Plate Boxes

Mom's jewelry, Dad's paper clips, or youngster's tooth fairy money—everything gets first class accommodations in these hand-crafted aluminum boxes. Make them with as little equipment as sharp scissors and a hammer. The aluminum is an offset printing plate from a printing shop which gives each box its own personality.

Materials
    One used offset printing plate
    Paper

Tools
    Ruler
    Sharp scissors
    Center punch or sharp instrument
    Length of scrap wood
    Hammer

Fine steel wool
Pencil

Directions
1. Draw and cut out a paper pattern of the box and lid, using the drawing as a guide.
2. With pencil, trace around the patterns on the back side of the aluminum sheet.
3. Cut out using sharp scissors.
4. Use center punch or sharp instrument and a ruler to scribe cutting and folding lines on the plate. See Photo A.
5. With sharp scissors, cut the flaps which become the sides and ends of the box. See Photo B. (**Note:** Keep cuts properly spaced or the box pieces will not be even.)
6. Fold flaps along pre-inscribed lines, using a length of scrap wood. See Photo C.
7. Fold flaps into the shape of the box. Extra flaps hold the box together temporarily. Final

folds will hold the box together permanently.
(**Note:** See Photo D for a guide to the sequence
of folding flaps.)

8. Use a piece of wood and a hammer as shown
in Photo E to crimp the edges of the box.

9. Rub the surface of the box with fine steel wool
to get a brushed finish.

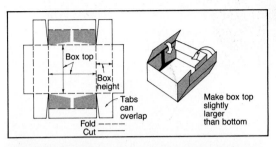

Box top

Box
height

Tabs
can
overlap

Fold - - - -
Cut ————

Make box top
slightly
larger
than bottom

C

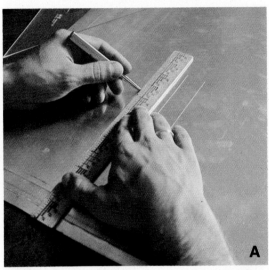

A

D

B

E

Funnel Light

Funnels are hardly what you consider glamorous home accessories—until a pair of them join forces and become a lamp like the one below. Two funnels, epoxied together and enameled bright red, serve as the housing for a large globe light. These funnels are decorating dynamite wherever they're used.

Materials

Two 8-inch metal funnels
Epoxy
Heat-resistant enamel
Lamp cord, socket, line switch, and plug
Four small rubber "feet"
Large globe light

Tools

Hammer
Block of wood
Paintbrush
Screwdriver

Directions

1. Remove cone ends of two funnels by placing a block of wood on the cone and hitting it sharply with a hammer. Cone will fall through.
2. Glue funnels together with epoxy.
3. Paint funnels with enamel. Let dry.
4. Attach a lamp cord to a weatherproof socket.
5. Feed the socket into the housing.
6. Glue the base of the socket in place, using epoxy. (Avoid gluing the upper half of the socket. This keeps it replaceable.) Let dry.
7. Glue small rubber "feet" onto the bottom of the funnel lamp. Let dry.
8. Install a line switch where desired.
9. Add a plug at the end of the cord.
(**Note:** For complete instructions on wiring a lamp, see pages 252-253.)
10. Screw in a large globe light.

Coat Hanger Cats

Even superstitious guests will take to this trio of black cats made from coat hangers swathed in fringed black crepe paper. These fantasy felines are the "purr-fect" centerpiece for a Halloween party and it's a sure bet that they'll bring you nothing but good luck.

Materials

One coat hanger per cat
Medium-weight wire
Newspaper
Cotton or polyester batting
Masking tape
Black crepe paper
Scrap of green paper
Cardboard
Glue
Three chenille bumps
Yarn for bow

Tools

Scissors
Wire cutters

Directions

1. Bend coat hanger in a long triangle with the hook at the top.
2. Cut a length of wire for ears and twist it along the top of the hook.
3. Pad body with newspaper, holding with tape.
4. Cut wire for the tail.
5. Cut two-inch fringed strips of crepe paper.
6. Pad tail and wrap with crepe paper strips starting at the tip of the tail.
7. Twist the tail wire to body hanger to attach.
8. Finish padding body with strips of batting.
9. Cut cardboard ears, tape to ear wire and cover with crepe paper.
10. Cut and stretch a 7-inch square of crepe paper for the face.
11. Glue to top part of padded body. Let dry.
12. Fringe more 2-inch crepe paper strips.
13. Wrap cat with strips, working from the base up. Overlap and glue strips. Let dry.
14. Outline face with fringe.
15. Twist three chenille bumps to form nose and mouth. Glue to face. Let dry.
16. Cut eyes of green paper, glue to face. Dry.
17. Tie yarn bow around cat's neck.

Typewriter Note Holder

The secretarial pool is no place for a standout like the typewriter at left. Instead, this old machine has joined the executive ranks and now functions as the most unique message center a family ever had. If you think painting a typewriter is a lot of work for just a message center, think of it as creating a piece of pop art—and sign it!

Materials
- One old typewriter
- Metal primer
- High-gloss enamel in various colors
- Chalk
- Clear varnish (optional)

Tools
- Paintbrush
- Vinegar or turpentine
- Cleaning cloths

Directions
1. Clean typewriter thoroughly, using a solution of vinegar and water or turpentine. Make sure keys have been cleaned well.
2. Allow machine to dry completely.
3. Paint entire machine with metal primer. Allow primer to dry thoroughly.
4. Draw design on typewriter with chalk. Plan to erase chalk as you paint each area. Don't try to paint over chalk marks.
5. Paint designs. Let dry.
- To keep colors from running together, paint one color at a time, allowing paint to dry thoroughly before applying the next color.
- For best results, paint two coats.
- For a hard edge design, use masking tape to define each area of paint.
- For quicker results, use a simple design. Paint the machine one bright color, let dry completely, and then trim with flowers, butterflies, or other design.
- For the completely unartistic craftsman, paint the machine a solid color, let dry completely, and then use letter stencils to paint a montage of letters over the machine. Let dry completely before proceeding.
6. To keep enamel from chipping, coat the finished painting with one or two coats of clear varnish. Dry completely between coats.

Type Drawer Shelves

Any collector of mini-memorabilia should have at least one of these printer type drawers. They're full of interesting niches for knickknacks—and they're still available at flea markets, house sales, or junk/antique stores.

Materials
- Old wooden type drawers
- Wood screws *or*
- Picture hangers and nails

Tools
- Drill
- Mineral spirits
- Screwdriver *or*
- Hammer

Directions
1. Clean old drawers, using mineral spirits. (Use in a well-ventilated room.)
2. Hang type drawers on wall:
- Drill holes through backs of drawers and attach directly to wall with wood screws. *Or,*
- Nail picture hangers to backs of drawers and hang from nails in the walls.

Metal Roll-Around Bar

Because of its mobility as well as its storage possibilities, this metal roll-around changed easily into a portable bar. You can turn a dusty derelict such as this into a conversation piece by making just a few basic alterations to bring out clean design lines of this 'outdated' piece.

Materials
Metal roll-around cart (discard shelves)
Primer
Bright yellow enamel paint
Four big chrome ball-type casters
¼-inch plate glass shelves (cut according to length and width of the roll-around used).(Allow an extra inch of length so shelves will sit securely on crossbars)

Tools
Coarse-, medium-, and fine-grade sandpaper
Paintbrush
Pry bar

Directions
1. Pry off the old casters. (Take them shopping to buy the correct size to fit the old caster sockets.)
2. Sand the roll-around,
• First use coarse-grade sandpaper.
• Feather any chipped edges with medium-grade sandpaper.
• Finish the job with fine-grade sandpaper.
3. Primer the roll-around. Let this prime coat dry completely before proceeding to the next step.
4. Paint the roll-around. Apply two or three light coats instead of one heavy coat of paint. (This way you will avoid drippy runs.) Let the paint dry between coats.
5. Attach the new casters.
6. Apply two self-stick foam pads to each crossbar as shown in the photograph below, so the glass shelves don't slip.
7. Position glass shelves on the roll-around.

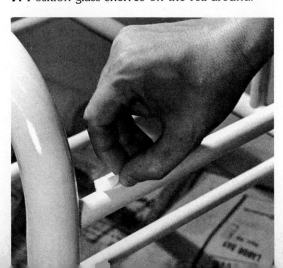

Correct casters for furnishings

Mobility is a bonus feature of many home furnishings. Knowing what casters to select for your projects will give them a professional finished appearance. Here are some common caster types.

Caster type	When to use
General-purpose 	Use on furniture ranging from lightweight desk chairs to medium-weight beds. Attach by tapping the grip-neck caster yoke into furniture leg for tight fit.
Adjustable 	Use when placing furniture on uneven floors or to compensate for uneven leg length. Attach to tubular metal leg or wooden leg. Adjust after furniture is placed where desired.
Ball-type 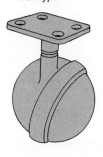	Use on furniture that will be rolled across carpeting or rugs since the ball-shaped caster doesn't dig into carpeting as much as other casters. Comes with plate-type mount as shown here or grip-neck mount as shown on the general-purpose caster.
Flat-plate swivel 	Use for hand trucks or heavy pieces of furniture that are moved frequently. Attach the plate-type mount by screwing it to flat surface. Soft rubber or powder iron is used for the wheels of this heavy-duty caster.

175

chapter 9

Cardboard Crafts

Youngsters who discover that a scrapped packing box is a great potential money-maker as a lemonade stand, are probably the first to learn that cardboard boxes and containers are just too good to toss. There's something better than sending them into obscurity with the garbage. Here's a sampling of some cardboard conversions that are not just better, but best!

Cardboard Tree Sculpture

Genuine metal sculptures cost an "arm and a leg"—and at least a slashed finger or two to make. But not the bold and colorful tree shown here. It's a "mock" metal sculpture created from lightweight cardboard, and it's easy on both budget and bandages.

Materials
Dry branch
One sheet lightweight cardboard
Acrylic paints (dark brown, red, and orange)
Plaster of paris
Masking tape or florist's clay
Epoxy
Spool of fine wire
Small wooden box
Pebbles (polished)
White paint

Tools
Scissors
Paintbrush

Block of florist's foam
Can for mixing plaster of paris

Directions
1. Anchor the dry branch inside the box with florist's clay or with masking tape.
2. Pour in plaster of paris. Let it harden.
3. Paint the branch dark brown. Let dry.
4. Paint the small wooden box white. Let dry.
5. Cut odd-shaped triangles of cardboard (altitude and base sizes ranging from 1 inch, 1½ inches, and 2 inches).
6. Glue 3-inch pieces of wire on each cardboard "leaf." Let dry.
7. Glue another piece of cardboard on the leaf to sandwich the wire. Let dry.
8. Trim second triangle to shape of first.
9. Stick free ends of wire into clay.
10. Paint both sides of the leaf and the edges in red and orange. Let dry.
11. Twist several leaf wires together and twist around the branches of the tree.
12. Glue joint where wires attach to tree. Let dry completely before proceeding.
13. Touch up wires with brown acrylic. Let dry.
14. Place pebbles around the base of the tree.

Centipede Table

Long on contemporary styling, this centipede table stands on its own as a creative accessory. The attractive legs (38 in this case) are made of heavy cardboard tubes from rolls of fabric or carpet. Use this clever table as an extra side unit to display favorite decorator pieces, but remember it's a decorative piece by itself.

Materials
    Three 8-foot 2x4s
    Two 8-foot 2x6s
    Eight 5½-inch machine bolts with washers
        and nuts to fit

    One 4x8-foot sheet of ¾-inch plywood
    1¾-, 2¼-, and 2½-inch diameter heavy
        cardboard tubes (once used as
        center of carpet or fabric rolls)
    Epoxy
    Varnish or shellac
    Latex enamel paint (two contrasting colors)
    Twenty 1½-inch wood screws (No. 8)

Tools
    Drill
    Adjustable wrench
    Paintbrushes
    Saber saw
    C-clamps

Directions

1. For the tabletop, place two of the 2x4s and the two 2x6s side by side in an alternating fashion (see sketch below).

2. Measure the exact width of the tabletop. Then cut the remaining 2x4 into four pieces to fit across the table width.

3. At each end of the table position a crosspiece above and below the top. Hold in place with C-clamps (or have someone help you hold them in place).

4. Drill four holes for machine bolts through all the thicknesses at each end of the tabletop. Then, secure the ends with the bolts, washers, and nuts (see sketch); and tighten bolts.

5. Cut a piece of plywood to fit underside of table (cut it two inches narrower on all sides).

6. For the legs, cut 38 9-inch lengths from the cardboard tubes.

7. Arrange the legs on the piece of plywood in a haphazard pattern to achieve the centipede effect. Mark the position of each leg on the plywood.

8. Drill pilot hole near the center of each marked area, then insert the blade of the saber saw and cut out the circles.

9. Turn the table upside down and center the plywood on the underside of the tabletop. Attach with the wood screws (use rows of four screws spaced every two feet).

10. Give the cardboard legs a prime coat of varnish or shellac. Let dry.

11. Paint the cardboard legs with latex enamel. Let dry completely.

12. Glue the legs in place in the holes in the plywood. Let dry.

13. Turn table right side up and give tabletop a coat of varnish or shellac. Let dry.

14. Paint tabletop with a coat of latex enamel in a color that contrasts with legs. Dry.

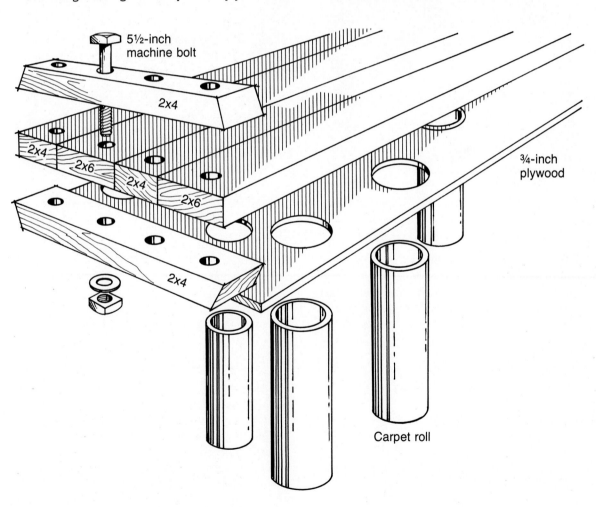

5½-inch machine bolt

2x4

2x4

2x6

2x4

2x6

2x4

¾-inch plywood

Carpet roll

Corrugated Characters

Cardboard gingerbread people are not what you'd serve at a Christmas coffee, but they certainly help you serve up a pert and pretty door decoration. And they're such fun to make. Mix up an extra "batch" for tree trims or packages.

Materials
One sheet lightweight cardboard
One sheet of cardboard corrugated on
  one side
Soft, heavy white string
Two brown paper bags
White glue
Acrylic paints (brown, pink, red, and white)
Clear varnish

Tools
Rubber bands
Scissors
Flat container

Directions
1. For each cookie character, cut two patterns from lightweight cardboard and three from corrugated cardboard. Use pattern on opposite page. (**Note:** To increase the textural effect, cut the corrugated pieces so that not all the corrugations run in the same directions.)
2. Hold all of the pieces together (corrugated pieces on the outside) with a rubber band at the neck and another at the ankles.
3. Cut a 5-inch piece of string to use for a hanging loop.

180

4. Tie an overhand knot in the ends.

5. Glue the hanging loop at the top of the head, with the knot ends tucked in between the layers of corrugated cardboard. Let dry.

6. Tear brown paper bags into strips and then into pieces about 1x2 inches.

7. Pour white glue into a flat container and dilute it with two parts water.

8. Dip the paper pieces in the glue solution.

9. Press the paper pieces onto the cookie edges, beginning at the top of the head on both sides of the hanging loop.

10. Paper from one side over the edge to the other side, continuing down the body (remove the rubber bands just before you add paper at the neck and the ankles.

11. Cover both the front and the back of the cookie with one layer of paper strips, overlapping the pieces slightly.

12. Hang the cookie up until it is dry.

13. Draw on details with a pencil.

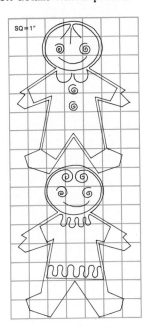

14. Using photo as an example, paint the clothing with acrylic paints. Let dry.

15. Dip a piece of string in the glue, squeeze out the excess glue, and outline the pencilled details. Let the string dry.

16. Cover both sides of the cookie with a clear varnish. Let dry.

17. Hang the gingerbread people on a background of green branches and add satin balls.

Paper Core Plant Stands

It's not hard for a discount store plant to look like a fancy flower shop special when you "stage" it on one of these brightly colored plant stands. They're made of cardboard tubes.

Materials
Cardboard tubes (6 to 10, depending on desired circumference of stand)
Glue
Heavy cardboard
Tissue paper
Lightweight cardboard
Gesso
Acrylic paint (assorted colors)

Tools
Spring-type clothespins
Knife
Paintbrush

Directions
1. Cut cardboard tubes in half lengthwise.

2. Glue together at edges, securing with spring-type clothespins until dry.

3. Cut round circle of heavy cardboard for top.

4. Glue cardboard disk to tube base. Weight down until completely dry.

5. Cover tube grooves by coating indentations with thin glue and applying tissue paper. Let dry.

6. Glue strip of lightweight cardboard around edge of disk; wrap twice for double thickness. Let dry completely.

7. Gesso all surfaces. Let dry.

8. Paint. Let dry.

Ice-Cream Carton Lamps

Treat your home to these colorful hanging lamps with shades fashioned from round ice-cream cartons. Cut out clever patterns in the shades, and watch the light cast a decorative glow throughout your room. You should have no trouble finding the containers at a local ice-cream specialty store.

Materials (for each lamp)
   Empty three-gallon ice-cream cartons (you need four cartons for lamp at left in

photo and three cartons for lamp at right)
Gesso
Acrylic paints in various colors
Clear varnish
1 yard 9-inch wide fringe
Electrical parts (15 feet of swag lamp chain, 20 feet of cord with a line switch, plug, 8-inch spider ring, two swag hooks, and candelabra socket)
⅛-inch IPS all-thread lamp pipe (cut to fit length of lamp)
Three threaded lock washers

One threaded lock nut
Canopy loop to fit lamp pipe
Scraps of yarn for connecting cartons (rug yarn or four-ply knitting worsted)
White glue
7½-watt light bulb to fit candelabra socket

Tools

Paintbrushes
Large sewing needle
Art knife with small pointed blade
Hole punch

Directions (for each lamp)

1. Enlarge patterns A, B, C, and/or D from the grid on page 184. (See grid system instructions on page 209.)

2. Cut out a hole in center bottom of one round ice-cream carton. (This carton will form the top shade of the lamp shown in the drawing. Make hole large enough for lamp pipe to go through.)

3. Cut out the bottoms of remaining cartons.

4. Trace desired pattern lightly onto the carton.

5. Cut out holes on the pattern design where desired so the light will shine through and throw the patterns on the wall.

6. Punch holes for yarn around carton edge just above or below rim, spacing holes about 1 inch apart. (Punch holes around the bottom edge of the top carton, both top and bottom edges of the middle carton(s), and the top edge of the bottom carton.)

7. Give each carton two coats of gesso. Let dry between coats.

8. Re-mark design as necessary. Then, paint the design with desired acrylic paint colors. Let dry.

9. Apply a second coat of paint, if needed. Let dry completely.

10. Give cartons a coat of varnish. Let dry completely before proceeding.

11. To lace the cartons together, use large needle to thread the yarn through holes around carton edge (for added strength and decorative effect, thread yarn in an X pattern).

12. Glue the fringe to the bottom edge of the shade. Let dry.

13. Run the all-thread lamp pipe through the hole in top carton.

14. Thread spider ring on lamp pipe and position against underneath of lamp top.

15. Secure the pipe with threaded lock washers

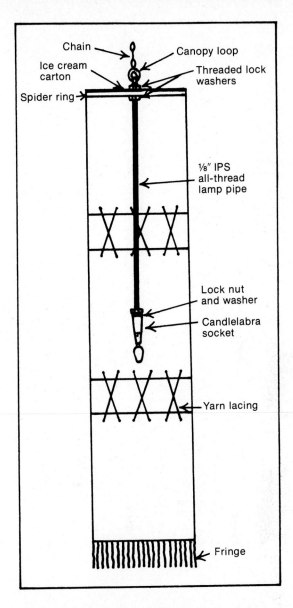

on each side of hole, as shown in drawing.

16. Weave cord through chain and attach one or two links of chain to canopy loop.

17. Screw the canopy loop onto lamp pipe.

18. Run cord down through lamp pipe.

19. Wire socket according to wiring directions given on pages 252 and 253. (Screw lock nut and lock washer onto pipe just before attaching socket, as shown in drawing.)

20. Drill holes in ceiling for swag hooks.

21. Screw the hooks into ceiling. (They come with a toggle bolt.)

22. Hang lamp by linking chain to swag hooks.

23. Screw in the light bulb.

(continued on next page)

1 space = ½ inch

Cardboard Pets

Want an ideal pet? Here's a menagerie guaranteed to be neat, clean, and housebroken. The tiger, elephant, and "snaka-gator" are made of interlocking pieces of posterboard. Don't let the leopard pillow fool you. Its frame is cardboard.

Materials
Tiger, elephant, and snaka-gator
  Poster board
    in appropriate colors
  Poster paints in various colors
    as shown in photo
  Felt-tip pen

(continued on next page)

Leopard pillow

8x16-inch heavy cardboard
½ yard animal print fabric
   45 inches wide
Matching thread
Polyester stuffing
Felt scraps for eyes and nose
Glue

A

Tools

Scissors or craft knife
Pencil
Paintbrush
Sewing machine
Sewing needle

Directions

Tiger **1.** For the body, cut a piece of poster board 6x17 inches.

2. Cut a groove where the tail fits (about ½ inch from the back of the body).

3. Cut groove for head 1 inch from other end of body. (See sketch A for placement of the cut pieces.)

4. On bottom side, cut 3-inch groove about 3 inches from end for back feet.

5. Cut a 3-inch groove 3 inches from other end for front feet.

6. Cut the head pieces 6 inches wide and 6½ inches tall.

7. Make a 2½-inch groove in the center of the head piece where the neck fits.

8. Cut neck 5x8 inches. (Cut end where head

fits to resemble a nose.)

9. Cut 2-inch grooves at front and back on opposite sides of neck for attaching to the head and body.

10. Cut ears 2x5 inches with a 3-inch long groove in the center.

11. Cut two leg pieces for the tiger 6 inches tall, 6½ inches wide at the bottom, and 2 inches wide at the top.

12. Center a 3-inch-long groove on top 2-inch side.

13. Draw features on tiger, following sketch A.

14. Paint features. Let dry.

15. Assemble tiger according to sketch A.

Elephant **1.** Cut two pieces of white poster board 8½x11 inches.

2. On both sides of the 11-inch piece, measure up 6 inches and in 1 inch. Cut this portion away to form ear shapes. (Top will now measure 8½ inches, bottom will measure 6½ inches wide.)

3. On 6½-inch edge, measure 2 inches in from each side.

4. Cut out a 2½-inch square for the legs.

5. On second rectangle, cut legs and trunk in stairstep fashion. (See sketch B.)

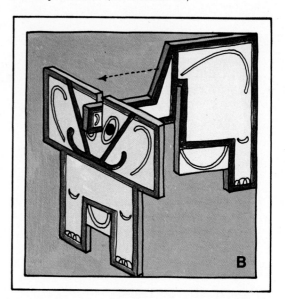

B

6. Cut one 3-inch-long slot in top of first piece for trunk placement.

7. Draw features on poster-board cutouts, following sketch B.

8. Paint features on elephant. Let dry.

9. Assemble elephant according to sketch B.

Snaka-gator **1.** Cut three 3x10-inch rectangles from each of two colors of poster board.
2. Cut two 4x6-inch rectangles from one of the colors. (These form the mouth.)
3. Cut a 4x6-inch rectangle from the second

color for the head.
4. Measure about 1½ inches from each short end on all six body pieces.
5. Cut slots 1½ inches deep at this point. (When fitting pieces together, slots of one color will be on top, other colors on the bottom. The pieces that are for the front section have grooves that fit two grooves to hold mouth.)
6. Cut grooves in two mouth pieces and in head piece, as shown in sketch C.
7. Draw the features on the snaka-gator cutouts, as shown in sketch C.
8. Paint on features. Let dry.
9. Assemble pieces to form snaka-gator, using sketch C as a guide.

Leopard pillow **1.** Cut a piece of cardboard 8x16 inches.
2. Cut two pieces of leopard print fabric 10x20 inches.
3. Cut eight small tabs for feet, four triangles for ears, and two long, narrow strips for the tail, as shown in sketch D.
4. With right sides together, sew feet, ears, and tail, and leave the edge that attaches to the body open for stuffing.
5. Turn the pieces and fill the leopard pillow

with the polyester. (See sketch D.)
6. Position ears, feet, and tail in seams of 10x20-inch rectangle.
7. With right sides together, sew body with the ears, feet, and tail in the seams. Leave front edge open for turning.
8. Turn right side out.
9. Slip in cardboard rectangle.
10. Stuff on either side with polyester.
11. Slipstitch front edge opening closed.
12. Glue on felt pieces cut for eyes and nose. Let dry completely.

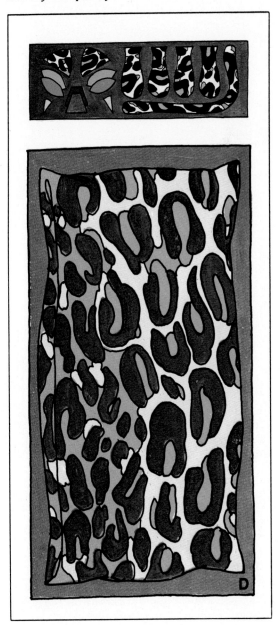

Cardboard Core Wise Men and Wall Tree

Christmas is full of traditions and one of its best ones is making use of throwaways. Here, three kings and a contemporary tree are the rewarding results of salvaging cardboard tubes.

Materials
Tube Wise Men
    Two 11-inch paper towel tubes per
      Wise Man
    Glue
    Paint (red, blue, green, yellow, brown,
      white, and black)
    Sequins and jewels

Braid
Gilt-embossed paper
Foil

Merry Christmas Tree
Three 11-inch paper towel cardboard
    tubes
Paint (red, orange, pink, green, white,
    and yellow)
Glue

Tools
Knife
Paintbrush
Scissors

Directions
Tube Wise Men   **1.** Cut 11-inch lengths of paper towel tubes in half lengthwise (use one-half of the tube for the center of the body).
2. Cut the remaining half in half lengthwise.
3. Glue a quarter-tube on each side of the body center, reversing the curve. Let dry.
4. Trim the upper part of the side pieces for tapered shoulders.
5. Cut slightly tapered sections of tube about 6 inches long for sleeves.
6. Paint sleeves and body. Let dry.
7. Glue on sleeves. Let dry.
8. Cut sections of tubes for the face, neck, hat, and decorations.
9. Paint figures as in the photo. Let dry.
10. Glue on necks, then heads (tilt back). Dry.
11. Decorate the robes and headgear by gluing on sequins, jewels, braid, gilt-embossed paper, and foil. Let dry.
12. For stability, glue short length of whole tube to back of each king at bottom. Let dry.

Merry Christmas tree   **1.** Slit two of the 11-inch paper towel cardboard tubes in half lengthwise.
2. Cut halves into 2-inch lengths.
3. Paint both sides of the tube sections. Let dry. (Use a variety of colors.)
4. On 21 2-inch lengths, draw the letters M, E, R, R, Y, C, H, R, I, S, T, M, A, S, and make seven star shapes.
5. Cut out the letters and stars. Leave some pieces plain.
6. Assemble and glue the parts. Let dry.
7. Paint a section of whole tube green. Let dry.
8. Glue to bottom of arrangment for trunk. Dry.

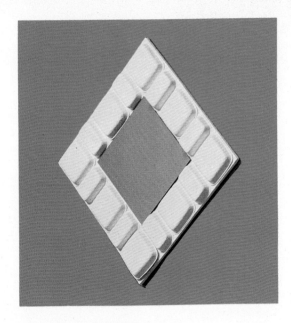

Produce Tray Frame

This produce tray mirror frame is a great look for thrifty decorators who have a flair for design. Just save your papier-mâché produce trays. The tray arrangement shown here creates a smart frame for a 12-inch mirror tile.

Materials
12-inch-square mirror tile
24-inch-square piece of ½-inch plywood
Produce trays (5 to 6-inch size)
White glue
Gesso
Paint

Tools
Saw
Paintbrush

Directions
1. Arrange produce trays, face down, around mirror centered on plywood background.
2. Mark location of trays and outside dimension of plywood.
3. Trim excess plywood around edges.
4. Glue trays to plywood. Weight while drying.
5. Coat with glue to strengthen, then gesso. Dry.
6. Paint, leaving space for mirror. Let dry.
7. Glue mirror in place. Let dry.

Ice-Cream Carton Storage

More ice-cream carton fun is in store for the decorator who wants extra storage space. The ice-
cream cartons are usually available from a bulk
ice-cream dealership.

Materials
    Six ice-cream containers
    Nine bolts fitted with nuts
    Instant papier-mâché
    Paper tape
    Gesso
    Paint
    Three common nails

Tools
    Knife
    Drill

    Paintbrush
    Hammer

Directions
1. Remove top metal ring of containers.
2. Cut containers on an angle (three long, two
medium-size, and one short).
3. Stack in pyramid, and mark spots where containers touch.
4. Drill holes at joining points.
5. Insert bolts. Tighten nuts.
6. Tape joining front edges of containers.
7. Cover surfaces of cartons with papier-mâché.
Let dry completely.
8. Paint with gesso. Let dry.
9. Paint with acrylic paints. Let dry.
10. Hang by resting unit on three nails in wall.
(Space nails to coincide with openings where
containers join.)

Egg Carton Animals

Anyone who loves animals will love these egg-carton cutups. They're fun to make—even more fun to display on your bookshelf. And they are certainly much easier to manage than their real-life counterparts.

Materials

Egg cartons (two kinds: one with tall center dividers; the other with dividers all the same level)
Contact cement or tacky glue
Acrylic paints
Two glass-head pins

Tools

Rubber bands
Craft knife
Scissors

Directions

Lamb **1.** Paint both sides of two lids white. Dry.
2. Cut into 1-inch squares; round off corners; then cut into spirals for "wool."
3. Form body, using a pair of end egg "cups" for the underside, another pair turned upside down for the top surface. Fill in any gaps by gluing on small pieces of carton to round out shape of body. Let dry. (Body measures 4 inches long.)
4. With craft knife, cut out four tall center dividers and glue to body to form legs. Dry.
5. Glue on a section of a divider for neck. Dry.
6. Glue on one complete egg cup for nose. Dry.
7. Cut two small pieces of carton for ears.
8. Paint lamb and ear pieces. Let dry.
9. Glue "wool" over body and back of head. Dry.
10. Glue on ears. Let dry.
11. Paint mouth. Let dry.
12. Insert glass-head pins for eyes.

Cat **1.** Form body and neck same as for lamb.
2. Use a section of carton with two egg cups inverted for face.
3. Cut shaggy strips on lower edge of face.
4. Cut pieces of egg cups for ears.
5. Glue on ears. Let dry.
6. Paint entire cat white. Let dry.
7. Cut narrow strips of carton lid for whiskers.
8. Paint whiskers, eyes, and nose. Let dry.
9. Glue on whiskers. Let dry.

Giraffe **1.** Soak egg carton lid in water to make it pliable.
2. Roll it into a slightly tapered cylinder. Hold with rubber bands until dry; then glue. Dry.
3. Construct body as for other animals.
4. Use eight tall divider pieces for legs. (Make back legs slightly shorter.)
5. Cut one tall divider so a portion of egg cups remains. Use this for face.
6. Cut hole in higher end of body for neck. Insert neck and let it protrude about 9 inches. Secure with glue.
7. Paint giraffe. Let dry.
8. Cut mane, tail, horns, ears, and "spots" from carton lids.
9. Paint horns and ears the body color. Paint mane, tail, and spots darker. Let dry.
10. Glue onto giraffe. Let dry.

Felt Bethlehem Village

On the surface, this brilliant miniature version of Bethlehem is a needlecraft masterpiece. Underneath the felt applique, things aren't so exotic. The underpinnings are throwaways. Here, a salt box, cardboard tubes, and a gallon milk carton serve as armatures for this simple, but striking and colorful needle art.

Materials
½-yard felt in royal blue
¼-yard felt in turquoise, cerise, and violet
Mylar (from a craft shop) or an aluminum baking tin
White glue
Cerise, turquoise, and royal blue sock yarn (to coordinate with the felt)
One gallon milk carton for the mosque
Two long pins with beaded heads for the tops of the domes
Two styrofoam balls (one 4 inches; one 5 inches in diameter)
Three or four assorted beads for the tops of the domes
Two cardboard cores from paper towels (for the minarets)
Two silver deodorant or cosmetic container tops for the tops of the minarets (each should be about 1½ inches in diameter)
One carton (3¾x3¾x11¼ inches) for main part of square tower
Lightweight cardboard
One decorative cosmetic bottle top for square tower top (this should be about ¾ inch in diameter)
One salt box (for the round tower)
1½ yards of decorative edging (¼-inch width; in matching shade of blue)

Tools
Tracing wheel
Carbon
Large embroidery needle
Scissors
Knife or razor blade
Hard pencil
Handsaw
Straight pins
Tape

Pattern Color Code
B—royal blue
T—turquoise
C—cerise
V—violet
M—mylar

Completed Sizes
Mosque (including minarets)
7x8x11 inches
Square tower
3¾x3¾x19 inches
Round tower
4-inch diameter
8½ inches tall

Directions
General applique instructions **1.** Enlarge the patterns on pages 194-197. (See general instructions for grid patterns on page 209.) Draw each pattern on a separate sheet of paper. (Each square equals 1½ inches.)
2. Press the felt pieces.
3. Tape the patterns to the appropriate pieces of felt. (Allow enough felt on the right side of patterns so you can move the patterns over to trace the third and fourth sides.)
4. Mark the edges of the building with carbon and the tracing wheel. (Broken lines on pattern indicate edges of building and corner folds.)
5. Place marks on the outside of the broken lines to indicate folds, but do not trace folds. Make enough marks to show placement of all design pieces within.
6. Untape patterns.
7. Reposition patterns. Move the pattern to the right side of the fabric, placing the left broken lines of patterns on marks.
8. Trace as before. Trace four sections for each dome and trace two minarets.
9. Working on one building section at a time, tape the patterns to the appropriate color felt and trace small design pieces. (Trace repeated shapes once, then use as models to cut the rest. Cut pieces that are smaller than 1 inch by eye. Position them on appropriate building parts as they are cut so you can keep track of them. Use a hard pencil to trace designs on mylar or foil.)
10. Cut out and position pieces.
11. Glue metallic pieces firmly in place. Let dry.
12. Glue all felt design pieces in place, using

(continued on next page)

a minimum amount of glue. Let dry for one hour.
13. Lift up pieces to make sure nothing falls off.
14. Reglue any loose pieces. Let dry.
15. Following dots on patterns, make French knots with contrasting colors of yarn.

Mosque **1.** Rinse the milk carton.
2. With a knife or razor blade, cut off the angled top. Dry thoroughly and turn upside down. (Bottom of carton will become top of mosque.)
3. Cut a 7-inch square of royal blue felt.
4. Glue this to the top of the mosque and fold excess felt over the edges. Glue to the sides and clip bulk from corners. Let dry.
5. Trim off upper and right edges of mosque piece, using broken lines as a cutting guide.
6. Wrap the design around the carton with corner marks on bottom edge lining up with corners of the carton. Glue in place. Let dry.
7. Trim off lower edge of excess felt.
8. Cut a 5-inch foam ball in half, using saw.
9. Glue four felt sections to dome with edges touching. Let dry. (Pin as you glue to make it conform to the round shape.)
10. Fold over and glue bottom edges to flat portion of the foam. Allow one hour to dry.

11. Remove pins and glue edging over seams. Let dry.
12. Place a long pin through one or two beads and place it into center top of the foam ball.
13. Center and glue dome to top of mosque. Let dry.
14. Trim the top edges from minaret pieces.
15. Wrap each one around a paper towel core, overlapping where side edges join.
16. Glue together on the seam. Let dry.
17. Trim off the lower edge.
18. Glue silver domes to the top of each minaret. Let dry.
19. Glue minarets to the two front corners of the mosque. Let dry.

Square tower **1.** Tape the tower roof pattern to lightweight cardboard.
2. Trace the outline.
3. Cut out cardboard roof shape. Use a knife to score it on broken lines. (If proper size carton is not available, make tower of cardboard, using pattern as guide. Position pattern twice as you did when tracing felt.)
4. Form roof into pyramid shape.
5. Glue together at underlap. Let dry.

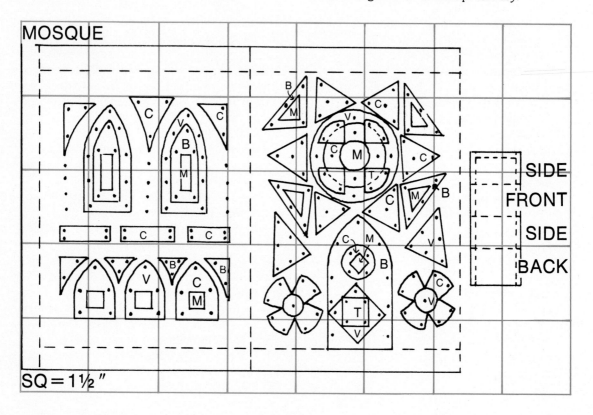

194

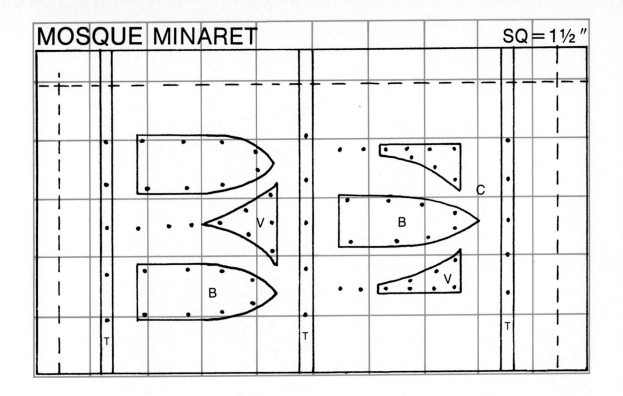

MOSQUE MINARET

SQ = 1½″

T · C · B · V

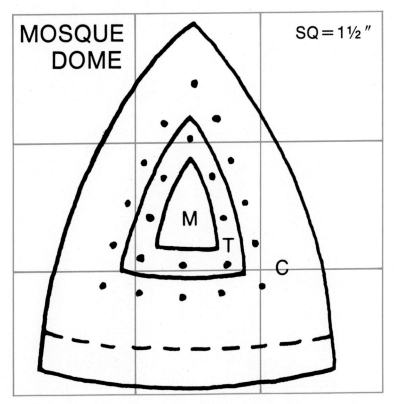

MOSQUE DOME

SQ = 1½″

M · T · C

(continued on next page)

195

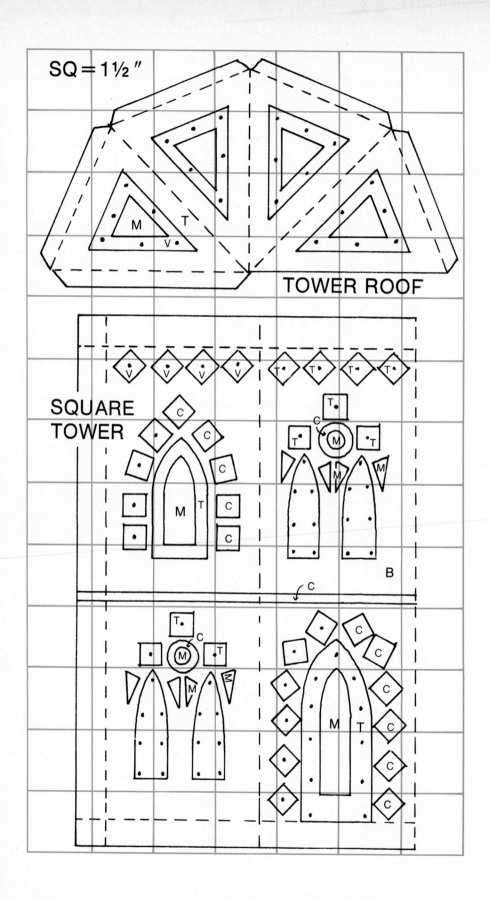

SQ = 1½ "

TOWER ROOF

SQUARE
TOWER

196

ROUND TOWER

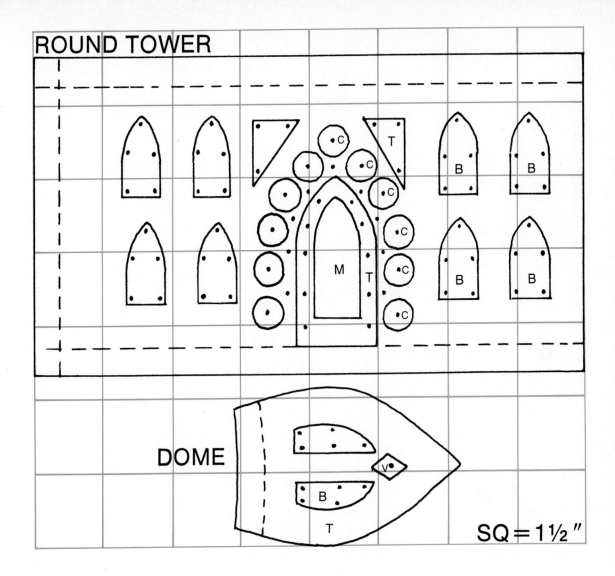

DOME

SQ = 1½ "

6. Fold lower edges under.
7. Form building and glue together at corner. Dry.
8. Wrap tower felt piece around building.
9. Glue at overlapping corner edges. Let dry.
10. Clip off corners and trim off lower edge of excess felt.
11. Glue appliqued felt piece to pyramid roof. Let dry.
12. Glue roof to top of building, placing glue along folded-under edges of roof top. Let dry.
13. Glue decorative bottle top to top point of roof. Let dry.

Round tower 1. Trim appliqued felt at top and right edge.

2. Wrap felt around salt box.
3. Glue along overlapping edge. Let dry completely before proceeding.
4. Clip upper edge of felt allowance, making clips about ½ inch apart.
5. Fold and glue clipped edge down to top of salt box. Let dry.
6. Trim away bottom edge of excess felt.
7. Cut a ¾-inch slice from 4-inch foam ball, and discard slice.
8. Glue the four felt sections to ball as you did in step 9 for the mosque. Let dry.
9. Glue edgings over seams. Let dry.
10. Pin beads to top.
11. Glue dome to top of round building. Let dry.

Chicken Bucket Lamps

Any chicken-eating family can collect buckets for these colorful light fixtures in rather short order. The round cardboard containers are painted and wired to give you caviar-class lights at peanut-butter prices.

Materials
> One empty chicken bucket per lamp
> One lid from cardboard ice-cream carton
> Gesso
> Paint
> Lamp cord and candelabra socket
> One 40-watt bulb

Tools
> Paintbrush
> Awl
> Screwdriver

Directions
1. Cover all surfaces of chicken bucket and ice-cream carton lid with gesso. Let dry.
2. Paint bucket one color and lid another. Dry.
3. With awl, punch a hole in the center bottom of the bucket and ice-cream carton lid.
4. Thread cord through holes in lid and bucket.
5. Attach candelabra socket to lamp cord. (See pages 252-253 for instructions.)
6. Wire lamp to existing ceiling fixture base.

Milk Carton Planters

Even the smallest sprouts in the family can enjoy carton gardening. All it takes is an empty milk, cottage cheese, or yogurt carton; adhesive-backed paper; some soil; and small plants.

Materials
> Half-gallon milk cartons *or* large
> cottage cheese container
> Clear plastic wrap
> Tape
> Adhesive-backed paper
> Drainage rocks
> Potting soil
> Seeds or seedlings

Tools
> Craft knife
> Scissors

Directions
Planter with windows **1.** Cut off carton top.
2. Cut a piece of adhesive-backed paper to cover outside surfaces of carton.
3. Smooth paper onto carton.
4. Mark position of window flaps.
5. Cut the sides and bottom edges of flaps.
6. Bend flaps up.
7. Line the carton with clear plastic wrap.
8. Tape plastic in place.
9. Plant according to instructions below.

Boat-shaped planter **1.** Cut milk carton in half from top to bottom. Place on its side.
2. Cut adhesive-backed paper to fit sides.
3. Smooth paper onto carton.
4. Cut out letters of solid-colored adhesive-backed paper and position on decorated carton.
5. Plant according to instructions below.

Round planter **1.** Cut paper to fit container.
2. Position paper 1 inch below rim.
3. If container slopes in at the bottom, make slashes in paper to ensure proper fit.
4. Plant according to instructions below.

Planting instructions **1.** Place drainage rocks in the bottom of the planter.
2. Add potting soil.
3. Plant seeds or small terrarium plants.

Milk Carton Mobile

There's more to be said for milk cartons than you think. Here, cardboard cast-offs are used to express some of the nicest words around—love, hope, and joy.

Materials
    Milk cartons
    Scraps of adhesive-backed paper
    Monofilament line
    Paper

Tools
    Pencil
    Craft knife
    Needle or awl

Directions
1. Wash and dry milk cartons. Cut off tops and bottoms. Open side and lay carton flat.
2. Draw a paper pattern of words. (Make sure letters touch so word is one piece.)
3. Trace around pattern on milk carton.
4. Cut out with a craft knife.
5. Peel backing off adhesive-backed paper and position cut-out word on top of it. Press down.
6. With knife, trim around letters.
7. Repeat steps 5 and 6 with the reverse side.
8. With needle or awl, puncture small holes in top of letters at either end of word.
9. Thread monofilament line through and tie.
10. Hang as mobile or use as tree trims.

Cardboard Tube Christmas Trees

Liven up your holiday table next time with the original and attractive trio of trees shown here. They're made of wood scraps and cardboard tubes, so they're easy on a tight Christmas budget.

Materials
    Three pieces of heavy cardboard or
        wood scraps (For each tree: two
        24x1½- and one 12x1½-inch strips.)
    Cardboard tubes with varying diameters
    Glue
    Heavy cardboard tube (3 inches in diameter)
    Wood or laminated cardboard circle (5 inches
        in diameter and 1 inch thick)
    Gesso
    Paint (red and yellow)
    One ½-inch dowel
    One sheet of light cardboard (for stars)

Tools
    Paintbrush
    Knife
    Drill

Directions
1. Glue the three strips of cardboard or wood together to form triangular frame. Let dry.
2. Slice cardboard tubes into 1½-inch lengths.
3. Lay frame on work surface and position tubes inside. Glue circles in place. Let dry.
4. Cut the trunks from a 3-inch-diameter cardboard tube. (Vary heights. The trunks in the photograph are 4½, 6½, and 8½ inches.)
5. Glue the wood or laminated cardboard circle base onto the tree trunk. Let dry.
6. Glue the trunk to the frame. Let dry.
7. Cut two stars from cardboard for each Christmas tree.
8. Coat all surfaces with gesso to seal. Dry.
9. Paint stars, dowel, tree base, and trunk yellow. Paint tree red. Let dry.
10. Glue two stars on opposite sides of a ½-inch dowel. Let dry.
11. Drill hole into top of tree frame. (Hole must allow dowel to extend down into the uppermost tube slice inside the frame.)
12. Insert the star-topped dowel. Glue. Dry.

Cardboard Tree Ornaments

Let these baubles and bangles decorate your Christmas tree for as little as the price of the beads. The bangles are cardboard tubes sliced and given a snow-white paint job.

Materials
Cardboard tubes
Assorted silver and red beads
Silver bead-stringing thread
Gesso
White paint

Tools
Craft knife
Beading needle
Paintbrush

Directions
1. Cut cardboard tubes into ¾-inch lengths.
2. Coat with gesso. Let dry. Paint white. Let dry.
3. Bead the ornaments, using photo as guide:
• Knot one bead at the end of a length of silver beading thread.
• Add the desired number of beads to drop from the bottom of the ornament.
• Draw needle through cardboard circle.
• Add more beads on string to fit inside opening of circle.
• Bring all beading threads out through center top of circle.
• Tie off all but one thread.
• Continue threading beads to form top of ornament.
• Tie off thread to create hanging loop.

Marbleized Boxes

Here's tangible proof that last year's gift boxes can look even better this year. After a resurfacing in hand-crafted marbleized paper, each spectacular design demands individual attention.

Materials
Three to four tubes of oil paint
Benzine
Gum turpentine
Medium-weight drawing paper
Assorted cardboard gift boxes
Rubber cement

Tools
Newspapers
Small tin cans
One large pan
Several watercolor brushes
Wooden skewer
Large-tooth comb
Scissors

Directions
1. Working next to a sink, fill the pan with one or two inches of cool water.
2. In a tin can, dilute 1 tablespoon oil paint in 1 tablespoon gum turpentine.
3. Stir with skewer until paint is completely dissolved.
4. Add 3 tablespoons benzine and stir until thoroughly mixed.
5. Dip brush in tin can and touch in water in five or six places. (Paint spots should expand in circles. If they don't, dilute the paint with more benzine and try again.)
6. Swirl paint spots in water with a comb.
7. While the water is still swirling, lower drawing paper held at diagonal corners onto the dye bath so that the center touches first. **(Note:** Add more paint spots to water after every second sheet. After every dozen prints, start over with fresh pan of water.)
8. Lift the paper immediately.
9. Turn over and rinse briefly under running water; spread on newspapers to dry.
10. Cut paper to fit neatly around boxes.
11. Wrap bottoms and lids of boxes separately, folding paper carefully over edges and gluing down securely. Let dry.

chapter 10

Classic Ways with Glass, China, and Clay

At one time, the best you could hope for from an empty bottle was to get your deposit money back. Now, you can do better than that. With a little ingenuity, cash in on empty bottles, unused flowerpots, test tubes, and even TV tubes as the raw materials for an array of interesting items. Here's a chapter loaded with ideas—all worth much more than the deposit money on all of those empty pop bottles.

Acid Bottle Terrarium

Gardening under glass becomes more and more popular every year especially for housebound gardeners. This handsome terrarium lets you capture a tiny, green environment. Get an empty water cooler or acid bottle from a chemistry lab or drugstore and use homemade tools like those shown in the left photograph on page 206 to plant the terrarium.

Materials
    One 5-gallon glass bottle
    One cork
    18 to 24 inches of rawhide thong
    Sand or fine gravel
    Granulated charcoal
    Potting soil
    Variety of terrarium plants
    Decorative rocks or figures (optional)

Tools
    Funnel
    Small plastic or metal spoons and forks
    Small sponge
    Several 36-inch-long ¼-inch dowel rods
    Knife
    Corkscrew
    Tape

Directions
1. Make long-handled tools for working inside the small-necked bottle:
- Flatten one side of wooden rods with knife.
- Trim utensil handles, if too awkward.
- Attach utensils to dowels by wrapping them securely with tape.
- Attach a small sponge to one wooden rod.

2. Wash bottle thoroughly. Let dry.

3. Mix charcoal and sand. With funnel, place a thin layer of mixture in bottom of bottle.

(continued on next page)

4. Add soil. (**Note:** A rough guide for the soil depth of the terrarium is about ¼ inch of soil for every inch of bottle height.)

5. Place plants:

• Dig out small areas of soil.

• Remove most of the soil from the plant roots before placing them.

• Make foliage and roots as compact as possible without damaging them.

• Slide them through the container top.

• Pack soil around roots, using tools as shown in the photo at bottom right.

• Plant container so the front or best side of each plant faces out.

6. Pour water carefully in the top of the bottle so it rinses down the inside. This will also moisten the soil. (**Note:** It will take some time to achieve the proper moisture content in most terrariums.)

7. With corkscrew, drill hole through cork.

8. Push both ends of rawhide thong through center of cork. Knot on bottom side. Attach to jar.

9. Arrange decorative rocks or figures among plants as desired.

Terrarium tips

Choose the right plants. Among the best terrarium plants are synogonium, dracena, pittosporum, Norfolk Island pine, artillery plant, boxwood, fittonia, variegated heart-leaf philodendron, English ivy, aluminum plant, croton, baby's-tears, partridge-berry, maiden hair and other ferns, mosses, and evergreen seedlings.

Moisture control is important. If there's too much moisture, condensation will form on the inside of the glass. Ventilation and air directed from a small fan will help remove the excess moisture.

Leave the top open until plants show they need moisture, which won't be often.

When terrarium seems to be drying out, replace the cork for a short time.

Place your terrarium where it will get light, but avoid direct sunlight.

Flowerpot Base Lamp

Finding just the right lamp to accessorize your home may be easier than you think—and less expensive. Although this lamp, which features three flowerpots stacked on end, is a snap to make, the end result is so good-looking that you can use it on almost any desk or end table.

Materials
Three clay flowerpots (8½ inch diameter)
Yellow latex paint
Blue latex paint
Paper lampshade
Epoxy
One 10½x10½x1-inch wooden base
Electrical parts (lamp harp, harp base, cord with molded end plug, and socket)
⅛-inch IPS all-thread lamp pipe (cut to fit)
Pebbles
60-watt mini globe light bulb

Tools
Screwdriver
Rabbet plane
Scissors
Drill
Paintbrush

Directions
1. Wash the flowerpots free of soil. Let them dry to their natural clay color before proceeding.
2. Glue the three flowerpots together as shown in the photo. (Line up the drainage holes.) Let dry completely.
3. Paint the flowerpots yellow. Let dry.
4. Trim the flowerpots with blue paint, as shown in the photo. Let dry.
5. Paint the paper shade and the wooden base to match the trim of the pots. Let dry completely before proceeding.
6. Drill a hole through the center of the wooden base for the lamp pipe.
7. With rabbet plane, cut a groove for lamp cord from center to edge of wooden base bottom.
8. To assemble the lamp,
• Run the lamp pipe through the drainage holes in flowerpots.
• Place a pile of pebbles on top of the wooden base to weight down the lamp.
• Fit the lip of the bottom pot over the pebbles and onto the wooden base.
• Fit the lamp pipe through hole in base.
• Glue lip of bottom pot to base. Let dry completely before wiring.
9. Run the cord through the pipe from the bottom up to the lamp socket. Wire the lamp according to directions on pages 252 and 253.
10. Fit cord into groove on base bottom so base will sit flat.
11. Position the shade.

How to use a rabbet plane

The rabbet plane is most commonly used to cut a recessed groove along the edge of a board. However, you can also use it with adjustable parts for other specialty woodworking jobs including cutting grooves away from the edge, as was done in this particular lamp project.

With the rabbet plane, you can make a cut as wide as the plane's bottom. To control the depth of the cut, adjust the plane's depth gauge. As you use the plane, each stroke deepens the recess until the desired depth is reached. For across-the-grain planing, attach a sharp spur.

Stained-Glass Bottles

Window accessories needn't cost a fortune. Here, ordinary glass bottles were converted into decorative pieces by capitalizing on their shapes and using glass stain and liquid leading in an imaginative way. To get luminous results as shown here, be sure to display your bottles on a windowsill where the sunlight will reveal the stained-glass colors most effectively.

Materials

Assorted clear or lightly tinted bottles (for your initial attempt, select bottles with flat fronts)
One tube liquid lead
Several colors of glass stain
Glass stain thinner
Resin and catalyst

Tools

Art knife
Paintbrushes (small, inexpensive ones)

Directions

1. Wash and dry bottle. (If you use the lid, wash and dry it.)
2. Prepare bottle surface for accepting lead:
• Mix the resin and the catalyst as directed on the package.
• Cover bottle with coat of resin.
• Let dry for about 20 minutes.
3. To soften the liquid lead, immerse the tube in hot tap water for five minutes. (**Note:** Practice squeezing the lead into a variety of designs on old newspapers. Squeeze the tube gently with even pressure. To make even, flat lines, always draw the tube toward you.)
4. Lay the prepared bottle on a newspaper-covered surface. (Prop up with wadded newspaper.)
5. Decorate one side of bottle with lead. (Create your own design, or enlarge pattern from grid on page 210 and mark it on bottle. Scrape off any lead smears or mistakes with art knife.) Let the leaded side dry at least one hour.
6. Turn the bottle and decorate other side with lead. Let dry several hours.
7. Set bottle upright. Then, cover each area completely with desired color of glass stain, brushing it slightly on top of all surrounding lead lines. (Use

---

How to make use of a gridded sketch

Whenever possible in this book, patterns are given full size. At times this just isn't possible. That's when the grid system comes in handy. It's the key that enables the "I-can't-draw-a-straight-line" craftsman to come up with a design drawn exactly to scale. Here's a little bit about the system and how to use it:

There are two parts to a gridded sketch: a graph formed by a combination of parallel horizontal and vertical lines, and the line drawing of the design superimposed on top of the graph lines.

To create the full-sized pattern, first look for the scale given with the grid. (For example, 1 square = ½ inch or 1 square = 2 inches.) This tells you what each square of the grid will measure when it has been enlarged to full size. Then, select paper large enough to accommodate the finished design (brown wrapping paper works well for large designs). Draw horizontal and vertical lines on the paper as far apart as the scale indicates.

Once you've ruled the paper into the full-sized grid, you are ready to transfer the drawing. As you look at the pattern, draw on the full-sized grid until you have reenacted the path of the line as it moves through the squares. Although it takes some practice, it won't take long for you to figure out just how the lines pass from square to square, and whether they move in a straight, curved, or diagonal line.

Use the same method, regardless of whether you wish to make a pattern smaller or larger. To alter the finished size of the design, simply vary size of grid scale.

---

a different brush for each color. Glass stain will not brush on completely smooth but tends to smear, giving an authentic glass-like effect.) Allow the stain to dry for at least two hours before moving the bottle. (If deeper color is desired, apply a second coat of stain. Let dry.)

(continued on next page)

8. Let the finished bottle dry for one day.
9. Seal with a coat of resin, as in step 2.
10. If using lid, paint it and let dry completely before use.

1 square = ½″

Wine Bottle Canisters

For years, people have been reluctant to throw out attractive wine bottles. So the empties ended up supporting dripping candles or drooping ivy. Now, there's a new twist. Use those with a lip as sure-to-be-commented-on canisters.

Materials
Two 36-inch-long pieces of 1x8-inch pine
Four 4-inch L-shaped shelf brackets
Paint primer
Paint
Eight wood screws
Eight fasteners to attach units to the wall (long wood screws, or toggle or expansion fasteners)
Eight empty half-gallon wine bottles

Tools
Saber saw or hole saw mounted on electric hand drill
Drill
Paintbrushes
Sandpaper

Directions
1. Measure for slots that hold wine bottles in place on the boards. (**Note:** The bottles shown here are spaced on 8-inch centers with 6 inches of board at either end. Change measurement to fit different size or shape.)

- Measure 6 inches in from one end.
- From that mark, make marks *every* 8 inches to accommodate the four bottles.
- You should have 6 inches of board left beyond the last mark.
- Repeat on second board.

2. Cut slots 1½ inches wide (centering slots on the marks) and 4 inches deep. With a hole saw, cut in from *edge* twice to intersect with hole. (**Note:** Make sure 1½ inches is the right width slot for the neck of your bottles to slip in but not through. Adjust measurements to fit.)

3. Sand rough *edges* of slots.

4. Sand all surfaces of boards. Wipe clean.

5. Drill holes and use wood screws to attach L-shaped brackets to underside of boards.

6. Paint all surfaces of the unit, including the bracket, with primer. Let dry completely.

7. Lightly sand wood of both boards. Wipe.

8. Paint boards and brackets. Let dry.

9. Apply another coat if *necessary* for a smooth finish. Sand lightly between coats. Let dry.

10. Position racks on wall. Leave space between top and bottom units for easy maneuvering.

11. Using fastener appropriate for the type of wall, attach the racks to the wall.

12. Wash eight wine bottles thoroughly. Let dry.

13. Slip necks of wine bottles into rack slots.

How to fasten things to any kind of wall

There are several types of wall fasteners. Since each situation calls for a certain one, learn them for safety's sake.

Ordinary nails and screws are the simplest and easiest fasteners to use. But you need something solid to fasten to, so locate wall studs, then fasten into them.

Suction cups, paste, or glue are adequate fasteners if the item you're fastening to a wall is light.

Flange-type fasteners are necessary for fastening to a hollow plaster or masonry wall. Choose toggle bolts or fasteners with casings that expand behind the wall as you screw the bolt into it.

Friction-held fastening devices are necessary for walls of solid masonry.

Clay Pot Bird Feeder

Birdwatchers can have almost as much fun with this clay pottery bird feeder as the birds themselves. Use three ordinary pieces of flower potting supplies to put together a first-class restaurant —specializing in inflight service.

Materials
    One 6-inch flowerpot
    One 9-inch saucer
    One 12-inch saucer
    Threaded ¼-inch rod (cut to size)
    Washers and nuts and rubber washers (or
        disks cut from rubber to pad between
        metal washers and clay)

Tools
    Drill with carbide drill bit
    Small wrench

Directions
1. Drill holes in center of saucer bottoms to receive the threaded ¼-inch rod..

2. Fill pot with bird seed.

3. Use nuts and washers to hold clay sections securely in place with rod down the middle, starting with the 9-inch saucer, then the inverted pot, and then the inverted 12-inch saucer. (**Note:** Leave enough space between pot and 12-inch saucer for seeds to fall from pot.)

Pop Bottle Carolers

These little street urchins will sing their hearts out on your mantel or tabletop. And the beauty of these pint-sized waifs is that they're made of pre-starched fabric draped over plastic foam balls and non-returnable pop bottles.

Materials

Pre-starched fabric (available at craft
    stores)
Scraps of fake fur (2- to 3-inch pile)
Gesso
Short sequin pins
Facial tissues
Glue
Short piece of wire
Paint

Large urchin
All materials listed above
Quart pop bottle
5-inch foam ball
Two 2-inch foam balls
4-inch foam egg
Two pear-shape headed corsage pins
18-inch length of 18-gauge flower wire
Cardboard

Small urchin
All materials listed for general construction
12-ounce bottle
4-inch foam ball
Two 1½-inch foam balls
3-inch foam egg
14-inch length of 18-gauge flower wire
Masking tape
Paper towels
Small buttons

Tools

Scissors
Paintbrush

Directions

Large urchin   **1.** Roll the larger foam ball along a table edge, pressing hard to make an indentation extending halfway around the ball. (See sketch A on page 214.)
2. Roll ball a second time, pressing one side of indentation flat for forehead.
3. Make a nose from a tiny part of one of the smaller foam balls. Fold and roll to about ½-inch

diameter. Position on head. Pin in place.
4. Scoop oval out of ball to form the mouth.
5. Cut a piece of fabric large enough to cover half of the ball.
6. Dip fabric in cold water, then remove. Do not soak or wring. (**Note:** Let starch in fabric soften for about 45 seconds before applying it to figure.)
7. Lay fabric over the face. Use short sequin pins to attach fabric around nose. (Push pins in until there are no bumps.)
8. Smooth fabric over the curves of the face.
9. Secure outside edges with pins.
10. Cut hair from fake fur. Pin and glue it to the front of the head. Let dry.
11. Coat hair and face with gesso. Let dry.
12. Push in corsage pins for teeth.
13. Form hands by cutting one of the smaller balls in half.
14. Notch side of each half, being sure to cut a right and left hand. (See sketch B.)
15. Wrap each hand with a 3½-inch circle of wet fabric. While wet, score with scissors point to indicate fingers. (See sketch C.)
16. Twist wire around top of bottle (sketch D).
17. Wrap each arm with tissue to pad it.
18. Secure arms with ¼-inch strip of wet fabric. Leave an inch uncovered at the bottom of each wire end. (Hands are inserted here later.)
19. Cut the foam egg in half lengthwise.
20. Cut an inch off the small end of egg half.
21. Glue egg "feet" to front of bottle. Let dry.
22. Cover feet and lower part of bottle with fabric. Make excess look like shoe soles.
23. Cut a piece of fabric 18 inches long and one inch higher than the bottle. Wet it.
24. Fold under a "hem"; gather the top together, and drape it around the bottle.
25. Wet an 8-inch square for each sleeve.
26. Turn under a hem at top and bottom.
27. Join sides to make a tube.
28. Slip sleeve over arm and pinch together at the top and bottom.
29. Arrange arms to hold a book. Let dry.
30. Attach head by positioning it over bottle and pressing down hard. Cut a hole in the head at the bottle mark. Spread thick glue over top of bottle. Press head down on the bottle and let it dry overnight.
31. Cut a 20-inch equilateral triangle of fabric for the figure's head scarf.
32. Push a wire into the back of the head.

33. Wet scarf and tie around urchin's head. Support scarf on wire. Then, remove wire when fabric is dry. (See sketch E.)

34. Cut a 7x30-inch fabric strip for muffler.

35. Wet. Fold sides under. Tie on figure.

36. Make front apron over dress by cutting fabric smaller than dress. Wet and drape.

37. Make the book from the cardboard. Cover with the pre-starched fabric.

38. Glue hands onto ends of arms. Glue book in hands. Let dry overnight before proceeding.

39. Coat completely dry figures with gesso. Dry.

40. Paint with acrylic paints. Dry overnight.

Small urchin **1.** Follow steps 1 through 16 as for large urchin. Eliminate teeth.

2. Tape a piece of folded paper towel to bottle to form the figure's chest.

3. Attach one half of a small ball to the bottle to form the back. (See sketch F.)

(continued on next page)

4. Continue, follow large urchin directions from 17 through 30 with the following variations:

- Pleat body fabric in front so it looks like two pant legs. Overlap in back.
- Attach a small square of fabric in front to look like a shirt.
- Cover upper back with another small piece of fabric.
- Do not gather sleeves.
- Add "hemmed" panels in front to indicate an open jacket.
- Make muffler as in Steps 34 and 35. Cut muffler slightly smaller than for large urchin.

5. Make stocking cap by cutting a 20-inch equilateral triangle of fabric, joining sides together to form cap. Push wire in head to hold wet fabric out while cap is drying.

6. Glue small buttons to jacket sides.

7. Add hands.

8. Coat dry figure completely with gesso. Let dry completely before proceeding.

9. Paint with acrylic paints. Dry overnight.

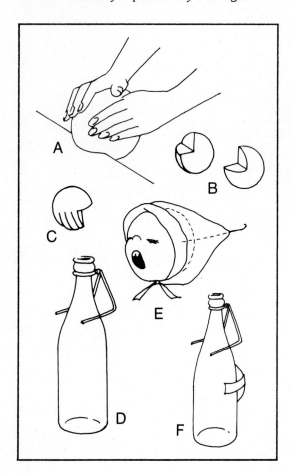

Jar Spice Rack

As anyone who has an infant will attest, baby food jars pile up at a furious pace. Here's a clever way to put three dozen of those jars back into circulation. Use them as containers in this spice rack.

Materials
    36 baby food jars
    ¼-inch pine in 2½-inch wide strips (twelve 14 inches long and two 14½ inches long)
    Wood glue
    14½ x 14½-inch piece of ⅛-inch hardboard or heavy cardboard
    Paint
    Model makers lacquer
    Pressure-sensitive letters (from art store)
    Clear plastic tape

Tools
    Saw
    Paintbrush

Directions
1. Glue the two long and two of the short wood strips together to form a 14½x14½-frame. Let dry completely.

2. Lap-joint interior dividers to form egg-crate effect. Glue to frame sides. Let dry.

3. Glue structure to backing material. Let dry.

4. Paint rack. Let dry.

5. Paint lids with model makers lacquer. Dry.

6. Apply pressure-sensitive letters as labels.

7. Cover letters with clear plastic tape.

Cracked Pot Planter

Hold it! Don't toss out those broken or cracked pieces of china. You can continue enjoying your favorite tableware—even in bits and pieces—in this smashing cachepot. It's a plain clay pot "tiled" with china shards.

Materials
    Large clay pot
    Waterproof tile mastic
    Pieces of chipped or cracked china
    Small shells, if desired
    White or tinted latex grouting
    Clear acrylic coating

Tools
    Putty knife
    Hammer
    Squeegee tool
    Paintbrush

Directions
1. Using gentle hammer taps, crack china into small, irregularly shaped "tiles."
2. Cover the clay pot with tile mastic.
3. Set the pieces of china into the mastic as closely together as possible.
4. Apply small shells or bits of china to the rim of the pot in the same manner. Let mastic dry.
5. Fill all cracks with latex grouting, using a squeegee tool. Let dry.
6. Apply several coats of clear acrylic finish. Let dry between coats.

Clay Pot Hanging Lamps

Clay products have never had it so good! Here, clay flowerpots, saucers, and tiles are used in various combinations to make highly serviceable lighting units. Once you've tried these ideas, create your own designs by combining other clay pot shapes.

Materials
For each lamp
    Swag lamp kit (includes 15 feet of chain, 20 feet of cord with a line switch, plug, set of swag hooks, and keyless Bakelite or porcelain socket)
    Epoxy
    Three threaded lock washers
    One threaded lock nut
    ⅛-inch IPS all-thread lamp pipe (cut to length needed)
    One canopy loop to fit lamp pipe
    60-watt mini globe light bulb

(continued on next page)

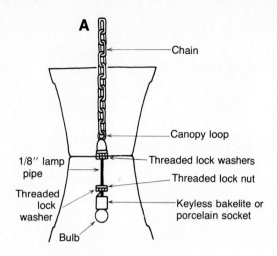

A

Chain

Canopy loop

1/8" lamp pipe

Threaded lock washers

Threaded lock nut

Threaded lock washer

Keyless bakelite or porcelain socket

Bulb

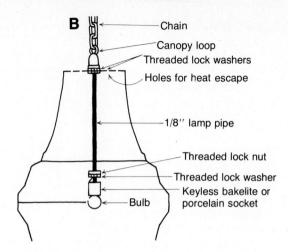

B

Chain

Canopy loop

Threaded lock washers

Holes for heat escape

1/8" lamp pipe

Threaded lock nut

Threaded lock washer

Keyless bakelite or porcelain socket

Bulb

Lamp number one
  Two medium-size clay flowerpots
Lamp number two
  One medium-size clay flowerpot
  One clay saucer
Lamp number three
  Two large clay flowerpots
Lamp number four
  One medium-size clay flowerpot
  One small clay flowerpot
  Four 3-inch-long, ¼-inch wooden dowels
Lamp number five
  One clay drain tile
  2-inch-thick wooden disk to fit inside
    drain tile
  Four 3-inch-long ¼-inch wooden dowels

Tools
  Drill with carbide-tip bit
  Hammer
  Chisel
  File

Directions

Lamp number one (see sketch A) **1.** Glue bases of pots together with epoxy, making sure drainage holes match. Let dry.
2. Run the lamp pipe through drainage holes.
3. Secure the pipe with threaded lock washers on each side of hole.
4. Weave cord through chain and attach one or two links of chain to the canopy loop.
5. Screw canopy loop onto lamp pipe.
6. Run the cord down through the pipe.
7. Wire socket according to wiring directions

given on pages 252 and 253. (Screw lock nut and lock washer onto pipe before attaching socket, as shown in sketch.)
8. Drill hole in ceiling for swag hook.
9. Screw swag hook into ceiling. (The swag hook comes with a toggle bolt.)
10. Hang lamp by linking chain to swag hook.
11. Screw in light bulb.

Lamp number two (see sketch B) **1.** Using carbide-tip bit, carefully drill six holes in bottom of pot. (These will allow heat to escape.)
2. To break out bottom of clay saucer,
• Slowly drill holes all around bottom edge, using carbide-tip bit. (While drilling, drip water on saucer occasionally to keep cool.)
• Carefully chisel and hammer out the bottom a little bit at a time.
3. To smooth surface area of pot rim and saucer rim for gluing, file top edges of rims.
4. Glue rim of saucer to rim of pot with epoxy. Let dry.
5. Wire the lamp as detailed in sketch B and steps 2 through 7 given for lamp number one.
6. Hang the lamp according to steps 8, 9, and 10 given for lamp number one.
7. Screw in light bulb.

Lamp number three (see sketch C) **1.** Carefully drill six holes in bottom of one flowerpot with a carbide-tip bit.
2. Break out the bottom of the other pot as in step 2 of lamp number two.
3. Drill holes for decoration in the sides of both pots. (Drill slowly and carefully.)

216

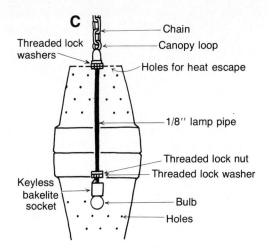

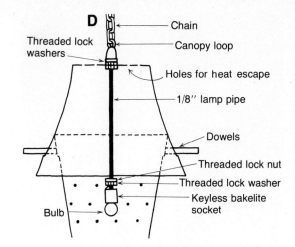

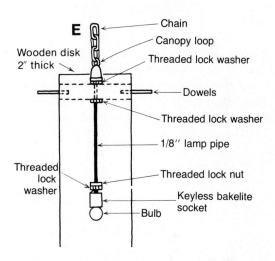

4. Wire the pot with holes in bottom, as detailed in sketch C and steps 2 through 7 given for lamp number one.

5. File across top edges of pot rims.

6. Glue the rims of pots together with epoxy. Let dry completely.

7. Hang the lamp according to steps 8, 9, and 10 given for lamp number one.

8. Screw in light bulb.

Lamp number four (see sketch D)   **1.** Carefully drill six holes in bottom of medium-size pot, using carbide-tip bit.

2. Drill holes in sides of small pot.

3. Drill four holes to accept dowels around side of middle-size flowerpot, spacing holes equidistant from each other.

4. Remove the bottom of the small pot according to step 2 given for lamp number two.

5. Glue the small pot inside the middle-size pot with epoxy. Let dry.

6. Push ¼-inch dowels into four holes in middle-size pot until they touch small pot. Glue in place. Let dry.

7. Wire the lamp as detailed in sketch D and steps 2 through 7 given for lamp number one.

8. Hang lamp according to steps 8, 9, and 10 given for lamp number one.

9. Screw in light bulb.

Lamp number five (see sketch E)   **1.** Drill hole in center of wooden disk to accept lamp pipe.

2. Drill four holes for dowels equidistant from each other near the top of tile, using carbide-tip bit to prevent shattering.

3. Insert wooden disk in top of drain tile, aligning with holes in tile. Then, mark position of holes on side of wooden disk.

4. Drill holes to accept dowels in disk side at marks. (Drill holes about an inch deep.)

5. Position disk in tile, aligning holes.

6. Run dowels through holes in tile and push securely into holes in wooden disk. Glue dowels in place.

7. Run the all-thread lamp pipe through the hole in the center of the wooden disk.

8. Secure the pipe with threaded lock washers on each side of the hole.

9. Wire the lamp as detailed in sketch E and steps 4 through 7 given for clay flowerpot lamp number one.

10. Hang lamp according to steps 8, 9, and 10 given for lamp number one.

11. Screw in light bulb.

Test Tube Bud Vases

These test tubes will never be part of any important medical research project, but they're a sure cure for the blahs. Turn a glass test tube into a handsome, contemporary bud vase.

Materials
    Scrap pieces of 2x4 pine
    Test tubes
    Wood stain

Tools
    Saw
    Drill with spade bit
    Jigsaw
    Coarse-grade sandpaper
    Paintbrush

Directions
Right vase   **1.** Cut wood block for base.
2. Drill a hole in the top of the block slightly larger than the diameter of the test tube.
3. Sand and stain to finish. Let dry.

Center vase   **1.** Follow steps 1 and 2 above.
2. Lay the wood piece on its side and jigsaw through the face of it.
3. Sand and stain to finish. Let dry.

Left vase   **1.** Do steps 1 and 2 like right vase.
2. Cut angles at top of base.
3. Sand and stain to finish. Let dry.

TV Tube Chess Set

Chess has replaced TV—at least as far as these TV tubes are concerned. They're back in business and more entertaining than ever. A check at any TV and radio repair shop will net you all the old tubes you want. Choose sizes and shapes to represent the six different chess pieces. Then attach them to clear acrylic plastic bases.

Materials
    32 assorted TV tubes
    One 12x12-inch piece of ¼-inch plastic
        (for the base)

Tools
    Power saw or plastic scribing tool and ¾-inch dowel rod
    Medium-grade sandpaper
    Fine-grade sandpaper
    Extra-fine grade sandpaper
    Electric drill
    Muslin and cotton flannel buffing wheels
    Fine-grit buffing compound

Directions
1. Measure plastic into squares for bases. (The ones shown here are 2- and 1-inch squares)
2. Cut bases for chess pieces:
• Do not remove paper backing on plastic.
• Saw plastic with power saw or cut with a scribing tool (**Note:** To cut with a scribing tool, lay a straightedge on your plastic and scribe along it four or five times—right through the paper backing. Lay the plastic sheet, scribed side up, with a ¾-inch dowel centered under the scribed line. Press on both sides until plastic breaks.)
3. Finish edges by sanding with medium-grade sandpaper.
4. To get a transparent edge, continue sanding first with fine-grade wet or dry sandpaper, then with extra-fine grade sandpaper.
5. Buff with an electric drill, using a muslin wheel and fine grit buffing compound.
6. Finish with a cotton-flannel wheel.
7. Mark position of TV tubes on bases.
8. Drill holes to hold prongs of tubes.
9. Remove paper backing from plastic.
10. Insert prongs of tubes into holes in each plastic base and glue in place to secure. Let dry completely.

One 1x6
One 1x8
Two 1x2s
Finishing nails
Six 2-inch-long wood screws
Six metal rods (diameter must match
    drainage holes in flowerpots)
Two inside corner braces (with four screws
    and four toggle bolts to fit)
Paint (flat finish in shade to match pots)
White glue
Epoxy

Tools

Paintbrush
Circular saw
Miter box
Furniture clamps
Square
Chisel
Screwdriver
Drill

Directions

1. To determine measurements of partition,
• Measure the length of top of unfinished chest
(measurement A).
• Measure height from top of chest to ceiling
(measurement B).
2. Cut lumber for frame:
• Cut the 1x6 the length of measurement A.
• Cut the 1x8 1½ inches shorter than measurement A.
• Cut both 2x2s the height of measurement B.
• Cut four pieces from the 1x2s—two pieces the
length of measurement A and two pieces 9 inches
long each.
3. To build the box that sits atop chest,
• Miter the corners of the 1x2s at 45° angle.
• Position one of the 9-inch pieces of 1x2 at each
end of the 1x8. Position one of the long 1x2s
along each side of the 1x8. Glue the 1x2s to
1x8 and glue mitered corners to form box, as
shown in the photo and the drawing.
• Clamp corners (use padding). Let dry.
• Nail finishing nails from side of 1x2s into 1x8
to secure. Nail three finishing nails from side of
each corner into joint to secure joint.
4. To make holes for metal rods,
• Inside box, position six large flowerpots evenly
apart. Mark position of drainage hole of each pot

Flowerpot Partition

Empty flowerpots have a strange way of accumulating. If a check of your basement or garage re-
veals an abundance of them, put them to work as
a partition, as shown here. Scrub the flowerpots
well before using them for this creative as well as
distinctive project.

Materials

Clay flowerpots (60 large size and 24 small
    size were used in the partition shown
    in the above photograph)
One unfinished chest
Drawer pulls for the chest
Two 2x2s

on box bottom. (You may want to use more or less than six pots, depending on length of box.)
• Make matching marks on one side of 1x6. (Be sure to measure exactly so space from ends and between pots is exactly the same on bottom of box and on 1x6.)
• Drill holes about halfway through the 1x6 and bottom of box to receive the metal rods that will hold the pots in place. (**Note:** The holes for the rods must be snug-fitting and bored true and square. Bore true holes by lining up the drill with a square.)

5. Make a half lap joint for bottom of partition:
• Lay 2x2 at right angle to end of box, 1 inch in from corner. Scribe width of box end on 2x2.
• Saw halfway through 2x2 to make cutout, as shown in drawing.
• Clean out the cut with chisel. (Check to be sure 2x2 fits down squarely over end of box, as shown in drawing.)
• Glue 2x2 in place. Clamp and let dry.
• Nail from inside through joint to secure.
• Repeat with other 2x2 on other end of box.

6. To make full lap joint for top of partition,
• Position 2x2 at right angle to center of 1x6.
• Mark the exact shape of the 2x2 on both faces and across end of 1x6.
• Cut out the marked shape.
• Clean out cut with chisel. (Check to make sure 2x2 fits securely in cutout.)
• Repeat on other end of 1x6.
• Slide 1x6, holes down, over 2x2s.

7. To attach frame to chest,
• With another person's help, position frame upright atop chest, aligning back edges.
• Drill holes for wood screws through box bottom and into chest top (put one near each corner and two in middle).
• Screw in wood screws.

8. To stabilize partition, attach inside corner braces to ceiling and 2x2s,
• Position braces and mark location of holes on ceiling.
• Drill holes in ceiling to accept toggle bolts.
• Remove end of toggle bolts and insert them through holes in braces.
• Replace end of toggle bolts.
• Screw them into ceiling.
• Screw braces to 2x2s.

9. Add pot pillars:
• String the pots on the rods as shown in photo.

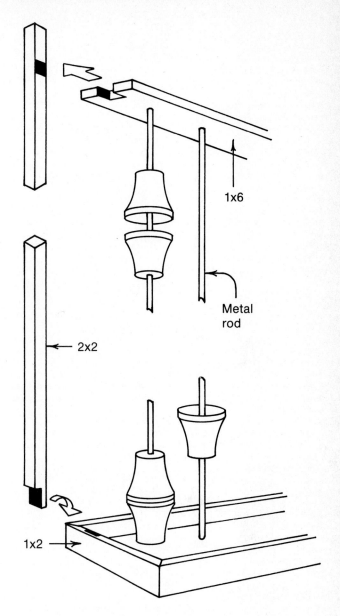

1x6

Metal rod

2x2

1x2

• Glue the pot rims and bottoms together with epoxy. Let dry.
• Slide the 1x6 almost to ceiling and clamp to hold.
• With another person's help, set the metal rods of the pot pillars into the prebored holes in the box bottom.
• Unclamp the 1x6, then slide it down and fit top of metal rods into prebored holes.
• Glue full lap joint. Let dry.

10. Paint the chest and frame to match the pots. Let dry.

11. Add drawer pulls to chest.

chapter 11

Plastic Potpourri

Plastic is to the modern man what fire was to the caveman. Can you imagine living without it? And now, you can discover still another dimension to this space-age material. Look what you can do with it the second time around!

Container-Lid Hanging

This attractive three-dimensional hanging may look expensive, but it isn't. Simply mount container tops, lids, and/or wood scraps on a plastic backing. Either spotlight the hanging or let the sun backlight the art piece.

Materials

Lids and tops of small cans and bottles, plastic foam cups, and wood scraps
¼-inch thick smoke-colored transparent or translucent plastic
Two pieces chandelier chain (cut to length needed to hang the art piece)
Flat latex paint
Dishwashing detergent
Swag hooks
Plastic cement

Tools

Electric drill
Circular saw with special blade for cutting plastic
Paintbrush
Coarse-grade sandpaper
Wet or dry medium-grade and fine-grade sandpaper
Buffing wheel (attached to electric drill)

Directions

1. Using circular saw, cut ¼-inch thick plastic to desired size.
2. Sand the edges of the plastic piece with coarse-grade sandpaper, with wet or dry medium-grade, then with fine-grade sandpaper.
3. Run the buffing wheel against the edges of the plastic until polished smooth.
4. Drill a hole near the top of each side of the plastic to fasten the chandelier chains. (Drill slowly to avoid chipping.)
5. Remove paper from both sides of the plastic; clean with mild soap and water.
6. Clean stamped prices off the lids and tops with kitchen cleanser or scouring powder.
7. Paint the lids, tops, cups, and wood scraps to be used with flat latex paint. (Add a few drops of dishwashing detergent to the paint to help it adhere to the lids.) Let dry.
8. Arrange the painted items on the plastic.
9. Attach the items to the plastic with plastic cement. Let dry.
10. Attach the chandelier chains to plastic.
11. Position art piece and drill holes in ceiling to accept swag hooks.
12. Screw in swag hooks (swag hooks come with toggle bolts).
13. Attach the chains to the swag hooks to hang the art piece.

Foam Tray Ornaments

A trip to the library provides you with design symbols to create a tree-full of these ornaments from meat trays. The symbols here are early Christian, Nordic runes, and alchemists' signs.

Materials
    Plastic foam meat trays (two for each trim)
    Glue
    Spackle
    Gesso
    Acrylic paints (assortment of colors)

Tools
    Paintbrush
    Craft knife

Directions
1. Cut out two circles for each ornament from the plastic meat trays.
2. Glue together. Let dry.
3. Spackle seams and any dents or holes.
4. Coat with gesso. Let dry.
5. Paint with acrylic paint. Let dry.
6. Paint on designs with black paint. Let dry completely before proceeding.

Plastic Cup Ornaments

Not all ripe dandelions raise the pollen count. These beauties, for instance, are as feathery and fragile as the real thing, but they are tree trims made from plastic cups. If you sneeze—you're allergic to Christmas.

Materials
> Two plasticized cups (the kind that fit into plastic holders)
> Monofilament line
> Glue
> Aluminum foil

Tools
> Scissors

Directions
1. With sharp scissors, cut the cups in thin strips from the outer rim to the center.
2. Glue two cut cups back to back. Let dry.
3. Cut circles of aluminum foil and glue to inner circles on both sides of ornament. Dry.
4. Tie monofilament line to base of two "spikes" at the top of the ornament.

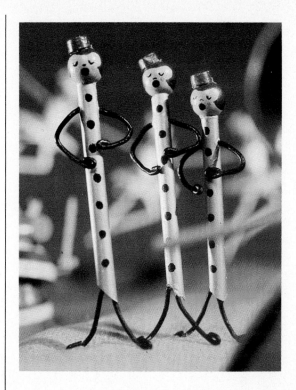

Drinking Straw Singers

This trio "con brio" is nothing more than three large plastic straws turned singers. What they may lack in musical brilliance, they make up in enthusiasm and whimsy.

Materials
> Malt-size drinking straws
> Wooden beads for heads
> Corks for hats
> Insulating wire for arms and legs
> Glue
> Paint

Tools
> Paintbrush
> Wire cutter

Directions
1. Cut and insert wire legs through the straw and into bead head.
2. Cut arm wires. Push through body of straw and bend ends for hands.
3. Glue cork on head for hat. Let dry.
4. Paint according to photograph. Let dry.

Corded Plant Hangers

Frozen dessert topping dishes and soft margarine containers have a tendency to stack up rapidly. If you have some that aren't delegated to a particular use, remember that they make excellent plant containers. Simply twist cording as directed to complete the conversion.

Materials (for each plant hanger)
   1-quart plastic container (6 inches in diameter and 3¼ inches deep)
   4-inch diameter plastic lid with ¼-inch deep lip
   1-inch curtain ring
   ½-inch wooden bead for each tassel
   8½ yards 3-ply twine or cord (12 yards if making double tassel)
   Black wool yarn
   Pebbles
   Masking tape

Tools
   One large-eyed needle
   Hole punch

Directions
1. Wrap the curtain ring with the yarn; tie off the end before proceeding.

226

2. Cut four 40-inch lengths of twine, and fold each in half.

3. Attach one folded length to the curtain ring with a lark's head knot (see sketch A). (**Note:** To make the lark's head knot, insert folded loop of twine through the center of the ring from the back. Bring the two loose ends around to the front of the ring and thread through the loop. Adjust the ends so they are the same length, pull, and tighten.)

4. Twist the two extending twine lengths together so they measure 14 inches. (Hold the twisted twine in place with masking tape.)

5. Hang the ring from overhead support in order to handle the work in progress easily.

6. Punch four holes equidistant from each other around the lip of the plastic lid.

7. With the needle, thread the ends of twisted twine through one hole in lid, threading from outside to underside of the lid.

8. Pull the twine ends through until the lid rests under the taped portion of cord.

9. Tie the twine into a knot directly under the lid edge.

10. Lay the remaining twine across the lid bottom just to the center, and tape. (You should have about two inches of twine left for attaching tassels.)

11. Repeat steps 3 to 10 for remaining three lengths of twine, threading each in hole in lid lip. (When all four are attached, they will form a cage as shown in photo.)

12. Use a short piece of twine to tie all extending lengths together directly under the center of the plastic lid.

13. To make a tassel,
• Cut five 8-inch lengths of twine.
• Unravel to make total of 15 one-ply strands.

• Make a bundle of the strands by tying them together in the center with an 8-inch length of one-ply twine (referred to as the "tie").
• Thread the two ends of the "tie" through hole in wooden bead. (The 15-strand portion hangs under the bead.)
• Cut eight 11-inch lengths of twine.
• Again unravel each length to make 15 strands of one-ply twine.
• Use ends of tie extending above bead to tie around center of these additional strands.
• Let these strands cascade over the bead to cover it evenly, and use a small piece of twine to tie strands together firmly under the bead.
• Wrap black yarn tightly around the strands under the bead until ½-inch length is covered.
• Trim the tassel ends evenly.

14. To attach tassels to plant hanger,
• Cut extending twine ends under the lid to 1½ inches. (For double tassels, separate the extending ends into two sections and tie. Then, attach a tassel to each section as follows.)
• Cut the tie on the tassel above the bead to 1½ inches.
• Tie tassel to extending twine ends so the tassel hangs below the plastic platform.
• Wrap the twine between the bead and the plastic lid platform with black yarn as shown in sketch B.

15. Remove the tape holdings.

16. Cover the bottom of the plastic container with pebbles to ensure proper drainage, then plant your greenery.

17. Position plastic container on plastic platform as shown in photo.

18. Hang the planter from a curtain rod or a swag hook.

A

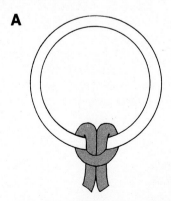

Lark's head knot on ring

B

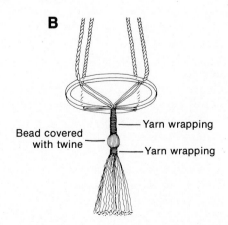

Bead covered with twine — Yarn wrapping
Yarn wrapping

Plastic Odds 'n' Ends Supermarket

Owning your own supermarket is probably the only way you're going to beat food prices. At least you can pretend you're lowering costs. This miniature market is stocked with interesting odds 'n' ends, making the supermarket as much fun to build as to play with.

Materials

One inexpensive pine drawing board
One sheet of wood grain poster board
½ sheet of ¼-inch plywood
One plastic berry box (for each cart)
Two plastic spray can lids
Two ice-cream carton lids
Blocks of wood for counters
Narrow strips of balsa wood
Paint (red, black, white, and silver)

Magazine cutouts for wall decorations
Glue
Small nails
Plastic letters spelling "supermarket" (from children's spelling set)
Miscellaneous items for "products"
  Beads
  Plastic straws cut to can-size lengths
  Small blocks of wood for boxes
  Colored popcorn
  Spices painted to resemble produce
  Whole red peppers cut in shreds and plastic wrapped for meat
  Round mints for angel food cakes

Tools

Saw
Craft knife
Paintbrush
Hammer
Scissors

Directions

Supermarket   **1.** Cut sides of plywood, using diagram below as cutting guide.
2. Assemble sides, using glue and small nails.
3. Face edges of supermarket with narrow strips of balsa. Glue in place. Let dry.
4. Paint interior and exterior surfaces of supermarket. Let dry.
5. Paint edges of drawing board black. Dry.
6. Cover with wood grain poster board.
7. Glue supermarket to surfaced drawing board. Let dry completely.
8. Glue magazine cutouts to walls for "ads." Dry.
9. Glue strips of balsa in place for shelves. Let dry completely.
10. Paint wood blocks and position for counters. Let dry completely.
11. Glue on plastic letters. Let dry.

Dump bins (see on sketch below)   **1.** Glue a spray can lid and an ice cream carton lid back to back. Let dry completely.
2. Paint bright red. Let dry.
3. Position on supermarket floor and fill with your choice of "products" listed on page 228.

Grocery carts   **1.** Cut through the center of a plastic vegetable basket.
2. Cut the two corner sections of basket that diagonally face each other so they slide together forming a small rectangle. (This gives the basket a double bottom.)
3. Glue corners together. Let dry.
4. Cut two 1-inch diameter wheels from leftover parts of basket.
5. Glue to cart. Let dry.
6. Cut remaining scraps to make push handle.
7. Glue handle to the cart. Let dry.
8. Paint with silver paint. Let dry.

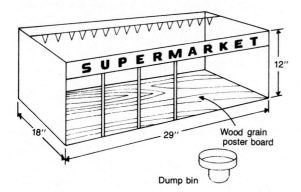

Dump bin

Bottle Top Ornaments

Christmas tree trims come in all shapes, colors, and prices. The beauties shown here are unbeatable in all three counts—particularly price. They're nearly free!

Materials
Two identical plastic bottles per ornament
Paint (at least three contrasting colors)
Glue
½ yard of cord per ornament
Felt pens (in colors to match paints)

Tools
Scissors
Large sewing needle

Directions
1. Cut off the tops of the two bottles.
2. Remove the plastic lid from one bottle top.
3. Thread a large needle with cord.
4. Heat the tip of the needle over a flame.
5. Perforate the top with the hot needle.
6. Thread the hanging cord through the hole and tie a knot inside of the cap to hold it.
7. Replace the cap on the bottle.
8. Paint bottle sections completely. Let dry.
9. Apply second color in excess so it will run. Let dry. (Apply additional colors the same.)
10. Glue tops together at cut edges. Let dry.
11. Add details to the ornament with felt pens.

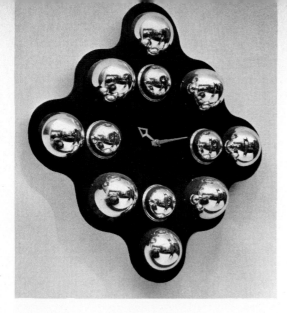

Topped Clock

Being a clock watcher is lots more fun when you count the minutes on a glittering contemporary clock like this one. It's domed with panty hose eggs and spray deodorant tops.

Materials
Eight shiny panty hose egg tops
Four shiny spray deodorant tops
One scrap of hardboard
Battery-powered clock works
12 wooden blocks (cut to size)
Black paint
Glue

Tools
Saber saw
Drill

Directions
1. Draw the clock face shape on hardboard.
2. Saw the piece to shape.
3. Drill a hole in the center. (This allows for attachment of the hands on the front of the clock and the battery-powered works on the back.)
4. Drill another hole near top to use as hanger.
5. Paint the hardboard black. Let dry.
6. For "numerals," arrange panty hose containers and spray deodorant tops as shown in the photograph. Mark their locations.
7. Glue blocks inside tops. Let dry.
8. Glue blocks to marked locations. Let dry.
9. Attach the face of the clock to the clock works according to package instructions.

Plastic Cup Jesters

If one court jester was enough to keep a king from melancholy, just imagine what this flock of funny fellows will do for your party. The clowns shown here are made of plastic cups covered with colorful adhesive-backed paper and topped with typical jesters' hats.

Materials
Plastic cups (two to four for each jester)
Adhesive-backed paper (orange, yellow, pink, blue, and black)
Lightweight cardboard
Gift-tie yarn matching jester's colors
Red yarn for hair
Glue

Tools
Scissors
Dowel or pencil

Directions
1. Roll a cup on adhesive-backed paper, drawing a line at top and bottom edges to form pattern.
2. Cut the pattern out and fit the paper to the plastic cup.
3. Cut hat from the same color paper as you use to cover cup. (**Note:** Use two pieces, back to back, so you will have a colored lining in the hat.)
4. Roll the points of the hat over a dowel or pencil to curl edges.
5. Cut a triangular piece of cardboard for nose.
6. Cover cardboard with adhesive-backed paper to match jester's costume.
7. Glue nose to unpapered cup. Let dry.
8. Cut mouth out of black adhesive-backed paper. Cut eyes out of blue.
9. Attach facial features to unpapered cup.
10. Cut 2½-inch long pieces of red yarn for jester's hair.
11. Fold each strand and glue to head at a place that will be just under the jester's hat. Dry.
12. Glue hat onto head. Let dry.
13. Stack and glue covered cups together to form jester's body. (Use from two to four cups, depending on the desired height.) Let dry completely before proceeding.
14. Cut 12-inch long pieces of yarn in colors to match jester's costume.
15. Tie yarn neckties around jesters' necks.

chapter 12

New Beginnings for Odds 'n' Ends

Any halfway accomplished scavenger ought to have enough raw materials in his or her attic to stay creative and crafty for a good long time. And if all you're lacking is good ideas, this closing chapter gives them to you.

Oz-ish Eggheads

"We're off to see the wizard"—or to be seen adding some fun to a tablesetting. Re-create the three famous Oz characters shown opposite with nothing more spectacular than eggs, cardboard, and a little fabric, paint, and yarn.

Materials
One blown egg (for each)
Tin man
  Lightweight cardboard
  White glue
  Silver paint
  Black and white acrylic paint
  Tape
Scarecrow
  Lightweight cardboard
  10x10-inch piece of white fabric
  White glue
  Rubber band
  Short length of rough twine
  4x8-inch piece of black felt
  Broomstraws

Black, white, and red acrylic paint
Tape
Lion
  Lightweight cardboard
  Tape
  10x10-inch piece of gold fabric
  Rubber band
  White glue
  Scraps of gold felt
  Gold yarn
  4½ inches fine wire
  Red bow
  Black and white acrylic paints

Tools
  Scissors
  Stapler
  Paper clips
  Paintbrush
  Wire cutter

Directions
Tin man **1.** Cut a 1x4-inch strip of cardboard.
2. Tape cardboard into circle to form stand.

(continued on next page)

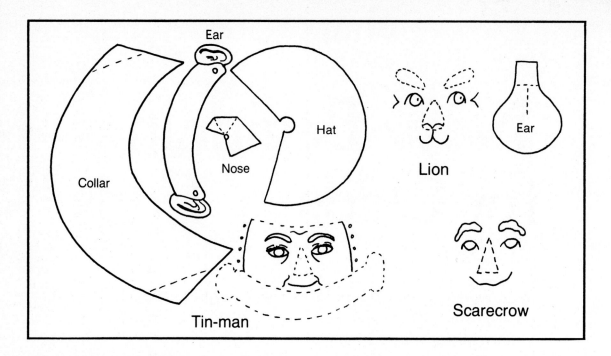

Ear

Collar

Nose

Hat

Lion

Ear

Tin-man

Scarecrow

3. Glue egg into stand. Let dry completely.
4. Cut collar, face, ears, and nose of cardboard, according to pattern above. Glue onto egg. Let dry. (Staple collar at base of back.)
5. Form a cone for hat. Cut off tip and insert a roll of cardboard. Glue onto egg. Let dry.
6. Cut a tiny strip of cardboard, form an open roll, and glue to hat for handle. Let dry.
7. Give the egghead several coats of silver paint. Let dry thoroughly between coats.
8. Paint on features and details with black and white acrylic paints.

Scarecrow **1.** Cut 1x4-inch cardboard strip.
2. Tape cardboard into a circle to form base for egg.
3. Glue egg on stand.
4. Cut a 10-inch-diameter fabric circle.
5. Brush glue on the egg and the stand.
6. Lay fabric over egg, gather the fabric at the neck and secure with a rubber band.
7. Tuck under raw edges, then glue. (Paper clips will hold them in place while drying.)
8. Wrap a piece of rough twine around neck of egghead. Tie in knot.
9. To construct hat,
• Cut two 3½-inch-diameter felt circles.
• Cut a pie-shaped piece out of one circle and lap over to form crown of hat.

• Glue the hat onto the egg.
• Cut 2-inch-diameter circle from center of second circle. Pull over hat to form brim.
10. Force pieces of broomstraw under hat.
11. Cut nose from cardboard, then paint it red. Let dry.
12. Glue to face. Let dry.
13. Paint features with acrylic paints. Let dry.

Lion **1.** Cut a 1x4-inch strip of cardboard.
2. Tape cardboard into a circle to form base for egg.
3. Glue egg on stand.
4. Cut a 10-inch-diameter fabric circle.
5. Brush glue on the egg and the stand.
6. Lay fabric over egg, gather the fabric at the neck, and secure with a rubber band. Let dry.
7. Remove rubber band from the neck.
8. Cut ears from felt. Fold on dotted lines. (See sketch above.) Glue ears to head. Let dry.
9. Cut 8-inch strips of yarn and glue strand by strand in curls onto lion head. (**Note:** Do several strands at a time and let dry before doing more.)
10. Cut three 1½-inch wire strips.
11. Twist together in the center.
12. Cut felt nose (see sketch). Glue to face with wire under the nose. Let dry completely.
13. Add yarn eyebrows and red bow.
14. Paint features with acrylic paints.

Jar Lid Picture Frames

It's a frame-up—but the kind that's fun for everyone. Why not start your own family rogues' gallery? Hang the frames down a strip of wide ribbon or group individual frames into a pleasing arrangement.

Materials
Canning jar rings
Lightweight cardboard
Corrugated cardboard
Flocked adhesive-backed paper or braid trim
Photographs
Glue
Red velvet ribbon
Glue-on picture hangers (or copper wire and masking tape)

Tools
Scissors
Craft knife
Wire cutter

Directions
1. Cut a circle of lightweight cardboard to fit inside the fruit jar ring.
2. Glue rim of photograph to cardboard. Dry.
3. To form colored mat around photo,
• Cut a circle of flocked adhesive-backed paper the same size as photo circle. Cut out center of flocked circle to form mat. Peel off backing and position mat on photo. Or:
• Glue pieces of narrow braid trim around the outside edge of the photo circle. Make sure you have enough braid bands to mat the photo when you place it in the jar ring.
4. Position matted photo circle in ring.
5. Cut as many corrugated cardboard circles as necessary to fill jar ring. (**Note:** Cut circles slightly larger than ring opening to allow for pressure-fitting them in place.)
6. Place corrugated cardboard circles behind photo circle in ring.
7. Add glue-on picture hanger to back. Or make your own hanger by bending a short length of wire into a circle. Slip a two-inch strip of tape through wire circle, fastening ends of tape to each other. Position hanger so only wire ring is above frame. Add more tape to secure.
8. Tie a bow. Position it and glue in place. Dry.

Candle Holders Galore

Here's your chance to use up not only some of the wood scraps left from your last woodworking project but also some of that multitude of plastic, glass, and cardboard cartons and containers you have on hand. Get the family together and work on several of these imaginative projects at one sitting. Then, for a special party, you can use a grouping of the candle holders as an eye-catching centerpiece.

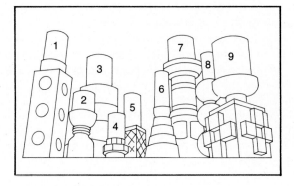

Materials
Mirror candlestick (1)
> Twelve 2¼-inch-diameter mirrors
> One tuna fish can
> Instant papier-mâché
> One 4x4 (11¾ inches long)
> Contact cement
> Tooling aluminum (36-gauge)
> One ½-inch wood screw
> Four small wooden door pulls

Glasses candle holder (2)
> Three wide, short glasses or small sherbets
> 1 yard gold cording
> Epoxy

Small Christmas ball ornaments (with wire on the end of each)
Jumbo candlestick (3)
> Cardboard box (9x9x5 inches)
> One 10½-inch-tall cardboard cylinder with tin top (made to store toy blocks)
> Gold foil
> Spray adhesive
> White and black tape
> Small brass tacks
> Raw umber transparent dye (buy at art store)
> White glue

Pipe union candlestick (4)
> Pipe union (3-inch diameter on the inside)

Primer
High-gloss enamel paint

Box-mirror candlestick (5)
24 1x1-inch mirrors
Cardboard box (3x3x6 inches)
Contact cement
Instant papier-mâché
Eight cardboard strips (¾x3 inches)
Cardboard ring from masking tape
Aluminum foil
Black enamel paint
¼-inch red auto stripping tape

Curled tin holder (6)
Five empty tin cans (two small and three graduated sizes, with tops removed)
6-inch stove bolt (⅛-inch diameter) with washer and nut to fit
Fine wire
Gold paint

Jug candlestick (7)
One 6-inch-tall cardboard carpet roll tube
One 1-gallon glass jug
Contact cement
Flowerpot tray (7 inches in diameter)
Aluminum foil
Spray adhesive
Eight wood pieces (½x1x2½ inches)
Leather strips
Six upholstery tacks
Raw umber transparent dye (buy at art store)
Red and brown tape

Triple-ball candlestick (8)
Three large white foam balls
Three wooden drapery rings
One small can to hold candle (top removed)
Wooden circle for base (cut to size)
Instant papier-mâché
White glue
Red, orange, and yellow acrylic paint

Jumbo square candlestick (9)
Cardboard or wooden box (6x6x6 inches)
Contact cement
16 wooden blocks (⅛x2x2 inches)
16 brass tacks
One 6-inch wooden salad bowl
Spray-can lid
Raw umber transparent dye (buy at art store)
Varnish

Tools
Paintbrush
Wooden or metal modeling tool
Tracing wheel
Craft knife or single-edged razor blade
7-inch tin snips
Round-nose pliers
Drill
Adjustable wrench
Medium-grade sandpaper
Knife or serrated grapefruit spoon

Directions

(1) Mirror candlestick **1.** Enlarge the pattern from the grid in sketch A on page 238. (See page 209 for instructions on how to work grids.)
2. Position pattern on one side of 4x4 and mark position of center of each of the three sunbursts. Repeat marking on other three sides.
3. Glue one of the mirrors at each mark, centering mirror over mark. Let dry.
4. Cut four 4½x12-inch pieces aluminum.
5. With a fine pencil, mark the pattern on each piece of tooling aluminum.
6. Working on a lightly padded surface, tool the pattern on both sides of the aluminum with the modeling tool.
7. Mix papier-mâché as directed on package.
8. Fill back of tooled areas with papier-mâché until level with the background. Let dry.
9. Glue one of the tooled pieces to each side of the 4x4 with contact cement. Press the aluminum against the wood and the mirrored surfaces, firmly bending and gluing the edges at top, bottom, and sides of the 4x4. Let dry.
10. If desired, use tracing wheel to texture the background of aluminum, as shown in photo.
11. To expose the mirrors, cut out the center of each sunburst with a craft knife or single-edge razor blade.
12. Clean glue off mirrors with a damp cloth.
13. Cut piece of tooling aluminum to fit top of the 4x4, and glue in place. Let dry.
14. Cut a strip of tooling aluminum to fit around the sides of the tuna can.
15. Tool desired design on this strip (see diamond design in photo).
16. Glue the strip to the can. Let dry.
17. Drill a small hole through center of can bottom and into center of candle holder top.
18. Screw can in place with wood screw.
19. For candle holder feet, glue one door pull at each corner of candle holder bottom.

(continued on next page)

(2) Glasses candle holder **1.** Glue bottoms of two glasses together with epoxy. Let dry.
2. Twist the wires of the ornaments together and arrange in a heap. Fill the remaining glass with the small Christmas ball ornaments.
3. Glue the top rim of the glass containing the ornaments to the rim of either of the other glasses. Let dry completely.
4. Trim with gold cord as shown in the photograph, gluing cord in place.

(3) Jumbo candlestick **1.** Cover box with gold foil, gluing in place with spray adhesive.

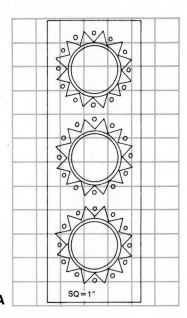

2. Trim box with black tape as desired.
3. Put tin top in position on cardboard cylinder, and glue in place. Let dry.
4. Cover sides and top of cylinder with gold foil, gluing in place. Let dry.
5. Trim cylinder as desired with black tape, white tape, and small brass tacks.
6. Center cylinder atop cardboard box and glue in place. Let dry.
7. Paint with several coats of raw umber transparent dye. Let dry between coats.

(4) Pipe union candlestick **1.** Scrub pipe union with soap and water to remove grease.
2. Prime the pipe union. Let dry.
3. Paint pipe union with several coats of high-gloss enamel. Let dry between coats.

(5) Box-mirror candlestick **1.** Glue six mirrors to each side of box in diagonal checkerboard pattern. Let dry completely.
2. Mix papier-mâché as directed on package.
3. Fill areas between mirrors with papier-mâché. Smooth the surface. Let dry.
4. Glue cardboard strips at top and bottom of each side of box. Let dry.
5. Glue the cardboard ring to the top of the box. Let dry. Line inside of ring with aluminum foil.

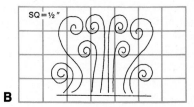

6. Paint plastered areas, box top, and cardboard with black enamel. Let dry.
7. Trim cardboard strips with red tape.

(6) Curled tin holder **1.** Remove the top rim of one of the two small cans:
● Cut through rim on one side of can joint with the tin snips.
● Cut around can just below rim, stopping at joint.
● Remove the joint by bending it back and forth until it breaks off.
2. Measure around can, then cut a 1-inch-wide strip of paper to fit can.
3. Fold the paper strip in half three times. Unfold paper and mark at each fold line for a total of eight sections.
4. Fit the paper strip around can and mark sections on can with ballpoint pen or crayon.
5. Cut on each line to bottom rim of can.
6. Cut one section of can into eight strips. (To make strips equal width, halve the section, halve each half, and then halve each quarter.)
7. With round-nose pliers, grasp the left strip at the bottom and turn the pliers so the strip is at a right angle to the can rim.
8. Repeat this procedure so first four strips are turned one way, then reverse procedure so next four strips are turned opposite way.
9. Using round-nose pliers, grasp one strip at tip and curl down. Repeat for remaining strips curling them to form design shown in sketch B.

238

10. Pinch the center four strips together and secure with fine wire.

11. Repeat steps 6 to 10 for the remaining seven sections. (Be sure to keep the pattern even.)

12. Cut and curl the remaining four cans, using the same technique.

13. Drill hole in center bottom of each can.

14. Put the two cans of the same size together bottom to bottom.

15. Put the stove bolt through the center holes.

16. Thread on next size can, bottom end up. (Bend strips of smaller can so they slope out and fit just behind rim of larger can.)

17. Thread on the remaining two cans.

18. Screw on the washer and nut and tighten with an adjustable wrench.

19. Paint gold. Let dry.

(7) Tall jug candle holder (see sketch C)

1. Glue carpet roll tube to top of jug. Let dry.

2. Glue flowerpot tray to top of tube. Let dry.

3. Measure around glass jug and cut a 4-inch-wide strip of aluminum foil to fit around jug.

4. Use spray adhesive to glue aluminum foil strip around the center section of the jug.

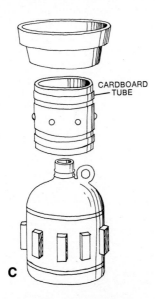

CARDBOARD TUBE

C

5. Glue the wood pieces to the foil, spacing evenly. Let dry.

6. Trim jug, tube, and tray with aluminum foil, tape, and leather strips, as desired.

7. Stud tube with upholstery tacks.

8. Paint the candle holder with raw umber transparent dye. Let dry.

(8) Triple-ball candlestick   **1.** Push the open end of the can into one of the foam balls, then remove it, leaving a circular mark.

2. With a knife or serrated grapefruit spoon, dig out a hole at the mark to surround can.

3. Push the can, bottom down, into the depression in the foam ball.

4. Glue a wooden drapery ring to the center of the wooden base. Let dry.

5. Glue one of whole foam balls to ring. Dry.

6. Glue another ring atop ball. Then, glue on the other whole ball, remaining ring, and the ball with can insert. Let dry.

7. Mix papier-mâché as directed on package.

8. Smooth a light coat of papier-mâché onto the foam balls. Wipe excess off drapery rings and base. Let dry.

9. Sand the candle holder until smooth.

10. Mask off rings and paint the foam balls. Dry. Remove mask.

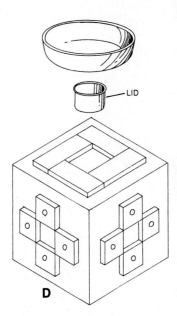

LID

D

(9) Jumbo square candlestick (see sketch D)

1. On each side of box glue four wooden blocks in a cross pattern, as shown in sketch.

2. Push a tack into center of each block.

3. Glue the bottom of the salad bowl to the bottom of the spray-can lid. Let dry.

4. Glue top of lid to top of box. Let dry.

5. Paint the entire unit with raw umber transparent dye. Let dry.

6. Finish with a coat of varnish. Let dry.

Carpet Tree Mural

Create your own one-of-a-kind wall cover without the expense that many store-bought treatments involve. Simply go to a carpet dealer near you and ask for some carpet scraps. Once you've completed the mural, keep it bright and clean by vacuuming occasionally.

Materials
    Texture paint (in a neutral color)
    Brown enamel paint
    Scraps of carpet in green and two other
        harmonizing colors
    Latex-base adhesive (for gluing carpet)

Tools
    Heavy scissors for cutting carpet
    Paintbrush

Directions
1. Paint the wall with texture paint as a background for the mural. Let the paint dry completely before proceeding.
2. Lightly pencil-in the outlines of the trunk and branches of the tree to get the overall design you want.
3. Paint in the outline of the tree, using brown enamel paint. Let dry.
4. Cut up carpet scraps for the foliage. (Use the orange and gold color scheme shown in the photo or work out another color scheme to harmonize with your room.)
5. Glue the carpet scraps in place on the wall to create the leaves and other foliage growing in the landscape scene.

Painting hints

Paint wall with brush or roller. When using brush, apply paint liberally to surface and brush from ceiling to baseboard in panels about 3 feet wide. Repeat procedure to finish by beginning next panel before top of first one dries.

With roller, make first stroke upward, cover same; follow with down stroke over same area crosswise. Blend laps starting from dry surface to last painted area.

Welded Hardware Wall Hanging

Unusual to say the least, this hanging is sure to spark conversation whenever someone sees it for the first time. Locate metal hardware such as these through wrecking companies or even in some antique stores or junk shops.

Materials
    Collection of door and drawer hardware—
        brass in this case (backplates, knobs,
        pulls, and knockers)
    Two L-screws
    Two large screw eyes
    Heavy-duty picture wire

Tools
    Drill
    Vinegar

Directions
1. Lay out your assortment of hardware into a design.
2. Have the pieces welded together professionally. (Also, have the screw eyes welded to the back of the piece for hanging.)
3. Treat the welded pieces with vinegar. (This will give the brass a greenish cast.)
4. Attach heavy-duty picture wire to screw eyes and twist ends securely.
5. Screw L-screws into wall studs and hang.

Mishmash Music Makers

Here's a rhythm band that ought to inspire the whole family to gather 'round the old upright. The featured instruments are a pine and rawhide tom-tom, washtub bass, tin-can maracas, rubber-band guitar, and wood xylophone—all made from odds 'n ends. Try other classics such as cardboard-tube kazooz, willow whistles, water-filled jars and spoons.

Materials
Rubber-band guitar
  ¾-inch pine boards
  ⅛-inch plywood
  Wood scraps
  Glue
  Nails
  Screws
  Long rubber bands
  Large screw eyes

Tom-tom
- 16 pieces of pine 2½x10¾ inches
- Two 14-inch rawhide circles
- Two ½-inch leather strips
- Masking tape
- White glue
- Blued carpet tacks

Xylophone
- Oak or other hardwood (enough for a strip ¼ inch thick, 1½ inches wide, and 31 inches long
- ¾-inch pine
- Two strips of plastic foam

Washtub bass
- Galvanized washtub
- Length of clothesline
- Four-foot length of closet pole or broomstick
- Eyebolt
- Two nuts
- Two washers

Maracas
- Two tin cans
- Two ½-inch dowels, 4 inches long
- Scraps of pine lumber
- Seeds or pebbles
- Nail

Tools
- Drill
- Hammer
- Table saw
- Screwdriver
- Sandpaper medium-grade
- Staple gun

Directions

Rubber-band guitar (See sketch 1 on page 244)
1. Make sides of 8x10-inch box from ¾-inch pine.
2. Cut two 8x10-inch pieces of ⅛-inch plywood for top and bottom.
3. Cut 3-inch hole in piece used for top.
4. Glue box together and let dry.
5. Cut ¾-inch pine to 2x18 inches for neck.
6. Make parallel cuts in neck to within three inches of one end.
7. Cut triangular bracket 1¼x2 inches.
8. Glue and nail bracket and neck to box.
9. Cut two bridges ¾x½x2 inches. Notch in four places and glue in place. Let dry.
10. Insert two screws at bottom of box to hold rubber bands.

11. Insert large screw eyes at top of neck to serve as "tuners" and attach rubber bands.

Tom-tom (see sketch 2 on page 244)
1. Cut long edges of the 16 pine boards 11¼ degrees to fit together. (Use table saw set at ¼ of 45 degrees.)
2. Lay down two strips of masking tape, adhesive side up.
3. Arrange wood on it, beveled side up.
4. Fill spaces with white glue. Let dry.
5. Lift ends of tape so pieces meet, forming a circle, secure with more tape. Dry overnight.
6. Remove tape and sand outside, rounding top and bottom rims (12-inch diameter circle).
7. Soak rawhide until soft and pliable.
8. Stretch over top and bottom.
9. Staple in place, working from opposite sides.
10. Tack leather strips in place, as shown in sketch (be sure to cover staples).
11. Trim excess rawhide. Let dry overnight.

Xylophone (see sketch 3 on page 244)
1. Cut oak strip into eight pieces. (Cut one piece three inches long, then cut the rest progressively ¼ inch longer.)
2. Make frame of ¾-inch pine. (Frame should measure 2¾x15 inches. Miter corners.)
3. Lay two strips of plastic foam on frame's long edges.
4. Pre-drill two holes two inches apart in each "key". Arrange keys on foam.
5. Use screws slightly smaller than holes to attach keys loosely to frame.

Washtub bass (see sketch 4 on page 244)
1. Notch end of pole to accept bottom rim of tub.
2. Drill hole near other end of pole for line.
3. Drill hole in center bottom of tub.
4. Rigidly fasten an eyebolt, two nuts, and two washers to tub.
5. Tie clothesline to bolt.
6. Set pole notch on rim.
7. Lean pole slightly toward center. Pull line taut, wrap around pole, and tie.

Maracas (see sketch 5 on page 244)
1. Cut wood disc to fit can. Drill ½-inch hole in disc.
2. Insert four-inch dowel in hole. Glue and dry.
3. Partially fill can with seeds or pebbles.
4. Press disk in place, flush with can end.
5. Secure with nail.

(continued on next page)

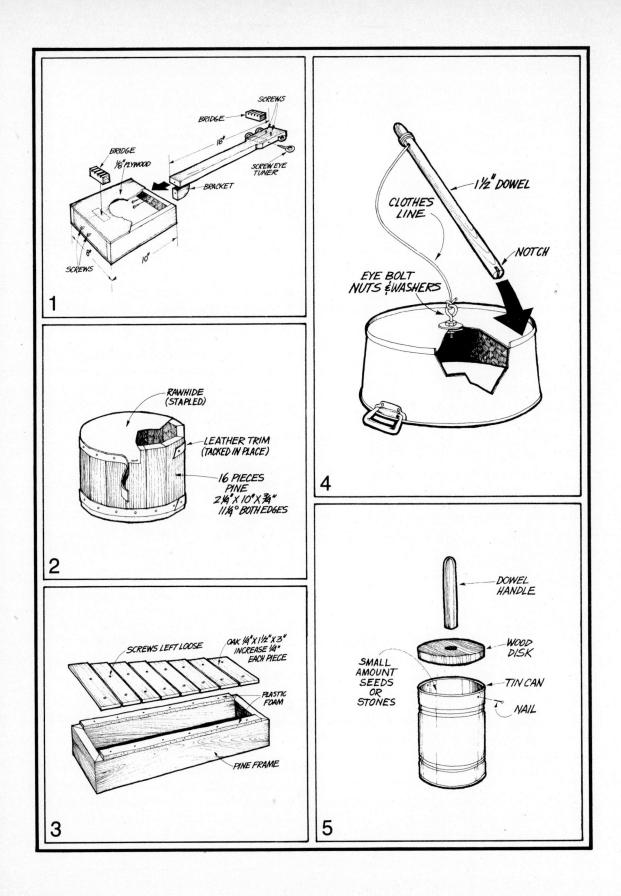

1

SCREWS
BRIDGE
BRIDGE
⅛" PLYWOOD
18"
SCREW EYE TUNER
BRACKET
8"
10"
SCREWS

2

RAWHIDE (STAPLED)
LEATHER TRIM (TACKED IN PLACE)
16 PIECES PINE
2⅛" X 10" X ¾"
11¼° BOTH EDGES

3

SCREWS LEFT LOOSE
OAK ¼" X 1½" X 3"
INCREASE ¼"
EACH PIECE
PLASTIC FOAM
PINE FRAME

4

1½" DOWEL
CLOTHES LINE
NOTCH
EYE BOLT
NUTS & WASHERS

5

DOWEL HANDLE
WOOD DISK
SMALL AMOUNT SEEDS OR STONES
TIN CAN
NAIL

Directions

1. Divide the top of the end table trunk into 64 squares (eight rows of eight, as shown) to form the game board. (If using rectangular trunk, measure width of trunk and mark a square that size in center of trunk top. Divide this large square into 64 small squares.)

2. Make paper pattern of the small square size.

3. Cut 32 squares from each piece of vinyl, using the paper pattern as a cutting guide.

4. Cement the vinyl onto the marked game board in a checkerboard arrangement.

5. To attach the casters to the trunk bottom,

• Mark in each corner of the trunk where you want casters to go.

• Center-punch at each mark, then drill holes.

• Secure the casters to trunk with bolts, washers, and nuts, as shown in drawing.

• Tighten nuts with adjustable wrench.

6. Paint the castellated nuts (half each color). Let them dry thoroughly.

Trunk Game Table

Sure, this is a fantastic game table—but that's not all. With its heavy-duty structure, the trunk will stand hard wear as an end table in your recreation room, too. When game time is over, stash the game pieces inside the trunk.

Here, large castellated nuts were used for game pieces, since they stack easily, but bottle caps or wooden blocks work as well.

Materials

One end table trunk or flat-topped trunk

¼ yard each of two contrasting colors of upholstery vinyl

Contact cement

Four plate casters with bolts, washers, and nuts to fit

Paint (two contrasting colors)

24 large castellated nuts

Tools

Scissors

Center punch

Drill

Adjustable wrench

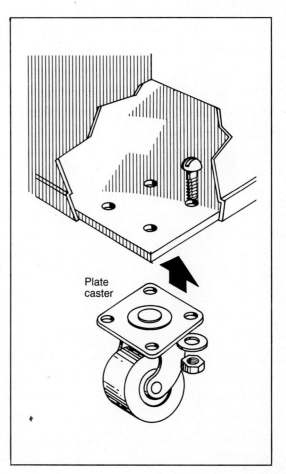

Plate caster

Feed-Sack Pillows

The results are strictly uptown—even though these pillows are put together from down-home odds 'n' ends. The bold labels of the feed sacks increase the visual impact of the decor at no extra cost. Check grain dealers and house auctions for sacks of this type.

Materials
> Feed sacks
> Matching thread
> Polyester fiber fill

Tools
> Sewing machine
> Needle
> Scissors
> Straight pins

Directions
(**Note:** If feed sacks are dusty, soiled, or smell old, machine-wash them before converting them to pillows. Avoid bleach or water that's too hot. Colors are not fast and designs may fade with washing.)
1. Iron feed sacks well.
2. With sewing machine, double-stitch around the three sewn sides of the sack. (This gives a knife-edge seam for a finished look. It also keeps original seams from pulling out.)
3. Stuff pillow with polyester fiber fill:
• With scissors, push fiber fill down into bottom corners of feed sack to even stuffing.
• Continue filling with polyester until pillow is as plump as you desire.
4. Fold raw edges of the top toward the inside.
5. Pin folded top edge of pillow closed.
6. With needle, hand-stitch top closed, using a slip stitch:
• Fasten thread on underside of folded edge.
• Work from right to left.
• Slip needle through one fold and pull the thread out.
• Slip needle through the other fold and pull the thread out.
(**Note:** The end of the first stitch and the beginning of the second are directly opposite each other. Threads are hidden in the folds.)
7. Shake filling down in pillow and with machine, double-stitch along top edge.

Boot-Tree Bookends

There's a brand-new version of bronzed baby shoe bookends. It's boot-tree bookends! The clever book holder you see here is engineered so the boot trees slide along a track to hold any number of books. Still, making it requires only a minimum of workshop expertise.

Materials
> One pair of wooden boot trees
> 1x4-inch board, 28 inches long
> Two wood screws
> Two washers
> Wood stain
> Clear varnish

Tools
> Coping saw
> Router with flat cutting bit and ⅛-inch bit
> Coarse-grade sandpaper
> Paintbrush

Directions
1. Round each end of 28-inch-long board.
2. From bottom side, use router and dado a channel ½ inch wide x ½ inch deep along the center of board, stopping one inch from each end.
3. From top side, use ⅛-inch router bit to make an opening through top of board to dado.
4. Sand wood. Stain. Finish with clear varnish.
5. Fasten boot tree with a washer and screw from underside. Screw into heel of boot tree.

Room Divider

Prolong the life of old doors by using them for this unique room divider. Besides being attractive, this divider has the added bonus of being movable from room to room.

Materials

One pair of interesting old wooden doors (doors must be no more than 4½ inches shorter than height from floor to ceiling of room you plan to put divider)

Water-base wood putty

Dark oil-base stain

Raw umber oil paint (buy at art or craft store)

Finishing nails

Two 1x2-inch pine strips as long as double doors are wide

Pronged washer/nuts

Carriage bolts to fit pronged washer/nuts
  (4 inches long)
Two thin strips of lattice molding as long
  as double doors are wide
Screw eyes
Strings of plastic beads

Tools
  Hammer
  Putty knife
  Coarse-grade sandpaper
  Paintbrush
  Hammer
  Drill
  Wrench

Directions
(**Note:** Strip the doors to bare wood before using.)

1. Give the doors a rough sanding.

2. Fill latch or hinge holes with water-base wood putty. Let dry.

3. Apply a coat of dark oil-base stain to the doors, the 1x2 strips, and the lattice molding, as shown in photograph A.

4. Wherever the stain won't take well, such as over the putty, touch up those areas with raw umber oil paint. Let dry.

5. Lay the doors side by side and nail one 1x2 pine strip across top edge and the other pine strip across bottom edge of doors.

6. To accommodate pronged washer/nuts, drill several deep holes through top strip and into doors. (Space holes three to four inches apart.)

7. Tap the pronged washer/nuts into the holes (see photo B).

8. Screw the carriage bolts down snug into the pronged washer/nuts.

9. With another person's help, stand the doors in place.

10. Unscrew the carriage bolts against the ceiling, as shown in photograph C. (Pressure from the bolts wedges the doors between the ceiling and the floor.)

11. To conceal bolts at ceiling, nail up strips of lattice molding. (Whenever you want to move the doors, just remove molding and loosen bolts.)

12. Position screw eyes at top of each window opening.

13. Hang strings of plastic beads from the screw eyes to fill openings.

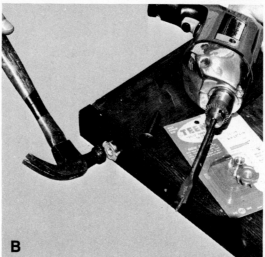

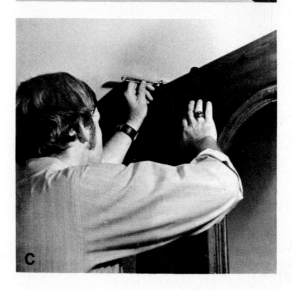

Hobby Block Sculpture

Not all hobbyists want to drag out a scrapbook everytime they're going to show off their collections. If that's your case, then what you need is a hobby block sculpture like the one shown here. The racing enthusiast who designed this one utilized a conglomeration of tickets, photos, and track memorabilia.

Materials
One ¾-inch piece of wood (6x6 inches)
One 6-inch long wooden dowel (⅜-inch diameter)
One wooden block (3x4¼x14 inches)
Enamel paints (red, white, and black)
Collector's items (This block uses gears from a car, photos, tickets, small model car parts, magazine clips, keys, and small parts from various cars)
Glue
Clear acrylic

Tools
Saber saw
Coarse-grade sandpaper
Drill
Paintbrush

Directions
1. Sand the wooden block.
2. Cut a 5-inch-diameter circle from the ¾-inch wood piece.
3. Sand the circle until smooth.
4. Drill holes for the dowel in the bottom of the block and halfway into the 5-inch diameter circle center as well.
5. Glue the gear pieces around the hole on the circle. Let dry.
6. Paint rectangular sides of block. Let dry.
7. Paint the circle. Let dry.
8. Dip the ends of the dowel in glue, and push the dowel into the hole in the block and the circle stand. Let dry. The dowel should measure about three inches from the block to the circle base.)
9. Glue pieces of models, photos, cutouts, and other assembled materials. Let dry.
10. Touch up the block with paint, as shown in the photographs. Let dry.
11. Coat the block sculpture with clear acrylic. Let dry. (This will preserve the project.)

Block Bookends

Wooden blocks bring a touch of nostalgia to these classic bookends. Though today's youngsters play with the plastic variety, these charming wooden ones are available at secondhand stores.

Materials
18 wooden blocks
White glue
One pair metal bookends
Six screws
¼-inch hardboard (2x2-foot piece)
Felt or flocked adhesive-backed paper
Paint

Tools
Saw
Drill
Screwdriver
Scissors
Paintbrush

Directions
1. Glue two groups of nine blocks together. Dry.
2. Cut hardboard to fit back and sides of the wooden block units.
3. Glue to blocks. Let dry.
4. Drill holes into metal bookends. Position on framed block units. Screw in place.
5. Paint hardboard and metal bookends. Let dry.
6. Line backs and bottoms with felt.

How to Wire Lamps

The sockets of all portable lamps, whether they are table, floor, or swag lamps, are wired in the same way. However, you will not use the lamp harp and harp retainer for the swag lamps. Here are the basic steps and precautions to consider when wiring lamps. (**Note:** The sketch is numbered for easier reference.)

Directions

1. Disassemble the socket:
• If the socket has two screws inside it, remove them with a screwdriver to free the base.
• If there are no screws, grasp the socket cover and pull to remove it.

2. Use hacksaw to cut all-thread lamp pipe to length of lamp. File off rough edges of pipe both inside and out to prevent cutting the lamp cord or scraping the insulation and exposing bare wire. (**Note:** ⅛-inch IPS all-thread lamp pipe is most commonly used for lamps. IPS is an abbreviation for Inside Pipe Size. The pipe is numbered on the sketch as an easy location reference.)

3. Screw a nut and washer on lamp pipe so about ½ inch extends below washer. Insert lamp pipe through hole in center of lamp base. Screw on another washer and nut, and tighten against bottom of base with adjustable wrench.

4. Put harp retainer on lamp pipe and screw on base of lamp socket. (Some sockets have a set-screw to hold socket in place.)

5. Thread cord from bottom of lamp base up through the pipe to socket base. (**Note:** Use a ready-made lamp cord, which usually comes in 8-foot lengths, with a molded-end plug. (Swag lamp cords are longer, but they're made the same way and are available as part of a swag lamp kit.)

6. Take hold of the cord at the top and pull it until about 2 inches extend above socket base. At this point, separate the two wires for a distance of 2 inches. (Most ready-made lamp cords have "zip" cords that are easy to pull apart.)

7. Strip the insulation off each wire for a distance of 1 inch, then twist the ends of each wire clockwise. As a safety precaution, make sure that there are no loose strands.

8. Loosen the two screws that are on either side of the socket mechanism.

9. Place the twisted end of one wire to the left side of one screw, wrap the wire end clockwise

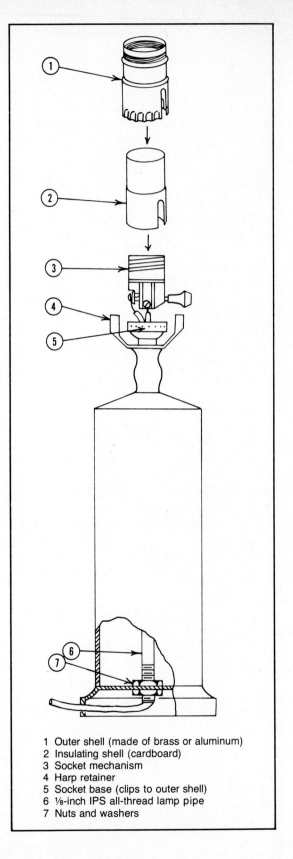

1 Outer shell (made of brass or aluminum)
2 Insulating shell (cardboard)
3 Socket mechanism
4 Harp retainer
5 Socket base (clips to outer shell)
6 ⅛-inch IPS all-thread lamp pipe
7 Nuts and washers

around the screw, and tighten the screw with screwdriver. (Be sure there are no strands of wire left out.)

10. Turn the socket around and attach the other wire to the second screw in the same manner as was done in step 9.

11. Gently pull the cord at the bottom of the base, to remove the slack below the socket.

12. Put the cardboard insulating sleeve inside the metal outer shell from the bottom up as shown in the drawing.

13. Put both over the socket mechanism and snap (or screw) the unit into the socket base. (Be sure to support the base of the socket when placing the cover on it.)

When to use what light bulb

With a variety of throwaways available for conversion to lamp shades, it is important from a safety standpoint to know what light bulb wattage is recommended for each type of shade.

Type of shade	Bulb wattage
Ready-made shades	50-, 100-, or 150- watt light bulb
Clay pot shades	60-watt limit; use small globe-shaped light bulb (mini-globe)
Heating duct shade (painted with heat-resistant paint)	60-watt showcase bulb (long bulb)
Funnel shade (covered with a heat-resistant plastic coating)	50-watt flood bulb or spotlight
Stove T lamp shade	25-watt mini-globe light bulb recommended; 60- watt safety limit
Cardboard food containers such as chicken buckets or ice cream containers	7½-watt bulb for maximum safety; use a candelabra socket like those used for Christmas tree light bulbs.

Lighting safety factors to remember

When wiring or repairing your lamps, there are certain safety rules you should follow at all times. Use the following list as a mental safety check:

• Do not attempt to do any electrical repairs until you turn off the power at the service entry. Unplug the lamp to be repaired or turn off the fuse box or the circuit breaker that supplies power to the circuits you are working on.

• Do not plug in the lamp until all of the parts are together.

• Observe the safety limit in use of light bulb wattage (see box opposite).

• To ensure stability, weight any lamp you make with pebbles or gravel. (Do not use sand, since it will cause moisture complications in the lamp.)

Specialized tools for electrical work

From safety and efficiency standpoints, it is important to use the correct tools whenever doing any electrical repairs or wiring. Check the following list, then select the tools that specifically apply to your electrical job before proceeding.

Screwdriver with a special clamp on the end to hold small screws is especially suited for inserting screws in tight places such as electrical boxes.

Neon lamp tester is a small light with two wires attached. If the light lights when you insert the wires into an electrical outlet, you know that electricity is flowing to the outlet.

Wire strippers enable you to strip the insulation from a wire without cutting the wire itself. (It is necessary to expose the bare wire this way when you are connecting two insulated wires.)

Multipurpose tool has many uses including cutting wire, stripping wire, and crimping terminal joints.

INDEX

Tip Boxes

Adhesives, when to use what, 69

Candle-making materials, 31

Candle-making safety reminders, 29

Casters, types of, 175

Continuous bias strips, 137

Cross-stitch, how to work, 125

Decoupage, basic tools and materials for, 146

Decoupage, how to prepare prints for use in, 147

Decoupage, surfaces you can and cannot, 147

Electrical work, specialized tools for, 253

Gridded sketch, using, 209

Hacksaw, how to use, 34

Light bulb, when to use what, 253

Lighting safety, 253

Lumber, guide to buying, 166

Metal to metal, attaching, 24

Metal, working with, 40

Molding, standard builders', 11

Painting hints, 241

Rabbet plane, how to use, 207

Sandpaper, different types to use, 89

Terrarium tips, 206

Wall-fastening techniques, 211

Wood, painting over stained, 87

A-C

ABC Cross-Stitch Rug, 124-125

Acid Bottle Terrarium, 204-206

Adhesives, 69, 211
  for metal, 24

Agitator Sculpture, 129

Animal figures:
  cardboard, 184-187, 191
  egg, 233, 234
  paper, 159

Animal figures (cont'd)
  tin can, 6-8
  wire, 171

Antique shops, 5

Appliqué, 192-197
  Armoires, 70-71
  Auctions, 4

Bank, 21, 23

Barrels, 44-53

Bars:
  rolling cart, 174-175
  Victrola conversion, 90

Beer Can Table, 27

Benches, 102-103

Bentwood chair, 66

Bethlehem Village, 192-197

Bias strips, cutting, 137

Bird Feeder, 211

Bird House, 35

Block Bookends, 251

Boat Prop Sculpture, 140

Bolts, 24

Bookends, 247, 251

Bottle cases:
  wall organizers, 51-52

Bottles, 212-214, 229
  "stained" glass, 208-210
  terrarium, 204-206

Boxes, 109
  aluminum, 168-169
  marbleized, 202
  for matches, 145, 147
  packing crate uses, 44-52

Breakfast Nook, 102-103

Button Necklace, 113

Candle holders, 236-239
  agitator, 129
  tin can, 28-31, 36-37, 43

Candle-making, 29, 30-31

Canisters:
  coffee can, 9
  wine bottle, 210-211

Cardboard, 176-203
  crates, 48-49
  stereo unit, 52

Cards:
  Christmas, 148-149
  wedding souvenir, 145, 146-147

Caroler figures, 212-214, 225

Carpet Tree Mural, 240-241

Casters, 175

Cat, 191

Cedar chest, 88-89

Centipede Table, 178-179

Chairs, 57, 59, 76-80
  handwoven, 60-65
  as planters, 66

Chess sets:
  spool, 92-93, 104-105
  TV tube, 218-219

Chests, 70-71, 88-89
  flowerpot room partition and, 220-221

Chicken Bucket Lamps, 198

China, 215

Christmas decorations:
  bottle figures, 212-214
  cardboard, 180-181, 188-189, 192-197, 200-202
  package display ladder, 143
  paper, 148, 152-153, 156-157
  plastic, 224-225, 229
  tin, 26, 32-33

Clay flowerpot uses, 207, 211, 215-217, 220-221

Clock decoration, 230

Clothespin Soldiers, 94-95

Clothes Tree, 97

Clothing, recycling of, 106-125

Coat hanger figures, 164-165, 171

Coffee cans:
  canisters, 9
  hat rack, 23-24
  pull toy, 21, 23

Container-lids:
  hanging, 222-223
  picture frame, 235

Crates, 44-52

Crochet rugs, 120-121

Cross-stitch, 124-125

D-G

Dandelion ornaments, 225

Decoupage, 144-147
  on tiles, 151

Desks, 86-87

254